STUDIES IN COMMUNICATION
General Editor: John Fiske

ADVERTISING
AS
COMMUNICATION

IN THE SAME SERIES

Introduction to Communication Studies *John Fiske*
Understanding News *John Hartley*
Case Studies and Projects in Communication
Neil McKeown
Key Concepts in Communication   *Tim O'Sullivan,
John Hartley, Danny Saunders and John Fiske*
An Introduction to Language and Society
Martin Montgomery
Understanding Radio *Andrew Crisell*
Popular Culture: The metropolitan experience
Iain Chambers

ADVERTISING

AS

COMMUNICATION

Gillian Dyer

METHUEN   LONDON AND NEW YORK

First published in 1982 by
Methuen & Co. Ltd
11 New Fetter Lane, London EC4P 4EE
Reprinted twice
Reprinted 1986

Published in the USA by
Methuen & Co.
in association with Methuen, Inc.
29 West 35th Street, New York, NY 10001

Printed in Great Britain by Richard Clay
(The Chaucer Press) Ltd, Bungay, Suffolk

British Library Cataloguing in Publication Data
Dyer, Gillian
Advertising as communication. – (Studies in
communication)
1. Advertising
I. Title   II. Series
659.1   HF5821

Library of Congress Cataloging in Publication Data
Dyer, Gillian.
Advertising as communication.
(Studies in communication)
Bibliography: p.
Includes index.
1. Advertising.   I. Title.   II. Series.
HF 5821.D89 1982   659.1   82-8134

ISBN 0-416-74520-2   AACR2
ISBN 0-416-74530-X (pbk.)

For my parents, Bertram and Gwen Dyer

CONTENTS

General editor's preface   x
Preface   xii
Acknowledgements   xiv
Introduction   1

   What is advertising?   2
   Commercial consumer advertising   4
   Mass communications   9
   Public relations   11

1 The origins and development of advertising   15

   Mercuries and newsheets   15
   An 'all-deafening blast of puffery'   28
   The break-up of the column lay-out
       in newspapers   30
   Slogans and catch phrases   32
   Bubbles   33
   Suggestions for further work   37

2 The new advertising   39

   Organizing the market   39
   The rise of popular journalism   41
   'Daddy, what did you do in the Great War?'   43
   The never-never   45

The nerve war   46
The home front   50
Note   53
Suggestions for further work   53

3 **The new media**   55

Post-war developments   55
Television   57
Commercial television   58
Commercial television and the BBC   60
Diversification   61
The pattern for the future   62
The press   63
Advertising sponsorship in the press   65
Advertising as a publishing authority   67
The crisis   69
Note   70
Suggestions for further work   70

4 **The effects of advertising**   72

Effects research   73˙
Market research   74
Sociological research   75
Advertising's effectiveness   78
Cultural effects   79
Images   82
The consumers   82
Notes   84
Suggestions for further work   84

5 **What do advertisements mean?**   86

Approaches to the study of meaning   87
Lines of appeal   92
Approaches to form and content   93
Props and settings   104
Analysing photographs   106
Content analysis   108

Notes   111
Suggestions for further work   111

✓ 6 **Semiotics and ideology**   114

Semiotics — concepts and methods   117
Iconic, indexical and symbolic signs   124
Syntagmatic and paradigmatic sign relations   126
Denotation and connotation   127
Codes   131
Notes   136
Suggestions for further work   136

✓7 **The language of advertising**   139

Words have feelings   140
The tone of voice   141
The role of advertising language   144
Language and the law   147
Key words   149
Figurative language   151
The 'absence' of language — calligraphy   155
Suggestions for further work   156

8 **The rhetoric of advertising**   158

A theory of rhetoric   159
Visual rhetoric   161
Suggestions for further work   182

Conclusion   183

Appendices   188
References   215
Bibliography   221
Index   227

GENERAL EDITOR'S PREFACE

This series of books on different aspects of communication is designed to meet the needs of the growing number of students coming to study this subject for the first time. The authors are experienced teachers or lecturers who are committed to bridging the gap between the huge body of research available to the more advanced student, and what the new student actually needs to get him started on his studies.

Probably the most characteristic feature of communication is its diversity: it ranges from the mass media and popular culture, through language to individual and social behaviour. But it identifies links and a coherence within this diversity. The series will reflect the structure of its subject. Some books will be general, basic works that seek to establish theories and methods of study applicable to a wide range of material; others will apply these theories and methods to the study of one particular topic. But even these topic-centred books will relate to each other, as well as to the more general ones. One particular topic, such as advertising or news or language, can only be understood as an example of communication when it is related to, and differentiated from, all the other topics that go to make up this diverse subject.

The series, then, has two main aims, both closely connected. The first is to introduce readers to the most important results of contemporary research into communication together with the theories that seek to explain it. The second is to equip them with appropriate methods of study and investigation which they will be able to apply directly to their everyday experience of communication.

If readers can write better essays, produce better projects and pass more exams as a result of reading these books I shall be very satisfied; but if they gain a new insight into how communication shapes and informs our social life, how it articulates and creates our experience of industrial society, then I shall be delighted. Communication is too often taken for granted when it should be taken to pieces.

John Fiske

PREFACE

This book is meant to provide some basic ideas, concepts and material for the study of advertising. It draws on work from a number of fields but revolves around the core concept of communication. Much of the book is in the form of a survey of existing material, and the second half in particular deals with questions of method and how to study advertisements rather than with extended examples of analysis. I hope that this provides enough groundwork for readers to pursue some of the issues raised in more depth, and especially to 'decode' one of the most ubiquitous and tenacious forms of communication and ideology in society. Advertising influences our thoughts, feelings and lives; we need to be aware of how it operates and equip ourselves with information and ideas on how far we think it a necessary and useful form of social communication. I hope this book contributes in some way to that project and will help people become more aware of the images and values perpetuated by advertising, and the forms and structures which carry and determine what they mean.

I would like to thank Julie Staniforth and Christine Barker for their excellent typing, a number of friends and colleagues who have helped with suggestions and ideas for this book, in particular Helen Baehr and David Child for their involvement and support. Clare Richardson kindly lent the newspapers from which the annoucements in chapter 1 were taken. Tim Bell of D'Arcy MacManus and Masius, and George Harrison of the History of Advertising Trust, also provided help with historical material and went to a great deal of trouble on my behalf. Special thanks should go to John Fiske, the general editor of this series, for his helpful advice and patience. I would also like to acknowledge a debt of gratitude to my parents for their general encouragement and interest in my work.

Gillian Dyer
1982

ACKNOWLEDGEMENTS

The publishers and I would like to thank the following for their permission to reproduce material: A, & F. Pears Ltd for plates 4 and 5; the Imperial War Museum for plate 6; Hamlyn Publishing Group Ltd for plate 7; Cadbury Typhoo Ltd for plate 8; Arthur H. Cox & Co. Ltd for plate 9; Jøtul Norcem UK Ltd for plate 10; Pendleton Woolen Mills and Danecraft International for plate 11; the International Gold Corporation for plate 12; Renault UK Ltd for plate 13; Lever Brothers Ltd for plate 14a; Philips Industries for plate 14b; Van den Berghs for 14c; Colman's Foods for plates 15 and 22; Birds Eye for plate 16; R.J. Reynolds Tobacco International, Inc. for plate 17; Rowntree Mackintosh Ltd for plate 18; Norman Craig & Kummel Ltd for plates 19 and 20; Kraft Foods Ltd for plate 21; John Walker & Sons Ltd and Parim Ltd for plate 23; Brandmark International Ltd for plate 24; White Horse Distillers Ltd for plate 25; Record Pasta Foods Ltd for plate 26; Young & Rubicam Ltd (International Distillers and Vinters Home Trade Ltd) for plate 27; Jacques Durand for table 1; the Advertising Association for tables 2–9 and Appendix IV; *Campaign* for tables 10 and 11. Every effort has been made to contact copyright holders, where this has not been possible we apologize to those concerned.

INTRODUCTION

Every day and for most of our lives we see and hear many advertisements. Even if you don't read a newspaper or watch television, and walk around the streets with your eyes down, you will find it impossible to avoid some form of publicity, even if it's only a trade display at a local store, uninvited handbills pushed through the letter box or cards displayed in the window of the corner newsagent. We usually take advertisements for granted because they are so pervasive, but many people, not least among them the advertisers themselves, claim that they are one of the most important influences in our lives. Not only do advertisements sell goods and services, they are commodities themselves, 'the most ubiquitous form in which we encounter commercial photography', according to a critic of advertising, Judith Williamson (1978, p. 57). In a sense advertising is the 'official art' of the advanced industrial nations of the west. It fills our newspapers and is plastered all over the urban environment; it is a highly organized institution, involving many artists, writers and film directors, and comprises a large proportion of the output of the mass media. It also influences the policies and the appearance of the media and makes them of central importance to the economy. Advertisements advance and perpetuate the ideas and values which are indispensable to a particular economy system. Advertisers want us to buy things, use them, throw them away and buy replacements in a cycle of continuous and conspicuous consumption.

Some advertisements are silly, inaccurate, misleading, or just plain irritating. On the other hand, we have probably all had occasion to say 'That's a good advertisement'. They can be skilfully designed and produced, very attractive, entertaining and funny. But we should not lose sight of their ideological function, which is linked to their economic function, nor of the real messages that lie behind their superficial gloss.

The primary function of advertising is, we are told, to introduce a wide range of consumer goods to the public and thus to support the free market economy, but this is clearly not its only role; over the years it has become more and more involved in the manipulation of social values and attitudes, and less concerned with the communication of essential information about goods and services. In this respect it could be argued that advertising nowadays fulfils a function traditionally met by art or religion. Some critics of advertising have even suggested that it operates in the same way as myths in primitive societies, providing people with simple stories and explanations in which values and ideals are conveyed and through which people can organize their thoughts and experiences and come to make sense of the world they live in. Varda Langholz Leymore, in her book *The Hidden Myth* (1975) argues that like myth, advertising reinforces accepted modes of behaviour and acts as an anxiety-reducing mechanism resolving contradictions in a complex or confusing society. She remarks, 'To the constant nagging dilemmas of the human condition, advertising gives a simple solution . . . [It] simultaneously provokes anxiety and resolves it' (p. 156). In a similar vein Raymond Williams (1980) has called advertising 'the magic system, . . . a highly organized and professional system of magical inducements and satisfactions functionally very similar to magical systems in simpler societies but rather strangely co-existent with highly developed scientific technology' (p. 185). And the critic Fred Inglis (1972) describes the advertiser as a modern-day shaman whose 'anonymous vantage in society permits him to articulate a novel magic which offers to meet the familiar pains of a particular society and history, to soften or sharpen ambition, bitterness, solitude, lust, failure and rapacity' (p. 78).

What is advertising?

In its simplest sense the word 'advertising' means 'drawing attention to something', or notifying or informing somebody of something. You can advertise by word of mouth, quite informally and locally, and without incurring great expense. But if you want to inform a large number of people about something, you might need to advertise in the more familiar sense of the word, by public announcement. If you put up a notice in a local newsagent's shop (preferably near a bus stop), design a poster or buy some space in a local newspaper, you are likely to attract the attention of more people to the information you wish to communicate than if you simply pass the word around friends and neighbours. You could go further and distribute leaflets as well, get someone to carry a placard around, even broadcast on local radio or organize a publicity stunt. However, you might not be content simply to convey certain facts, such as, for example:

For sale: four 6-week-old kittens
Contact M. James Tel. 324810

and leave it at that. You might wish to add a bit of emphasis to your message by proclaiming:

Adorable, fluffy kittens (house-trained) need a good
home. Black and white. An opportunity not to be
missed. Phone 342810. Hurry, only a few left!

There is a certain temptation, if we have anything to say or something to sell, to draw attention to our notice by exaggerating the facts or appealing to people's emotions:

Troubles at home? Marriage under strain?
These kittens will change your life, and
will bring joy and peace to your family.

And this is of course where all the controversy about advertising arises.

People who criticise advertising in its current form argue that advertisements create false wants and encourage the production and consumption of things that are incompatible with the fulfilment of genuine and urgent human needs. Advertising, it is claimed, is an irrational system which appeals to our emotions and to anti-social feelings which have nothing to do with the goods on offer. Advertisements usually suggest that private acquisition is the only avenue to social success and happiness — they define private acquisition and competitiveness as a primary goal in life, at the expense of less tangible rewards like better health care and social services. The consumer economy is said to divert funds from socially useful and human needs and make us greedy, materialistic and wasteful.

On the other hand, those who defend advertising say that it is economically necessary and has brought many benefits to society. It contributes to society's wellbeing and raises people's standard of living by encouraging the sales of mass-produced goods, thus stimulating production and creating employment and prosperity. Those people who would do away with advertising are accused of trying to deny cheaper goods and services to the majority, and of being puritanical, élitist and economically shortsighted. Furthermore, the champions of advertising say that people are perfectly free to ignore advertisements and that ads do not brainwash people because a number of advertising campaigns fail to attract customers.

Indeed it is perfectly true to say that consumer goods have brought comfort and pleasure to a large number of people and have alleviated want and hardship. I would not wish to argue that this is morally bad. In a complex society such as our own, consumer goods are necessary and important and on the whole have been a welcome development of the modern world. But along with commodities we need information about them: about their price, function, durability, quality, etc. This kind of information will help us make wise and rational consumer choices.

The question we have to ask ourselves is whether consumer advertising gives us enough, or indeed *any* accurate information, and whether the economic function of advertising is so vital that we cannot afford to do without it whatever the cultural, social and personal drawbacks. We also need to ask who is ultimately benefiting from the advertising of consumer goods — society as a whole (as it is claimed), or a few powerful commodity manufacturers and business corporations.

Commercial consumer advertising

There are many kinds of advertising: commercial consumer advertising is perhaps the kind most visible in our society. It commands more expenditure, space and professional skill than any other type and is directed towards a mass audience. It therefore provides the focus of this book. However, the other types are worth mentioning briefly:

Trade and technical advertisements are usually confined to special interest magazines like *Hi-Fi News, Amateur Gardener* or *Engineering Today*. They are aimed at the expert, professional or hobbyist. Most trade advertising is informative and useful — the customers are usually well able to evaluate the claims of cost, value, use and so on. The advertiser/supplier probably regards the customer as a 'user' and not a 'consumer' — a crucial distinction first proposed by Raymond Williams (1980) in his authoritative critique of advertising.

Prestige, business and financial advertising is a growing sector of the advertising industry. Ads for large companies or the publishing of yearly financial results in newspapers are usually designed to promote public confidence and favourable business images. Such advertising is not usually intended to influence sales directly. You will often see ads on television for such enterprises as the giant petrochemical firms or the large clearing banks which present themselves as disinterested pieces of public information and which are designed to make us think of these private corporations as benevolent, public-spirited and socially responsible. The inherent message in this type of campaign is the promotion of the capitalist enterprise and the values of the acquisitive society.

Small ads are usually straightforward and informative and have long since been relegated to the small print of the classified sections of newspapers or to such journals as *Exchange and Mart.*

Government and charity advertising is usually non-profit making, but often uses the persuasive techniques of commercial advertising. However, we should remember that an organization like the Health Education Council has a very small amount of money to promote anti-smoking in comparison with the giant tobacco firms who spend a great deal on encouraging us to smoke and thereby, by all accounts, to damage our health.

How then is advertising related to the economic systems of modern society? The sheer volume of goods or commodities which flow from modern factories would cause serious problems for the manufacturers unless they were quickly consumed and unless the general ideology of society was in tune with acquisitiveness and the 'way of life' associated with the consumer society. Advertising is one of the means used by manufacturing and service industries to ensure the distribution of commodities to people in society at large and is designed to create demands for such goods and services. It helps the manufacturer or business to secure a section of the market by organizing and controlling people's tastes and behaviour in the interests of company profit and capital growth. Advertising works not only on behalf of specific goods and services, it also assumes certain characteristics which are less directly connected to selling. It tries to manipulate people into buying a way of life as well as goods.

In the words of the economist J. K. Galbraith (1970), advertising keeps the atmosphere 'suitably consumptive'.

The more abundant goods become and the more removed they are from basic physical and social needs, the more open we are to appeals which are psychologically grounded argues Galbraith. Although the goods on display in shops and supermarkets do not usually relate to our urgent needs, we nonetheless desire them. Advertising's central function is to create desires that previously did not exist. Thus advertising arouses our interests and emotions in favour of goods and more goods, and thereby actually creates the desires it seeks to satisfy. Our desires are aroused and shaped by the demands of the system of production, not by the needs of society or of the individual. It is thus the advertiser's task to try to persuade rather than inform.

It is not really surprising that advertisements are unreliable as sources of information when one consideres that they come from biased or interested quarters, namely the producers of the advertised products. The producers are hardly likely to provide us with neutral information. An analogous situation would be if the authors of books or the directors of films wrote their own reviews in the newspaper columns, instead of 'disinterested' journalist-critics. And because the advertisers ('reviewers') subsidize the press this probably has the effect of restraining proper professional commodity 'reviews'. Information about commodities is valuable if it is impartial and objective, and this can only be achieved if the writers of advertisements which convey that information are financially independent of the product advertiser; but this is not the case with our present press and commercial TV systems. It could be argued that if the subsidy of the media by advertising had not developed in the way that it has, then newspapers and possibly television would have devoted more space and time to giving consumer information in the same way that they provide reviews of cultural events, and information on horse races or the Stock Exchange. In fact, advertising not only provides deficient and suspect information; in addition its development in the media has indirectly led to the suppression of other channels of information about commodities. In a famous essay on the economics of advertising, Nicholas Kaldor drew an important distinction between the informative and the persuasive element in advertising. His description is worth quoting here in full:

We must sharply distinguish here, of course, between the purely informative element in advertising and the persuasive element

6

(which belongs to another branch of the argument). If, to take an example, XX Ltd spend large sums annually on advertisements, saying 'XX is good for you', this may be an effective method of increasing the sales of XX beer, but the informative content of the advertisement is merely this: 'XX Ltd believe that the consumption of XX is beneficial to health'. Whether this is a valuable piece of information or not, its information value is exhausted as soon as the public are first told of it. Any further repetition of the message, and its display in prominent form, does not serve the purpose of information but of persuasion, it serves the purpose of inducing the public to believe it as well, and to keep it in the foreground of consciousness. While as a means of persuasion it may be very effective, its information value is zero. (Moreover assuming the message to be true, it might reach the public in many other ways — through the recommendation of doctors, for instance — it does not necessarily follow that without the advertisement the public would have remained ignorant of it.) (1950/1, p. 111)

One of the major criticisms of advertising is that it makes us too materialistic by persuading us, for instance, that we can achieve certain desirable goals in life through possessing things in a cycle of continuous and conspicuous consumption. But, paradoxically, modern advertising shows that we are not materialistic *enough*. If we were, presentation of the objects being sold would be enough in itself. But consumer advertising presents its goods along with other personal and social aspirations, and as Raymond Williams argues:

We have a cultural pattern in which the objects are not enough but must be validated in fantasy by association with social and personal meanings which in a different cultural pattern might be more directly available. (1980, p. 185)

If we were sensibly materialistic, then, as Williams points out,

beer would be enough for us, without the additional promise that in drinking it we show ourselves to be more manly, young in heart or neighbourly. A washing machine would be a useful machine to wash clothes, rather than an indication that we are forward looking or an object of envy to our neighbours. (1980, p. 185)

The reason that we have to be 'magically' induced to buy things through fantasy situations and satisfactions is because advertisers

7

cannot rely on rational argument to sell their goods in sufficient quantity.

The roots of this situation can be traced back to the coming of large-scale industrial production which, since the end of the last century, has been capable not only of supplying us with essential goods but also of swamping us. These goods have to be smoothly and effectively distributed or else the production system would clog up and collapse beneath the weight of surplus and unwanted products. Markets have to be found and created in order to absorb the perpetual flow of goods coming from factories. The producers have to be able to predict demand for goods, so that expensive capital equipment and plant is not risked, factories do not lie idle, and profits fall. Advertising is one of the mechanisms used by modern industrial capitalism to organize and ensure markets for its goods. This has the overall effect of taking decision-making about goods away from customers where it is not subject to control and of shifting it to the producers where it is under their control. Despite the fact that there is an enormous number and range of goods available, the real decisions about products — what should be produced, in what quantity and quality and at what price — lie not with us, the consumers, but with a small and powerful minority of businessmen, industrialists and entrepreneurs — a group which the sociologist C. W. Mills (1956) has aptly called 'the power élite' in his book of that name.

However, advertisers will argue that the great quantity and range of goods produced in a competitive free-market economy guarantees the consumer 'freedom of choice' and that choice is a basic human freedom. But perhaps advertisers are using the words 'choice' and 'freedom' in a rather restricted sense, referring mainly to commodities and meaning no more than a mechanistic reaction to them. Of course on the face of it there are any number of choices to be made in the marketplace. But does the choice that we have to make between ten brands of similar toothpaste really constitute choice and guarantee freedom? And are not the differences between the toothpastes, shampoos, televisions and so on, often trivial and unnecessary? And when it comes down to it, are we, the consumers, ever consulted whether we want toothpaste with blue stripes or green stripes of 'added ingredient X' in the first place? We are offered a 'choice' once all the real decisions about a product have been made. In addition, most commodity manufacturers are organized into conglomerates or monopolies who divide up the market between them and are more interested in profits than in genuine consumer choice. So what looks like a choice between different brands of a commodity on a super-market shelf is not really what it seems, because the different brands are probably produced by one or two manufacturers (who, incidentally, are also possibly involved in a price-fixing cartel which makes prices uncompetitive).

Now of course manufacturers want to produce successful products and do indeed spend a lot of money on market research in order to test consumer preferences and the possible market reaction. In this sense they are influenced by what members of society claim to want and need. But it is more likely that decisions about what goods to produce and market will be influenced more by questions of industrial viability and profit than by questions of longer-term economic stability and social need. If we, the public, were offered a genuine choice of goods and services, then most of us would be perfectly capable of judging private consumption against other pressing priorities, like better health services and schools or more recreational facilities. But our economy is not really geared towards the social services, and our real freedom of choice is by and large sacrificed to the flow of chocolate, shampoos, breakfast cereals and dog foods which gushes out of the factories. Our needs as human beings, our aspirations and weaknesses, can indeed be met by consumer goods when they are aroused by advertisements but these are met at the expense of more pressing, socially-based needs. Advertisers tend to think that consumer choice is equivalent to other kinds of choice and would no doubt be surprised if someone decided that resources should be spent on a new youth club rather than producing yet another kind of shampoo. Producers and consumers are more often than not trapped in the illusion that more and more consumer goods automatically guarantees choice and freedom.

Mass communications

In order to survive, powerful commercial interests must keep in almost constant touch with the mass public and continually try to persuade them. To these ends advertisers use the media of mass communication: commercial television and radio, the national and local press and magazines. Originally advertising was used by news-paper owners as a necessary and manageable support cost. Today it suffuses the whole system of mass communication and some econ-

9

omists argue that the media are in fact not just a part of the economy but its servants. The media convert audiences into markets, and because they exist through 'selling' audiences to advertisers, they generally preclude the services that the media could perform such as providing adequate consumer information to the public.

Advertisements not only influence overall media policy (although this influence is very subtle), they also affect or modify the 'look' of media production. According to Fred Inglis 'What we find [in the media] . . . is the harmonious interaction of advertising and editorial styles; styles which consistently reproduce and endorse the consumer's way of life' (1972, p. 16). Sunday newspaper colour supplements provide a good example of the 'harmonious interaction' between advertisements and feature material. Advertising has increasingly come to dominate presentation on TV; the insertion of adverts into TV programmes has altered the nature of TV as a sequential experience and has created entirely new visual rhythms. As Williams argues, 'it is possible to see TV of this kind as a sequence in which the advertisements are integral rather than as a programme interrupted by adverts' (1974, p. 69).

Many TV commercials consist simply of spoken announcements with an accompanying picture and caption. Those which are networked over the whole nation, rather than transmitted locally or regionally, are usually more complex. They draw on existing styles in print and poster advertising, of course, but also contain more emphasis on visual and aural styles drawn from non-advertising material. The most successful contain:

1. Concentrated dramatic sequences or 'playlets' in which some problem is realized and overcome through the recommendation and use of a branded product. These commercials are often meant to portray 'slices of life' and are similar in style to the kinds of drama common in programmes.
2. Popular/light entertainment sequences — comedy sketches, music and dance routines drawn from variety programmes and TV or film spectaculars.
3. Actors, actresses, celebrities and sports personalities endorsing products in a way that allows their allure or social standing to attach itself to the product. Whether they are 'acting' or being themselves, these famous people perform a dramatic function.
4. Cartoon and animated sequences either borrowed from another

10

source (Walt Disney films for example) or created specially for a product image (remember Esso's cartoon tiger?). Animals, young children and other 'numinous' objects are similarly used in an attempt to place the product in a flattering light.

5. Documentary sequences of everyday life, particularly family life, travelogues and industrial films featuring the use of a product.

Public relations

Whereas advertising is primarily about the selling of goods, general publicity or public relations (PR) has developed into a business for the selling of persons or companies. PR uses many of the same techniques as advertising; the main difference being that advertisements are booked and paid for, whereas PR relies on arranged incidents, spontaneous happenings, product or company anniversaries being reported by the media as ordinary news. The aim of PR is to promote positive and favourable images of people or firms in public life, without actually appearing to do so. Certainly it is difficult to tell the difference between an event or a photograph presented in the ordinary course of professional journalism and one which has been arranged by a publicity agent. Many personality pieces which appear in the popular press have landed there through the offices of a PR agent and their publication is paid for by some means or another — not always with money. Show-business personalities are not the only ones to benefit from this system: PR has entered the literary and political worlds as well. No political campaign is undertaken nowadays without the services of a publicity consultant, a fact, it is argued, that accounts for the rise and success of the Social Democratic Party (SDP) in Britain during 1981.

Although advertising agencies were used to 'sell' Dwight Eisenhower as long ago as the 1952 American presidential election, the coming of television and increasingly sophisticated PR techniques have put the political–PR relationship on a regular footing. The 'publicity boys' rehearse politicians before they go in front of the cameras; they advise on the timing and content of speeches; they stage-manage walkabouts, the opening of buildings, visits to supermarkets and the kissing of babies, all for the benefit of the mass media. Politicians and campaigns are marketed like soap. In the US, politicians can buy time for TV 'spot' commercials during an election campaign, the tones and rhythms of which are barely distinguishable from those of shampoo or laxative ads.

In this introduction I have tried to outline a general critique of advertising within the dominant context of its economics. In the following chapters I shall examine the broad historical context and growth of advertising in relation to the modern capitalist economy. I shall also look at the relationship between modern advertising and the system of mass communication within which it lodges and for which it provides the main impulse.

Chapter 4 is concerned with the persuasive power of advertising and its presumed 'effects'. This is an intriguing aspect of advertising because although we assume it to be powerful it is often difficult to pin down precisely what we mean by the power and influence of advertisements. Advertisers spend a lot of money and time making ads memorable and effective and trying to discover the best way of advertising a product to a particular group. One assumes that on the whole their messages are successful and effective. Social scientists are also interested in the power of advertising and have developed some elaborate methods to test the effectiveness of advertising on individuals and society at large, some of which will be discussed in this chapter.

Even more difficult to answer but probably more important is the question of what advertisements are like. Is life like the pictures that the advertiser creates? Are advertisements mirrors which reflect life? Are they a form of harmless escapism? Do they present an honest and legitimate picture of human values and aspirations? In chapters 5, 6 and 7 we will examine what advertisements say and what devices and techniques they use to appeal to us and get their messages across.

It is not possible in a book of this length to cover every aspect of what is in fact a complex industry and powerful form of social communication. A notable omission is any consideration of the actual work of an advertising agency and the people who make advertisements, the ad executives, the copywriters, the artists, etc. It would be interesting to go behind the scenes, so to speak, to find out how and why ads get made in the way that they do, how much they cost, what considerations influence the 'creative' people, and what advertisers think about their work and about their public.

A great deal of thought, research, planning and money goes into an advertising campaign; probably more than into any comparable form of communication. The purpose of creating advertisements is

12

to persuade and convert potential consumers. Thus advertisements are deliberate and consciously articulated messages. However, as in all forms of human communication, there are bound to be some 'unconscious' aspects of the creative process. That is to say the person who produces or creates an ad will not think in minute detail about every single word or image that goes into it. He or she takes for granted some things about communication assuming that the audience will understand the ad's message because both communicator and receiver share a common culture or common frame of reference. The advertiser employs language, images, ideas and values drawn from the culture, and assembles a message which is fed back into the culture. Both communicator and receiver are products of the culture — they share its meanings. However, compared to an average citizen, advertisers are in a position of considerable power. They spend a lot of time and money on the production of advertisements. They also have access to powerful channels of mass communication, unlike most of us. And although they draw on common assumptions and meanings, and reflect trends, popular types and the social scene, they do not draw on reality in any simple way. Producing an advertisement involves a mixture of market research, 'professional' skill, personal knowledge, and intuition, particularly the last. Advertisers might feel they are in touch with consumers, but they tend to be selective about the 'reality' they portray and present the values and ideals most familiar to them. Like anyone in a body of professionals in contemporary society, an advertiser works in a narrow world; he or she is circumscribed by the standards of a close-knit body of workers within the ad world or agency, which is a particular inward-looking social sub-group within metropolitan cities. Ads are usually highly selective and stereotypical; certain ideas and styles are emphasized or reinforced, others are ignored. The implicit message in most ads is 'this is how things/you should be'. They present what appears to be, without argument, the only ideal and desirable way of living. They *define* what is style and what is good taste, not as possibilities or suggestions, but as unquestionably desirable goals. The world of ads is the world of the carefree and the well-off as seen through the eyes of the advertisers. This small group has become the arbiter and judge of taste and the messenger for the 'good life'.

In the bibliography I have suggested some sources of information and reference material on the subject of advertising agencies, professional advertisers and planning advertising campaigns. Appendix IV contains tables and codes of practice used by the professionals. Readers will probably find that these sections give some insight into the world of advertising and provide guidelines for the analysis of advertisements themselves.

Ads are an inescapable and powerful part of our environment. Some are banal, others attractive, entertaining and amusing. It might be worth your considering what life would be like without them.

It is important to remember that however attractive or amusing ads are, they perform both economic and ideological functions in our society. Even if we don't actually believe what they say about this or that product, their influence is nevertheless strong. Advertisements provide pictures of reality and define the kinds of people we could be and the kind of lives we could lead. It is hard to break with the values and ideals supplied by advertisements although there are signs that some groups — and I am thinking particularly of the women's movement — are trying to campaign against the worst forms of misrepresentation in ads. It is doubtful whether advertising can accommodate criticism of its way of communicating other than in small, superficial ways. It is a powerful tool of existing economic and social relations and as such has to purvey the values which perpetuate and endorse the current socio-economic structure — a structure which frequently pays scant regard to alternative values such as a fairer redistribution of resources and power in society, and the ways of achieving this; ways which could be more humane and democratic and less wasteful of valuable resources.

1 THE ORIGINS AND DEVELOPMENT OF ADVERTISING

In order to understand advertising as a form of communication and as an influential social institution, it is important to see it as part of an historical and social process firmly linked to the economies of western industrialized nations. Modern advertising is effectively no more than a hundred years old, dating from a period when the capitalist system of production underwent major changes. Before this time advertising was a relatively simple system of proclamation and announcement on the periphery of the national economy. Today advertising is an enormous and highly organized institution controlling vast sums of money, highly profitable in its own terms as well as being a vital component of capitalist economies. In order to understand the social meaning of advertising and assess its place in modern society, we need to look at why and how it has developed from a simple to a sophisticated system of communication from the few (the producers) to the many (the consumers).

Mercuries and newsheets

Advertising is consistent with most types of human society and in fact was not unknown in ancient Greece and Rome. The public crier, who shouted out the wares of local traders and shopkeepers, was a well-known figure in medieval times. But advertising as we recognize it did not start until the seventeenth century. It was at about this time that newspapers began to circulate, although broadsides and

15

newsbooks had occasionally been produced in the Elizabethan era. By the middle of the seventeenth century newsheets or mercuries, as they were sometimes called, began to appear on a regular basis in the large towns of Britain. Merchants and traders needed regular information on prices, stocks, imports and exports and access to the new 'middle-class' readership whose appetite for news had been stimulated by the Thirty Years' War in Europe. The mercuries contained some foreign news, shipping timetables, lists of imports and exports and small announcements from booksellers, wig-makers and merchants. These announcements became increasingly important to the newsheets and in some were displayed prominently. During the English Civil War the demand for 'news' increased and more mercuries appeared under a variety of extravagant titles. As well as news and announcements of the recent publication of books (by, among others, John Milton), mercuries carried notices for the markets and fairs popular at the time. If one looks at these notices, one finds a frequent preoccupation with the freaks and human curiosities who were put on public display and whose deformities were relished by audiences of the time. Mercuries also printed ads for lost horses and runaway slaves, and offered rewards for their capture. Perhaps the most significant ads, however, were those for the earliest patent medicines and 'miraculous' cures. These looked like what today we would call classified or small ads.

The range and type of advertisement began to change from about the middle of the seventeenth century. The following notice, which appeared in a *Mercurius Politicus* of 1658, reflects this change, being much more direct and less restrained than ads before this time.

> That excellent, and by all Physicians, approved China drink, called by the Chineans Tcha, by other nations Tay, alias Tee, is sold at The Sultaness Head Cophee-House, in Sweetings' Rents by the Royal Exchange, London.

And even more enthusiastic is this advertisement of 1660 for tooth-paste:

> Most excellent and approved Dentifrice to scour and cleanse the Teeth, making them white as ivory, preserves from the Tooth-ach; so that being constantly used, the Parties using it are never troubled with the Tooth-ach; It fastens the Teeth, sweetens the Breath, and preserves the Gums and Mouth from cankers and Impothumes;

... and the right are only to be had at Thomas Rookes, Stationer

The reference to 'Physicians' and glowing phrases such as 'most excellent and approved' make this ad very similar to some of today's. Indeed, these early examples of advertising rhetoric should really be seen as part of a process of development from conventional recommendation to contemporary examples of persuasion and propaganda.

In England, the 1665 plague gave a considerable boost to the sales of patent medicines. Street posters and handbills proliferated which harangued the public into buying 'infallible preventative pills', 'never failing Preservatives against Infection', 'Sovereign cordials against the Corruption of the air', 'Anti-pestilencial Pills' and 'The Only True Plague-water'.

In the eighteenth century the number of people who could read grew steadily, as did the time available to do so among the middle and leisured classes. The newspaper and publishing trades flourished and in 1702 the first daily newspaper in Britain, *The Daily Courant*, appeared. 'Social' journalism came next, aimed particularly at women readers — the *Tatler* was first published in 1709 and the *Spectator* in 1711. The volume of advertising in newspapers increased despite the introduction in 1712 of an advertisement tax which was imposed by the government of the day with the aim of curbing the activities of the press. Each advertisement, whether it was a line or a column long, was charged one shilling, and if this was not paid within thirty days the charge was trebled. Many publications closed as a result of this tax and also because of the imposition of a newspaper stamp duty.

Advertisements of the time were still printed and laid out like classifieds and were rarely illustrated. On the whole they were directed at the wealthy clients of the coffee houses where the newspapers were available. A typical newspaper would carry ads for wigs, tea, coffee, books, wine, lottery and theatre tickets — and of course the inevitable purges and 'cosmatiks'. It was very rare to see ordinary household goods advertised, although there were offers to engage servants and slaves. In plate 1 you can see a typical range of ads of the time taken from eighteenth-century journals and mercuries.

In order to attract a reader's attention, the advertisers would occasionally use simple illustrative devices. For instance, sailing announcements might display a small woodcut of a ship at the top

17

To the A R M Y.

Gentlemen,

HAVING had the Honour of ferving thirteen Years, I am encouraged by many of my military Friends and Acquaintance to entreat your Protection and Support, to carry into Execution a Plan I have long formed to facilitate Promotions throughout the Army. By Means of a well eftablifhed and regular Correfpondence, I flatter myfelf that I fhall be able to procure the beft Intelligence refpecting Vacancies, wherefoever they happen, in his Majefty's Dominions; fo that thofe who may be difpofed to purchafe, fell, exchange, retire from Full to Half Pay, or quit the Service, fhall have immediate Opportunities of entering into Treaty with each other, without the ufual, though unneceffary, Delays, and the Terms be known only to the Parties concerned.

Such Gentlemen as honour me with their Commands, will find Punctuality and Defpatch at the Military Promotion Office, No. 8, Suffolk-Street, Charing-Crofs, where Letterc (Poft paid) will be inftantly attended to, by,

Genttemen,

Your moft obedient, and moft humble Servant,

London, Jan. 1, 1782.   JAMES BURNE.

TRENT NAVIGATION.
Bell Inn, Carlton upon Trent,
Friday, Jan. 4, 1782.

AT a Meeting of the Proprietors of Land, on the Banks of the River Trent, for the Purpofe of taking into Confideration, a Plan propofed to them " For improving the Navigation of the faid River, between Wilden Ferry and Gainfborough, by removing the Shoals therein, and allowing the Navigators the Liberty of towing their Boats with Horfes, &c."

P R E S E N T.

Lord George Sutton	felf and Sir W. Anderfon, Bt.
Sir Gers. Clifton, Bart.	Mr. Fletcher, for his Grace
Anthony Eyre, Efq.	the Duke of Portland
George Nevile, Efq.	Mr. Falkner, for Pen. Neale,

Plate 1 A range of typical announcements for different products, taken from eighteenth-century newsheets

(a) from *St James Chronicle* or *British Evening Post*, 17–19 January 1782

WANTED, at the School of Armagh, in Ireland,

An ASSISTANT, who muſt be a member of one of the Engliſh Univerſities, and well acquainted with the Greek and Latin Languages.

Eighty Pounds a year will be given to a perſon who can produce ſufficient teſtimonials of his abilities and good conduct.

Other particulars may be known, by applying to the Rev. Mr. Carpendale, at Armagh.

LIFE ANNUITIES.

PROPOSALS for granting a TONTINE or LIFE ANNUITIES, to increaſe by ſurvivorſhip, in ſhares of 100l. each, adapted to all ages, and to be ſecured on a very large Freehold Eſtate, may be had of Meſſ. Ranſom, Morland, and Hammerſley, Bankers, in Pall-Mall; Mr. Morgan, at the Equitable Aſſurance Office, near Black-friars-Bridge; of Mr. Lock, Tokenhouſe-Yard; and of Meſſ. Shepheard and Gibbon, Solicitors, No. 10, Boſwell-Court, near Lincoln's-Inn; at all which places a book is opened to enter the names of perſons willing to ſubſcribe.

M U S I C K.

A Young man, between 17 and 18 years of age, would be glad to engage himſelf as an aſſiſtant to a Cathedral Organiſt, having been bred very early to that duty, and has done the whole of it occaſionally four years in a Cathedral of great repute. He expects very little more than his board and lodging with the gentleman who employs him, for his attending the Cathedral duty.

N. B. A Cathedral would be preferred, but no particular objection will be made to parochial duty, &c. within 150 Miles of London.

Letters, poſt-paid, to Mr. Ireland, No. 29, Surrey-ſtreet, will be duely anſwered,

---

GLAMORGAN SOCIETY.

For the Encouragement of Agriculture, &c.

TWENTY GUINEAS will be given to the owner of the beſt, ſtrong, active BAY STALLION, fit for hunting or the road, not more than ſeven years old, that ſhall be produced at the Bear, at Cowbridge, on Friday the 1ſt of May next, at Two o'Clock, and attend ſuch markets as the Society ſhall then appoint, during May and June, and cover at one Guinea each mare for the ſeaſon.

The Members of the Society are requeſted to attend, and the Majority then preſent are to adjudge the ſaid premium.

JOHN FRANKLEN, Treaſurer.

Lanmihangle, March 25, 1789.

(b) from *St James Chronicle*, 4–7 April 1789

MARRIED.] Thursday, at South Lutten-
ham, Rutlandshire, Edward Boodle, Esq. of
Brook-street, Grosvenor-square, to Miss Cle-
mentson.

DIED.] Monday, Mr. J. K. Sherwin, En-
graver to his Majesty and the Prince of Wales.

St. THOMAS's HOSPITAL.

MR. CLINE will begin his COURSE of
ANATOMICAL and SURGICAL LECTURES,
on Friday, the 1st of October, at One o'Clock.

STOLEN or STRAYED, out of the grounds
of JOHN CAVE, Fletching, Sussex, on Friday night,
the 17th of September, 1790,

An aged CHESNUT GELDING, about thirteen hands
and a half high, of the saddle kind, strongish made, some
white down his face, and a snip on his nose, is full eyed, has
not been nicked.

Whoever will give information of the said horse, so that
he may be had again, if strayed, shall be paid One Guinea
reward, and reasonable Charges—if stolen, on conviction of
the Offender or Offenders, shall be paid a reward of Three
Guineas.

By JOHN CAVE.

N. B. The shoes are marked B.

NEW WORKS.

Will be published the first of next month, in quarto, to
be continued monthly, No. I. (containing three interesting
prints, and an engraved tittle) of

THE ELEGANT REPOSITORY,

AND

NEW-PRINT MAGAZINE,

Including Engravings, from original Pictures, of the most
pleasing Subjects furnished by the arts of Design. Price 1s.

2. No. I. of The ADVENTURES of TELEMACHUS,
Son of Ulysses, from the French of Fenelon, Archbishop of
Cambray. To be compleated during 1791, in 25 octavo
numbers, each containing one book, and a most elegant
print, price Sixpence.—N. B. A very excellent edition in
4to, 1s. each No.

3. No. I. of SURVEYS of NATURE, Historical, Moral,
and Entertaining, exhibiting the principls of Natural Science, and Natural History in various Branches; with near
200 plates, small quarto, complete in 32 numbers, One
Shilling each. Second edition.

(c) from *St James Chronicle*, 23–5 September 1790
(d) from *Aris's Birmingham Gazette*, 11 March 1799

4. *No.* I. The ARTISTS REPOSITORY, and *Drawing Magazine*, exhibiting the polite Arts in the moſt familiar Manner, with 250 plates. Complete in 39 numbers, or One Shilling each. Fourth edition.

5. No. I. of The CABINET of GENIUS, complete in 42 numbers, One Shilling each. Tenth edition.

6. A firſt pair of elegant Hiſtorical Engravings, ovals, from deſigns by Shelley. Price Half-a-Crown.

⁎ May be had any numbers together, weekly or monthly.

London, printed for C. TAYLOR, No. 10, Holborn: and ſold by N. Rollaſon, Printer and may be had of his Newſmen.

Propoſals at large may be had of all Bookſellers and Printſellers; where alſo the works may be ſeen.

This is Day publiſhed, Prit 6d. to be continued weekly.

No. I. OF THE

WONDERS of the LITTLE WORLD;

OR, A

General Hiſtory of Man.

DISPLAYING the various Faculties, Capacities, Powers and Defects of the Human Body and Mind, in ſeveral thouſand moſt intereſting Relations of Perſons remarkable for *Bodily Perfections* or *Defects;* or for the extraordinary *Virtues* or *Vices* of the *Mind;* or the uncommon *Powers* or *Weakneſs* of the *Senſes* and *Affections.*

Together with Accounts of the *Invention* of *Arts;* the *Advancement* of *Science;* ſurpriſing *Eſcapes* from *Death* and *Danger; Strange Diſcoveries* of long-concealed *Murders:* And a vaſt Variety of other Matters equally curious.

Forming a complete *Syſtem* of the *Mental* and *Corporeal Powers* and *Defects* of *Human Nature.*

The whole collected from the Writings of the moſt approved Hiſtorians, Philoſophers, and Phyſicians, of all Ages and Countries.

By NATHANIEL WANLEY,

Late A. M. and Vicar of Trinity Pariſh Coventry.

LONDON: Publiſhed by R. FAULDER, Bookſeller to his Majeſty, New Bond-ſtreet; E. JEFFERY, Warwickſtreet, Golden-Square; T. THORNTON, Southampton-ſtreet, Strand; and C. TAYLOR, No 10, oppoſite Brook-ſtreet, Holborn; ſold by N. Rollaſon, Printer, and may be had of his Newſmen.

The acknowledged Merit of Mr. WANLEY's Work (the only one of the Kind ever attempted in any Language) renders Encomium unneceſſary. It forms a complete Epitome of Univerſal Hiſtory, the Reſult of more than Forty Years laborious Reſearch; in which every Thing extraordinary that could be collected relative to MAN or WOMAN, is exhibited in the greateſt Variety of wonderful Relations ever ſelected; comprehending a moſt copious Fund of Knowledge, and furniſhing inexhauſtible Matter for amuſing and inſtructive Converſation.

By the very great Quantity given in each Number the Whole will be compriſed in thirty two; in the Courſe of which will be given ſix very highly finiſhed Copper-plates, the expence of one of which would defray that of ſeven of thoſe uſually given.—They will form a complete Set of Subjects, and if framed will make a moſt elegant Decoration to the firſt Drawing-Room in the Kingdom.

of a poster or small ad, and the minute figure of a man looking over his shoulder might be placed at the head of a runaway notice. The eighteenth-century essayist Joseph Addison, commenting on these devices, remarked

> Asterisks and Hands were formerly of great use for this purpose. Of late years the N.B. has been much in Fashion; as also were Cuts and Figures, the invention of which we must ascribe to the author of Spring Trusses. I must not here omit the blind Italian character, which being scarce legible always fixes and detains the eye and gives the curious reader something like the satisfaction of prying in a secret. (quoted in Turner, 1952, p. 26).

The drawing of an anodyne necklace (plate 2) comes from an ad for the cure of children's 'fits', 'fevers' and 'convulsions'. Another famous eighteenth-century figure, the critic and humorist Dr Johnson, accused a similar ad, which 'warned every mother that she would never forgive herself if her infant should perish without a necklace', of trying to scare mothers into buying the product (a tactic not unknown today).

Dr Johnson was generally critical of the growth in advertising and of the methods which were beginning to be used to appeal to the public. 'They are very negligently perused', he said of advertisements, '. . . and it is therefore become necessary to gain attention by magnificence of promises, and by eloquence sometimes sublime and sometimes pathetic. *Promise, large Promise is the soul of an advertisement . . .*' (quoted in Turner, 1952, p. 30). He also wrote that 'the trade of advertising is now so near to perfection that it is not easy to propose any improvement' (ibid.) a judgement not borne out by the extent to which advertising has developed since his time. Johnson appealed for higher standards and more truth in advertisements, and was particularly concerned about the practice among advertisers of 'censoring [their] neighbours', a practice which today would possibly be called 'knocking copy'. Addison, too, noted how rival merchants accused each other of 'base impositions' and 'fallacious subterfuges'.

However, by today's standards most ads were straightforward and informative. Their style and language tended to be formal, respectful and ceremonious as can be seen in this advertisement from *The Times* of 1788, placed there by a retailer of imported goods:

Vickery respectfully informs the ladies that he has now for sale

Plate 2 An eighteenth-century advertisement (from *Fog's Weekly Journal*, 20 November 1736)

The PROPRIETOR of

LEAKE's PATENT PILLS,

So long, and so justly celebrated for their superior Efficacy in curing VENEREAL, SCORBUTIC and CUTANEOUS AFFECTIONS, submits the following Letter to an impartial Public.

Little Wenlock, near *Bridgnorth*, *Shropshire*,
SIR, *May* 14, 1788.

A Friend of mine has long been infected with the Venereal Disease, insomuch, that he has not been able to get out of his Bed for these five Years, notwithstanding he has been Salivated, and every Means used by many learned Men of the Faculty, but all their Endeavours were without Effect. At length, hearing your most Excellent, indeed, I think Incomparable PILULA SALUTARIA, I advised him to try it, and in the Course of a Month, this poor emaciated Wretch was restored to perfect Health.

I think it Justice to you, and indeed to all Mankind, to make this public for their Benefit, if ever any of them should be afflicted with the like Disorder.

I am,
With the utmost Respect and Gratitude,
Sir,
Your most obedient,
And obliged humble Servant,
HENRY BATEMAN.

The above Medicine is prepared and sold by the sole Proprietor, Thomas Taylor, Member of the Corporation of Surgeons, London, at his House, No. 9, New Bridge-Street, where he will give Advice, without a Fee, to Persons taking these Pills, and will answer Patients Letters, if Post paid, on the same Terms, observing in all Cases the most inviolable Secrecy.

N. B. Two back Doors, and Lights in the Passages at Night.

They are also sold by his Appointment, for the Convenience of those living at a Distance, by N. ROLLASON, Printer of this Paper, opposite the End of Broad-Gate; Mess. Pearson and Rollason, Birmingham; Morgan, Litchfield; Gregory, Leicester; Harrold, Harborough; Marshall, Northampton; Cullingworth, Daventry; Sharp, Warwick; by one Person in every considerable Town in England, and may be had of the Newsmen. In Boxes of 2s. 9d. each, sealed up, with copious Directions, whereby Patients of either Sex may cure themselves

Plate 3 'Quack' eighteenth-century advertisements (from *Coventry Mercury*, 14 February 1791)

For DISORDERS of the HEAD,

The CEPHALICK SNUFF.

WHICH has been found by long Experience a very grateful and effectual Remedy for most Disorders of the Head, especially the common Head-Ach. It removes Drowsiness, Giddiness, and Vapours; relieves Dimness of Sight; is excellent in curing recent Deafness; and has been of great service in hysterick and paralytick Complaints; as also in restoring the Memory when impaired by Disorders of the Head. Persons who visit the Sick, unhealthy Places, or Hot Climates, will find this Snuff an admirable preventive of Infection; and it is particularly serviceable in those Complaints of the Head which Painters, &c. are subject to. Those also who take much of the common Snuffs, may prevent their bad effects by mixing with them a proportion of this excellent Cephalick.

It is sold by F. Newbery, at the only Warehouse for Dr. James's Powder, No. 45, at the East-end of St. Paul's, nearest Cheapside, London—and by B. C. Collins, at Salisbury; in Bottles, Price 7½d each. And as a security against Counterfeits, the Name of F. Newbery is engraved in all the Stamp Lables, by Order of the Commissioners of the Stamp Office. No others are genuine.

FREAKE's TINCTURE of BARK.

THIS Tincture contains every active property of the BARK, divested of its woody fibres (which are so apt to overload the stomach); and is found to be far more efficacious than any other preparation.—It may be given in smaller quantities than are usually prescribed of other tinctures; it often succeeds when other forms fail; and it is peculiarly serviceable in curing Agues, Putrid Fevers, Nervous Complaints, and all others for which the Bark is so celebrated.

The following CASE will be a proof of its superior Efficacy.

"Mrs. HOLLINWORTH, aged 68, about a year ago was inclined to a Dropfy—after using proper remedies for that complaint, she remained extremely relaxed, and was desired to take the bark; but that medicine, neither in substance, nor in any of the usual preparations, would fit easy on her stomach, and she was therefore advised by her physician to try FREAKE's TINCTURE. This perfectly agreed with her; and after taking two or three bottles, she was so much relieved as to induce her to continue it till she recovered. Since that time she had occasion to make use of it again, and with the same good effect as before; and she thinks it her duty to give this publick testimony, with the earnest desire that such a valuable Medicine may be more generally known.

"Newman-Street, No. 85,
"March 27, 1790."

Sold by A. Freake, Apothecary, No. 3, Tottenham-Court-Road; and by F. Newbery, at the only warehouse for Dr. JAMES's POWDER, No. 45, St. Paul's Church-Yard, London, in bottles, Price 4s. each, duty included, or the quantity of six bottles in one for a Guinea.

25

By his MAJESTY's LETTERS PATENT,

Leake's PILULA SALUTARIA ;

Or, SOVEREIGN REMEDY

In all VENEREAL and SCORBUTIC DISORDERS

For the Efficacy of this Medicine, the Public are referred to the following recent Case.

(C O P Y.)

GARRETT IVORY, now living at Mr. Clarke's, No. 1, Church-lane, Strand, had laboured under a Veneral Complaint seven years, for which he underwent a variety of means, and was at length salivated, but without effect. After the latter operation he was seized within the space of a few weeks with a most violent pain in all his limbs, a dreadful oppression of the stomach, general angour, total loss of appetite, and such agonies in the night, as not only entirely derived him of rest, but emaciated him in such a degree, that he could not even walk without support. He was then an In and Out Patient in several hospitals, without deriving any essential benefit, and on his dismission from one of them, was assured that every probable means had been tried, which reduced the unhappy sufferer to a state of despair. In this truly deplorable situation he applied to the proprietor of LEAKE's PATENT PILL, and to his great surprize as well as comfort, found himself after taking one box able to walk without support ; and in the course of three boxes the pains gradually subsided, the oppression of the stomach was removed, his appetite restored, and his health re-established ; insomuch that he now follows his business with usual alacrity, and is in every respect perfectly re-covered.

May 16, 1774.   GARRETT IVORY.

Witnesses to the Cure,

WM. COOLING, Shoemaker, Church-Lane, Strand.
ISAAC SILCOCK, Glazier, Church-Court, St. Martin's in the Fields.

N. B. Many others might be referred to for attestation ; but it is presumed the cure is too well known to need enumeration of witnesses.---The patient was put under no restraint or confinement during the whole course.

Sold in Boxes of 2s. 6d. each at the Patentee's, in Bride-Lane, Fleet-Street, London ; and by Appointment sold by Mr. Piercy, Bookseller, in Coventry ; Mr. Keating, Stratford and Warwick ; Mr. Marshall, Druggist, Northampton ; Mr. Wilcox, Bookseller, in Towcester, and on Market-Days at his Shop in Stoney-Stratford ; Mr. Clay, Bookseller, in Daventry, and on Market-Days at his Shops in Rugby and Lutterworth ; Mr. Aris, Printer, Birmingham ; Mr. Morgan, Bookseller, in Lichfield ; Mr. Gamble, Grocer, in Leicester ; Mr. Harrod, Book-seller, in Harborough ; and may be had of the Newsmen with proper Directions sealed up.

A NEW MEDICINE.

BEAUME DE SANTE,

For Coughs, Colds, Catarrhs, Asthmas, &c.

THE publication of this celebrated Medicine is owing to its unexampled success in very extensive practice; as it never failed in a single instance, where Medicine could afford relief. It effectually removes every recent Asthmatic or Consumptive Affection of the LUNGS; immediately allays that Tickling Sensation which occasions continual Coughing and Restless Nights, and speedily eradicates every stage of the HOOPING-COUGH.

It is a Medicine elegant in its composition, pleasant to the palate, grateful to the stomach, and certain in its effect. The dose to a grown person but a Teaspoonful, for a child a few drops.

A very few doses will cure a common COLD.

The BEAUME DE SANTE, with copious instructions for using it, is sold in bottles, at half a crown each, by J. Bew, No. 28, Paternoster-row; W. Davis, Piccadilly; and W. Davenhill, No. 30, Cornhill: Sold likewise at Oxford, Cambridge, Bath, York, the Printers of this Paper, and by one Person in most of the capital towns in England.

N. B. Sold wholesale by J. Bew only.

SUBLATA CAUSA, TOLLITUR EFFECTUS.

MR. HARPUR, at the Right Hon. Lord ROBERT BERTIE's had been afflicted with the confirmed STONE in the BLADDER many years, and had taken almost every medicine commonly prescribed in such cases without any good effect, as he had at times suffered such excruciating torture as rendered his life extreemly burthensome. in this melancholy condition he reflected on the operation of the knife, but was advised (though with great reluctance) first to try ADAMS's SOLVENT, and by taking only three bottles, he was a great deal better: as he began to discharge the rough Lamina of the stone which enabled him to walk with but little pain, and by continuing the medicine sometime longer, the stone was entirely dissolved, and he can now ride fifty miles a day, with as much ease as if he never had the stone. Besides the above, and many other astonishing cures effected by the Solvent, any person desirous may be referred to one of the first Dukes, and other noble Personages of this kingdom, as testimonals of its efficacy and safety to the most tender constitutions. Sold in bottles at 10s. 6d. and 5s. 6d. by the Proprietor, in Argyle-street, three doors from Oxford-street; and to exempt the Proprietor from the imputation of an empiric, he has certificates from St. Thomas's Hospital, and Dr. Mackenzie and Smith. For a further account of its operation and cures, see the Fourth Edition of his Disquisition, price 2s. Two bottles only will frequently cure the Gravel, and prevent the Stone.

The above Medicine is sold by the Printers of this Paper, and may be had of the Newsmen.

an extensive and admirable assortment of Transparent Tetes. . . .
The taste, fancy, elegance, convenience and accomodation of
these articles have already rendered them the greatest favourites
of every court of Europe and of numbers in Asia, Africa and
America. . . . Ladies who order these beautiful articles are requested
to describe whether for young, middle-aged or elderly ladies.

It is worth remembering that the eighteenth century was an age
of quacks, 'empirics' and tricksters. These were men who enjoyed a
considerable influence and social standing. They both made and
peddled an alarming variety of pills, purges, solvents and elixirs for
which extravagant claims were made. The quacks attracted attention
to their wares by indulging in the most repulsive details of the
diseases and scourges they claimed to be able to cure. Their promises
were matched by spurious testimonials elicited from miraculously-
cured sufferers, who were preferably 'dukes and other noble personages of this kingdom'. The use of snob appeal and 'puffs' can be seen
in the copy of the ads in plate 3.

No lesser claims were made for tobaccos and snuffs which were
said to be good for the 'Head, Eyes, Stomach, Lungs, Rheumatism
and Gout, Thickness of Hearing, Head-ach, Tooth-ach or Vapours'.
And it was even alleged that a person 'may never come to wear
spectacles' if he used a certain tobacco. The quacks were to have a
lasting impact on advertising, and subsequent generations of advertisers have perfected the art of puffery and persuasion. By the end of
the eighteenth century the quacks were on their way to giving advertising what the critic Raymond Williams has wryly described as a
'more specialized meaning' (1980, p. 172).

An 'all-deafening blast of puffery'

'Classified' types of advertising continued well into the nineteenth
century, but the use of handbills and street posters increased. Billposting was in fact a large and organized trade; both men and vehicles
were hired to display boards and posters. Later in the century advertisers even used hot-air balloons to advertise their products. Although
the newspaper ads of the time were discreet by today's standards
and confined to specific sections of a publication, some traders felt
that it was not respectable to advertise. One local newspaper stated
in 1859 that 'Advertising is resorted to for the purposes of intro-

28

ducing inferior articles into the market', and Thomas Carlyle, writing in 1843, disapproved of what he called the 'all-deafening blast of puffery' (quoted in Turner, 1952, p. 55). He argued that advertising was against nature and ungentlemanly and that a 'hat-maker' is degrading himself if he speaks of 'his excellence and prowesses and supremacy in his craft'.

During the 1800s there was, of course, an expansion in trade and a substantial increase in manufacturing. The abolition of the advertisement tax in 1853 and the newspaper stamp duty two years later, resulted in a growth in the volume of advertising and an increase in newspaper circulation. By this time advertisers were beginning to pay a bit more attention to the design and lay-out of their ads. Long sentences, superfluous linking passages and the generally long-winded style of eighteenth-century advertising language were being replaced by words set out in blocks, more spacing between sentences and by contrasting type sizes. The playbills published by theatres in the early nineteenth century show how advertisers were becoming aware of the need to communicate quickly and decisively. The 'art' of copywriting also sprang to life, making a noteworthy contribution to the language in the coining and inventing of new words.

Clumsy Latin compound words and Greek neologisms were especially popular. No doubt the public were impressed to know that teeth could be filled with 'mineral marmoratum' or 'mineral succedaneum', that a raincoat was a 'siphonias', and hair cream an 'aromatic regenerator'. There was also Rypophagon Soap, Olden's Eukeirogenion, Elme's Arcanum and Winn's Anticardium. Traders even hired poets to write stanzas in praise of their products, and one boasted in an ad that 'we keep a poet'. A saucemaker 'kept' a poet who produced the following lines:

> The goose that on our Ock's green shore
> Thrives to the size of the Albatross
> Is twice the goose it was before
> When washed with Neighbour Goodman's sauce.

The following piece of florid prose was written in 1843 for Parr's Life Pills:

The spring and fall of the leaf has been always remarked as the periods when disease, if it be lurking in the system, is sure to show itself. The coldness of winter renders torpid the acrimonious fluids of the body and in this state of inactivity their evil to the system is not perceived; but at the spring these are aroused, and if not checked mix up and circulate in the blood, and thus the whole system is contaminated. . .

Another favourite device of advertisers was the fashion of printing some eye-catching statement in bold type, followed by the remainder of the message in smaller type, thus:

A Beautiful Young Girl Strangled
a cry of admiration when she saw our new blouses

or:

The Duke of Wellington Shot
a glance of admiration at our hats

The majority of advertisements still came from local traders, and in tone and style they were very similar to those of the eighteenth century. However, a more general kind of household product was beginning to come onto the market. The first nationally advertised product was probably Warren's Shoe Blacking, followed by Rowland's Macassar Oil, Spencer's Liquid Hair Dye and Morrison's Universal Pill. The techniques used to promote these products had been pioneered by the eighteenth-century quacks, but the use of 'puffs' was extended. The crowned heads of Europe and all ranks of nobility were being signed up to give testimonials – the Tsar of Russia recommended the use of Revalenta Arabica while an ad for the Balm of Syriacum boasted that it was used in Queen Victoria's household.

The break-up of the column lay-out in newspapers

Advertising steadily expanded from 1850 to the end of the century. After the newspaper stamp duty was dropped in 1855, the circulation of newspapers increased and many new ones were founded. Newspaper editors were on the whole reluctant to open their papers to new-style advertisements, particularly to those which were designed to extend beyond the width of a standard newspaper column as it was thought that they would disrupt the design of the page. The more persistent 'quacks' pressed editors to abandon column rules and to take 'display' ads, featuring large, black typefaces and even pictures of 'voluptuous' women. Some editors argued, as it turned out quite rightly, that this type of advertisement would possibly favour bigger traders at the expense of the smaller ones.

Ingenious, if tedious, methods were employed by some manufacturers to exploit and no doubt ridicule the editor's fear of bold type and display lay-out. For example, some advertisements consisted exclusively of repetitions of a firm's name or its product, and the repeat could run for as many as one thousand lines:

John Smith and Son
John Smith and Son
John Smith and Son
John Smith and Son

Phrases were printed in small type in eye-catching patterns which still preserved the column rule. In response *The Times*, for one, imposed a rule against the endless repetition of words or phrases. Each line had to have some description after it. There then followed a spate of advertisements like this one:

Rossetter's Hair Restorer
                    is not a dye
Rossetter's Hair Restorer
                    contains no oil
Rossetter's Hair Restorer
                    prevents hair falling
Rossetter's Hair Restorer
                    promotes the growth of hair

Another trick was to build up large capital letters out of groupings of smaller letters:

```
TTTTTTT    HH      HH    EEEEE
TTTTTTT    HH      HH    EE
   TT      HHHHHHH       EEEE
   TT      HHHHHHH       EEEE
   TT      HH      HH    EE
   TT      HH      HH    EEEEE
```

The names of products could be spelt out using this method. For instance CUTICURA was spelt out one letter to a column across the top of an eight-column page of a paper, and subsidiary headings were constructed on a smaller scale. A trader might even demand that his product be shaped by letters in his advertisements. Thus a hatter could have a hat made out of letters, the oculist, a pair of spectacles.

Because they faced restrictions in the columns of the press, many manufacturers turned to outdoor advertising where there were no such limitations on their creativity and ingenuity. At one time in London billposting was so popular that it seemed you might never get to see a building at all. The following quotation is a description of billstickers in the 1850s.

> The billstickers never heeded the notices to beware, and cared nothing for the privacy of 'dead walls', or, for the matter of that, of dwelling houses or street doors. Though he himself was rarely seen, his disfiguring work was a prominent feature of the metropolis. Early morning was his busy time, and if he could cover up the work of a rival, so much the better . . . (Quoted in Marland, 1974).

Slogans and catch phrases

In the US there were no newspaper or advertising taxes so the press grew swiftly during the eighteenth century. Newspapers cost less than in Britain and sometimes over half the space was devoted to advertising. At the beginning of the nineteenth century most advertisements were largely like those in Britain; for sailing departures and arrivals, books, plays, patent medicines, and also for the slave trade. There were also restrictions on large type and multiple-column displays in American newspapers. One publisher grew exasperated at this and decided to extend the technique of repetition he had seen in *The Times* of London. He leased entire pages in a rival newspaper (he never advertised in his own), filling the columns with repetitious phrases. Sometimes he bought a whole page only to leave it blank in order to attract the reader's attention. On occasions he would even fill the pages with the opening chapter of a new serial story, cutting it off at the crucial moment and then notifying the reader that the continuation could be found in *his* paper.

Typographical restrictions and the ban on illustrations were lifted by most American newspapers by 1895, so the vogue of repetition, no longer needed, died out. Compared to their British counterparts, American advertisers used more colloquial, personal and informal language to address the customer and also exploited the uses of humour to attract attention to a product. New-style department stores grew rapidly in America from the 1850s onwards and quickly became large advertisers. Later, manufacturers of the new patent foods and mechanical inventions joined them as major advertisers.

As the device of repetition became more and more unfashionable, advertisers had to think of new ways of attracting the public's interest; they turned to the invention and use of slogans and catch-phrases. Two of the more unforgettable, if primitive, British examples of such devices were Beecham's pills' 'Worth a Guinea a Box' and Pears Soap's 'Good Morning! Have you used Pears soap?' In America the habit was no less effective: Kodak's 'You press the button we do the rest' proved to be memorable, while a slogan for Ivory soap boasted: 'It floats — It's 99 44/100ths pure!'

Bubbles

The food processing industry was launched around the middle of the nineteenth century and thanks to advertising, names like Bovril, Nestlé, Cadbury, Fry and Kellogg soon became household words. Like their predecessors in the pills and potion trade, the patent food advertisers also used testimonials from famous people of the day, and they went to a great deal of trouble to stress the pure and healthy nature of their products.

On the heels of the new foods came such mechanical inventions as bicycles, sewing-machines and typewriters and these too were advertised widely but with more restraint than the patent foods.

Because advertising was expanding so rapidly in the new products area, the advertisers of older products like soaps and pills were forced into thinking up fresh ideas for their advertisements. A & F Pears, for instance, one of the pioneers of catch-phrases, decided to use more extended campaigns for their soap. The company hoped that by constantly repeating the name of the product and the catch-phrases in the press and on public hoardings, the public would 'automatically' ask for Pears when they went into a shop to buy a tablet of soap. Pears also used riddles and puzzles to catch the attention of readers: plate 4 comes from a Pears annual, a publication started in 1891 to bring reproductions of paintings, serialized stories and of course advertising to the public.

Two important trends in advertising emerged in the 1880s. First, a number of advertising agencies transferred their loyalty from the newspaper to the advertiser. The agencies had originally established

A CONUNDRUM.

Question :

What is the difference between

and an Arab Steed ?

Answer :

One washes the Beautiful, and the other Scours the Plain.

Plate 4 A Pears conundrum (from *'Bubbles': Early Advertising Art From A. & F. Pears Ltd*, edited by Mike Dempsey, 1978).

themselves in small shop premises with the purpose of selling space for the newspapers. However, the increase in the number of newspapers during this period made the manufacturer's job very difficult because he had no way of knowing who the readers of the paper were nor, indeed, if his ads were reaching the right potential customer. But if the advertiser channelled his work through a specialist agency, the latter was able to assess the usefulness of a particular publication and feed this information back to the client.

This new breed of agent tried to convince reluctant traders and publishers of the benefits of agencies. One of them, Samuel Deacon, urged newspaper proprietors to announce their circulation figures (a move which does, of course, benefit advertisers), thus starting a campaign that was to last fifty years.

The second trend that emerged at this time was that some editors decided to relax their strict rule about single columns and began to allow display ads in their papers. Larger typefaces were used and the ads sometimes spanned two or more columns. Towards the end of the century even *The Times* was permitting advertisements onto their pages 'in type which three years ago would have been considered fit only for street hoardings' (quoted in Turner, 1952, p. 153).

Newspaper editors must have been influenced by the many street posters to be found lining the streets of Victorian England, and also by the introduction of illustrated advertisements in the magazines from the 1880s onwards. Some of these ads would look crude to us today but others established features which are still used. One rather stilted technique was the inclusion of the name of a product or a slogan into the drawing of the people or the setting in the ad itself. So there were many ads where the lettering ran along the edge of a table cloth or along the bottom of curtains and the product's name could even be found printed on the bare chest of a woman. One famous ad of the day, the Borax nude, showed the naked figure of a woman rising from waves, brandishing a wand at unclean shapes labelled 'disease' and 'decay'. She was called the 'Spirit of Purity' in order to counter any criticism of her nudity. Just as today, pictures of scantily dressed young women were used to advertise a whole variety of products ranging from combinations to cigarettes.

Established painters also contributed to the 'art' of publicity although, unlike in France where poster art was highly regarded, British artists were initially unwilling to venture into the world of commerce. In 1886 A. & F. Pears bought a picture by Sir John Everett Millais, who was unquestionably the richest and most popular painter in late Victorian England. The company wanted it for their exclusive use in promoting Pears soap. The painting was, of course, 'Bubbles' (see plate 5). Millais was apprehensive about the commercial use of his work but warmed to the idea because of the quality of the engraving Pears intended to reproduce. Many members of the public were hostile to this prostitution of art, and as late as 1899, three years after Millais's death, *The Times* still carried letters on the 'debate'.

Pears spent £30,000 on the 'Bubbles' campaign and, even today,

Plate 5 'Bubbles' by Sir John Everett Millais

the picture is one of the most instantly recognizable advertising symbols ever devised. This was perhaps the first example of advertising which associated a product with (high) culture (represented by Bubbles who, incidentally, was the artist's grandson). It is a combination which characterized the Pears image for many years. The company brought out the Pears annual until 1920. Much of its material would strike us as unashamedly sentimental. However, Pears were astutely catering for contemporary taste, and indeed children, animals, flowers and young women are still the common denominators of advertising appeal.

By the end of the nineteenth century advertising had reached new heights of boldness and confidence — not to say impertinence. Whereas ads in journals had previously been confined to special sections, they now proliferated throughout the pages. Many people were shocked to find theatre safety curtains displaying ads. Buildings disappeared behind outdoor hoardings and an American patent food company even had the audacity to erect a signboard halfway up the white cliffs of Dover. The writer Rudyard Kipling voiced the annoyance of many people when he accused railway stations of 'the beplastering of railway platforms with every piece of information in the world except the name of the station' (in Turner, 1965).

Partly as a response to these developments and to the many advertising eyesores and publicity stunts, the Society for the Checking of Abuses in Public Advertising (SCAPA) was founded in 1898. The crusade of SCAPA was instrumental in defining the now familiar arguments between the defenders of 'taste' and the 'needs' of commerce. But just as the battle 'for' and 'against' advertising was gathering momentum, the very nature of the object of their passions was radically changing.

Suggestions for further work

1. It is interesting to compare older style advertisements with contemporary examples although it is not always easy to get hold of old ads. If you are interested in rummaging around junk shops or secondhand bookshops you might be able to find some old magazines, newspapers or posters; even train tickets, trade cards and book markers used to carry ads. Some museums have exhibits of advertising ephemera.

Other sources of historical material There are surprisingly few books on the history of advertising but the History of Advertising Trust (see p. 214) is an educational foundation and a useful source of information and material. The trust has compiled a catalogue and index of significant advertising material. Some of the larger companies keep collections of their old advertisements (A. & F. Pears, for instance, have a collection of their early publicity), and advertising agencies sometimes keep examples of their earlier work. The British Newspaper Archive (Colindale Newspaper Library, Colindale Avenue, London NW9) keeps a collection of old newspapers so this is also a useful place to go to look at advertisements.

2. If you can get some older ads, study their design and layout and the methods used to persuade potential customers.
3. Compare some early examples of patent medicine advertising with today's. How similar are they? What are their lines of appeal? Compare how the images of women in ads have changed over the years.
4. Consider the most significant changes that occurred in the nine-teenth century which affected the purpose and face of advertising.

2 THE NEW ADVERTISING

Fundamental and far-reaching changes in the British economy, which were responsible for the transformation of advertising, took place at the end of the nineteenth century.

Organizing the market

During the early stages of the Industrial Revolution, advertising was a relatively straightforward means of announcement and communication and was used mainly to promote novelties and fringe products. But when factory production got into full swing and new products, e.g. processed foods, came onto the market, national advertising campaigns and brand-naming of products became necessary. Before large-scale factory production, the typical manufacturing unit had been small and adaptable and the task of distributing and selling goods had largely been undertaken by wholesalers. The small non-specialized factory which did not rely on massive investment in machinery had been flexible enough to adapt its production according to changes in public demand.

But the economic depression which lasted from 1873 to 1894 marked a turning point between the old method of industrial organization and distribution and the new. From the beginning of the nineteenth century until the 1870s, production had steadily expanded and there had been a corresponding growth in retail outlets. But the depression brought on a crisis of over-production and under-

39

consumption — manufactured goods piled up unsold and prices and profits fell. Towards the end of the century many of the small industrial firms realized that they would be in a better position to weather economic depressions and slumps if they combined with other small businesses and widened the range of goods they produced so that all their eggs were not in one basket. They also realized that they would have to take steps to ensure that once their goods had been produced there was a market for them. This period ushered in the first phase of what economists now call 'monopoly capitalism', which, roughly speaking, refers to the control of the market by a small number of giant, conglomerate enterprises.[1] Whereas previously competitive trading had been conducted by small rival firms, after the depression the larger manufacturing units and combines relied more and more on mass advertising to promote their new range of products.

A good example of the changes that occurred in manufacture and distribution at the turn of the century can be found in the soap trade. From about the 1850s the market had been flooded with anonymous bars of soap, produced by hundreds of small manufacturers and distributed by wholesalers and by door-to-door sellers. Competition grew steadily throughout the latter half of the century and eventually the leading companies embarked on more aggressive selling methods in order to take custom away from their rivals. For instance, the future Lord Leverhulme decided to 'brand' his soap by selling it in distinctive packages in order to facilitate recognition and encourage customer loyalty. In the 1880s, Pears were spending between £30,000 and £40,000 a year on advertising and in the 1890s they and Lever Brothers spent £100,000. In 1907 this figure had risen to nearly £500,000 a year but by 1919 the 'soap war' had died down with the merger of the leading companies.

Lord Leverhulme was one of the first industrialists to realize that advertisements should contain 'logical and considered' arguments as well as eye-catching and witty slogans. Many advertisers followed his lead and started to include 'reason-why' copy in their ads. For instance, one contemporary Pears soap ad went into great detail about how the product could enhance marital bliss by cutting down the time the wife had to spend with her arms in a bowl of frothy suds. And an ad for Cadbury's cocoa not only proclaimed its purity but also detailed other benefits: 'for the infant it is a delight and a support; for the young girl, a source of healthy vigour; for the young miss in her teens a valuable aid to development . . .' and so on. As the writer E. S. Turner rightly points out, the advertising of this period had reached the 'stage of persuasion as distinct from proclamation or iteration' (1952, p. 133). Indeed, advertise or bust seemed to be the rule of the day as bigger and more expensive campaigns were mounted and smaller firms who did not, or could not, advertise, were squeezed or bought out by the larger companies.

New inventions were entering the market at a rapid rate during the early years of the twentieth century and were introduced and popularized by advertising. Among them were the first motor cars, although these were not widely advertised until Henry Ford extended his publicity methods to the British market. Perhaps the most expensive and chauvinistic campaign of this period was one launched in 1901 by leading British cigarette companies under threat from the American Tobacco Company. One advertisement in this tobacco war covered four pages in the *Star* newspaper and boasted that it was the 'most costly, colossal and convincing advertisement ever used in an evening newspaper the wide world o'er'. One of its slogans was:

> Don't be gulled by Yankee Bluff
> Support John Bull with every Puff

The American firms retaliated and the campaign was a long and costly one. It was another early example of what has become one of the persistent features of advertising and marketing — the ad war.

The rise of popular journalism

Around the turn of the century advertising expanded rapidly alongside other innovations in marketing and trading. The new advertising agencies benefited from this growth, and revelled in their new found status and importance. By the beginning of the twentieth century they were offering a more comprehensive service to manufacturers than just selling space in newspapers, although some agencies continued to do this. However, they were hindered by the fact that the newspaper publishers were still reluctant to announce the net sales of their papers and so agents could not advise their clients as to which newspaper or magazine reached the greatest number of people. In 1900 the Advertisers' Protection Society was formed in order to bring more influence to bear on newspaper publishers, as well as to help the construction of better campaigns and to defend advertising against the attacks of critics like SCAPA.

41

Varied consumer goods, especially foodstuffs, were flowing into the country from abroad and, at home, manufacture was expanding further which meant that the traders' and producers' need for mass markets became increasingly urgent. So they turned to the ideal medium of communication — the mass popular press.

A number of popular papers and periodicals had been launched during the second half of the nineteenth century, helped by the Education Act of 1870 which raised the level of literacy in Britain considerably. In order to attract readers in a highly competitive market, the newspaper owners devised all sorts of gimmicks and publicity stunts. Competitions and treasure hunts became popular and the serialization of stories also proved to be a good method of capturing and keeping an audience. By 1900 the *Daily Mail* had reached a circulation of 700,000 and the *News of the World* 1,250,000. But the cost of producing newspapers was rising and many proprietors turned to advertising for an 'independent' source of finance and support. Alfred Harmsworth, later Lord Northcliffe, was a pioneer in this respect, and very early in the century he decided that advertising was 'news' in itself. The front page of his *Daily Mail* was soon devoted to display advertisements, particularly from drapery shops and the new department stores. It was not unusual to see pictures in the papers of women parading underwear and 'combinations'. Advertising proved such a useful source of revenue that Northcliffe — sometimes called 'the innocent genius of newspapers' — decided that through it he could reduce the price of his newspaper and thereby increase sales (despite the fact that he had reservations about the 'vulgar' drapery ads). He also decided to publish the *Daily Mail*'s circulation figures and challenged other newspaper proprietors to do the same. In doing this he effectively ushered in the industrialization of the British press and altered its entire financial base. From this time newspapers have become increasingly dependent on advertisements for revenue.

This period was a particularly buoyant one for the popular press. Printing techniques were improved, readership expanded and the new railways made the national distribution of daily newspapers possible for the first time. The less formal style of American journalism was beginning to be adopted by British journalists, and this together with the other developments made a great impact on the advertising trade.

'Daddy, what did you do in the Great War?'

As the twentieth century progressed, advertising moved nearer to the centre of the nation's economy, discarding its marginal and 'amateur' status on the way. People were even talking of advertising as a 'profession' and a 'public service'. New ways of appealing to and persuading people, many of them based on American techniques, were adopted, including the use of the new 'science' of psychology. For instance, a branch of psychology based on the principle of human instinct provided advertisers with the technique of 'association'. An American 'instinct' psychologist gave this piece of advice to advertisers:

> an advertisement should be presented in such a way that a reader would associate it with his own experience, which was best done by appealing to his ruling interests and motives. These included the desire to be healthy, to hoard, to possess, to wear smart clothes, to get something for nothing, to be more like the privileged and successful classes. (in Turner, 1952)

He stressed that advertisements should be cheerful, and products should be linked to prosperity, social status and attractiveness. These 'positive', idealized ads drew this sarcastic comment from the magazine *The New York Evening Post* in 1909: 'In the literary pages (of magazines) the world is the worst of all possible worlds, in the advertising supplements it is the best of all conceivable worlds.' Psychologists also suggested that advertisers use scare tactics to motivate people.

Psychological methods were also used to great effect during the First World War to recruit volunteers to the armed services. There are many famous posters deriving from this period; perhaps the most celebrated is the one entitled 'Daddy, what did you do in the Great War?' (plate 6). As a poster it is simple but effective, and is a great contrast to the crudely drawn and jingoistic 'Yankee Bluff' ad mentioned earlier and the mawkish and sentimental ads used by Pears. The drawing of the family group is detailed and closely observed — the little girl on her father's lap and the boy playing with toy soldiers on the carpet at his feet. The scene is domestic and not only represents an appeal to patriotism but also plays on basic human relationships and anxieties. Having aroused these anxieties and potential guilt feelings, the poster offers the message that they can be relieved by

Plate 6 Using psychology

joining up and helping to win the war in order to preserve the family values portrayed.

The never-never

With the end of the war in 1918, the factories once again turned their attention to the production of consumer goods. In America, more reliable cars became available by the thousand, as did radio sets, refrigerators, washing machines, and water closets. One way of getting people to buy vast quantities of goods, and thus to close the gap between the rate of industrial growth and people's purchasing power, was to offer credit and allow people to purchase things by instalment. But this did not really make long-term, life-long consumers out of people, so more manipulative methods had to be devised. People had to be made to feel guilty if they did not buy a new car or radio set, and were taught that it was unpatriotic not to discard things every year in order to buy the latest model of any item.

Advertisers had learnt a lot from the propaganda posters of the First World War and after the war they joined forces with the forces of management and social psychology to create a new generation of consumers in order that the wheels of industry could keep turning. One way of getting people interested in consumer commodities was to make them dissatisfied with themselves and to play on their insecurities. An American advertising trade journal of the 1920s summed up the advertiser's task in this statement: 'Satisfied customers are not as profitable as discontented ones'. The advertisements of the 1920s in America encouraged self-criticism and distrust: 'sneaker smell', 'paralysed pores', 'vacation knees', 'office hips', 'underarm offence' and 'ashtray breath' had Americans running to the nearest store for the latest preventative or cure. The public were taught through the ads that they could consume their way out of any trouble or misfortune, real or invented. And set against the afflictions that could visit people day and night, and untrustworthy friends and neighbours, the advertisers posed the paternalistic corporation as a substitute friend and family. A critic of the advertising of the period, Stuart Ewen, remarks: 'The authority of industry was being drawn as a sustaining father figure while traditional areas of social intercourse and the possibility of collective action were pictured as decrepit, threatening and basically incapable of providing any level of security' (1976, p. 102). The 1920s was a period overshadowed by 'patriarchal corporatism' and 'Fordism', terms used by the Italian social critic Antonio Gramsci (1971) to describe how industrialists entered into and directed the nation's family matters. Ford had pioneered not only the mass production of the motor car but also the extension of industrial authority over family relations. Many industrialists of this period assumed a right to administer family life in order to bring it into line with the demands of industrial production.

The power of business corporations and the new advertising techniques did not escape public criticism. The advertising industry responded with attempts to regulate its activities but by and large these efforts were mere window dressing because misleading assertions, deceptions and psychological manipulation continued. A code of ethics drawn up by the International Advertising Corporation (IAC) in 1924 pledged the industry to 'seek the truth and live it', a maxim taken very seriously by some ads: a New York department store proclaimed 'Gimbels Tells the Whole Truth'.

Fearing that advertising might be getting a bad name, the industry launched a campaign to advertise advertising. One example of this campaign which appeared in *Life* magazine in 1925 featured a young man saying 'I begin to see that it's advertising that makes America hum. It gives ginks like me a goal. . . . I guess one reason there is so much success in America is because there is so much advertising — for things to want — for things to work for.'

The nerve war

The economic depression of the late 1920s and 1930s meant that manufacture was cut back again and consequently the activities of many advertisers as well. But for some, business flourished because this was a period of 'nerve warfare'. At a time of economic gloom and uncertainty, the pedlars of nerve tonics, vitamin pills and mouthwashes came into their own. And the nerve war gave advertisers plenty of scope for their talents of invention: readers were told of the dangers of contracting hitherto unknown conditions such as 'halitosis', 'summer sluggishness', 'tell-tale tongue', 'listlessness', 'night starvation' and 'body odour'. The ads were often as lurid and exaggerated as the 'quack' advertising of the eighteenth century and were filled with pseudo-scientific argument. People were sent into a frenzy over threats to health, jobs, marriages and social status and words like 'protection' and 'confidence' took on new meanings. Plate 7 is a compilation of ads from the period all using the theme of bodily functions or 'dysfunctions'.

In Britain the advertisers appealed to patriotism and guilt. This scolding address was made to readers of *The Times* in 1920:

Do you know that
nearly £10,000,000 was spent last year
by our own people in these Islands for
FOREIGN MOTOR PRODUCTS?
A colossal loss to British trade and British Workers
No government can cure unemployment
if this sort of thing goes on
Do you realize this? You should.

The following notice appeared in *Advertisers Weekly* in 1931. It was from the producers of a tonic wine and displayed a somewhat cynical attitude to the nation's plight.

Rising unemployment figures, it seemed, were inevitably reducing our market; yet we refused to be intimidated by this. Consideration of the matter showed that even those who drew unemployment benefit represented a potential market and one likely to be productive enough if approached in the right way. So instead of neglecting the unemployed, we visualized them as a prospective market of 2,500,000 people.

There seemed to be no limit to the virtues of tonic wine. It could recreate married bliss, patch up quarrels, end nagging, etc.

The growing effrontery and absurdity of many ads drew the scorn of critics and writers of the 1930s. Even advertising men were disillusioned with the sensationalist and unscrupulous practices of some colleagues. The American magazine *Ballyhoo*, published in the early 1930s, was launched as a response to inflated advertising. It debunked the world of advertisers and among other attempts at ridicule it gave a glossary of advertising terms which included the following:

Delicate membrane   any part of the body
Lubricate the skin texture put on grease

Plate 7 A selection of advertisements from the 1920s and 1930s (from *The World of Small Ads*, Lippa and Newton (1979))

Pore-deep cleansing	washing the face
Harsh irritants	all the ingredients of a competitor's product
Great scientist	anyone who will sign an endorsement
Lifetime	until the new model comes in
Exclusive	expensive

A number of muckraking books were published in the 1930s which aimed to expose the tricks of advertising and alert the public to its 'confident absurdities'. By way of response to the criticism and the satire, many ads of the day began to display a certain kind of self mockery and cynicism. Raymond Williams sums up this development in his comment on

> the development of knowing, sophisticated, humorous advertising, which acknowledged the scepticism and made claims either casual or offhand or so ludicrously exaggerated as to include the critical response. Thus it became possible to 'know all the arguments' against advertising, and yet accept or write pieces of charming copy (1980, p. 181).

In Britain, so desperate were advertisers to attract the public that many revitalized the older methods of the 'quack' and the sandwich-board men. In America, advertising copywriters turned their skills to inventing their own language, or 'word magic'. In many cases it replaced the words of the English language that copywriters had previously devalued. Tight skirts were described as 'stem-slim classics of lethal grace . . . panther-sleek and fabulously disciplined'; lace was 'a wicked whisper'; there were 'moonstruck rayons' and 'parody-pearls trilling with pride'. More irritating was the advertiser's habit of using baby talk to describe various food products. Words like 'yummy', 'tangy', 'zippy', 'chewy', 'crispy', 'crunchy' or 'Krispy' and 'Krunchy' littered magazine copy. Hyphenated words like 'jiffy-quick', 'oven-hot' and 'sun-sweet' became all the rage. Stretch became s-t-r-e-t-c-h, cool became c-o-o-l; eating became an adjective as in 'a wonderful eating cheese' and then, not surprisingly perhaps, 'eatingest' appeared in some copy.

As the depression eased some advertisers decided that the only way to gain or regain a reputation and to stimulate interest in advertising was to offer an additional service. Borrowing techniques from sociology and psychology, advertisers tried to persuade their clients that market research was a way of ensuring that their money was 'scientifically' spent. The initial impetus for market research came from doubts over the 'readability' of word magic which, some said, had been written to please the seller not the buyer. Readability tests were devised to find out if word magic was easy or difficult to read, and consumers were recruited to test advertising copy for memorability, emotional arousal, credibility, etc. Market research was also beginning to be used to test and measure media/advertising influence and consumer motivations.

By the end of the 1930s advertising had become an accepted adjunct of the national economy. But the advertising of patent medicines still gave cause for concern. The advertising industry, mindful of its reputation, decided to clean up or throw out some of its more dubious associates. In both America and Britain, legislation was passed during the subsequent decade, designed to curtail or ban misleading and dangerous advertisements, especially those for drugs and patent medicines.

The home front

Nevertheless, the Second World War provided the advertisers of tonic wines, aspirins and bed-time drinks with a field day. 'War worry' and 'black-out nerves' had to be conquered and the home front had to be kept brave and cheerful. The advertisement for 'peace-time sleep' (plate 8) is typical in that it plays on a number of wartime themes. The reader is asked if she is 'war-proofed', the graph illustrates the need for 'scientifically sound sleep', and added to all this, the drink would help 'Mr Churchill' in the war effort. Wireless manufacturers, too, played on the nation's patriotism; one ad urged people to buy radios to prove their 'freedom to listen'.

Many ads of the war era stressed economy and self-denial. Readers were told to 'wage war on waste', to 'go easy with . . .', to 'save . . .', and 'please use . . . sparingly'. Firms boasted of their own efforts and sacrifices in order to encourage their customers. Campaigns were launched to make the best use of resources and materials in short supply, which included anything from paper and rags to fats and metals. Men were encouraged to use certain long-lasting razor blades and help save the nation's steel. A Rinso soap ad announced 'if

Plate 8 'Peace-time sleep'

BLACKOUTS WON'T GET YOU DOWN—ONCE YOU'VE BOUGHT A TIN OF

'Peace-time Sleep'

OH, I'M SICK OF ALL THIS!

Depression is a sign too, of ILLNESS — nerve-illness. Sound sleep is the greatest nerve-doctor of them all.

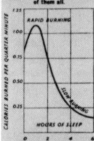

Are you war-proofed?

This chart shows how in the early restless hours of sleep you are burning up energy at a high rate. If your nerves aren't sound this persists all night — you wake up feeling a rag — it's done you no good, and it won't do for war-time. *Moral* : Take Bourn-vita. Start to-night.

Fortify your nerves for a reasonable price

If you wake up feeling like a duck in a desert you won't be much help to Mr. Churchill in 'uplifting the downcast'. Come on, brace up, put your nerves in order with a sound, natural sleep every night.

Scientifically sound sleep — not a tossing and turning half-insomnia, *nor* a drugged unconsciousness — is Nature's nerve-builder. Are you sleeping properly ?

You *can*. 'Peace-time Sleep' is helped by *Bourn-vita* — and at the same time *Bourn-vita* has Phosphorus, Calcium, Vitamin B — and these are all nerve-restoratives.

9d PER ½ LB

1/5 PER ? LB

CADBURY'S BOURN-VITA

Still at PEACE-TIME Price

everybody can prolong the life of garments by only one third then reduced supply will meet all our needs'. An American poster urged people to 'Save waste fats for explosives. Take them to your meat dealer'. Food ads invariably provided hints and recipes to make rationed food go further. Housewives were instructed how to make cakes without eggs, to make one rasher of bacon go round the whole family, to save gas and electricity in their cooking and to cook emergency meals for a hundred people in an air-raid shelter!

Since women were so vital to the economy outside, as well as inside, the home during the war, their advertising images underwent a fundamental change. Instead of being shown as passive consumers mainly interested in their appearance and the shine on their furniture, women in wartime ads were depicted more realistically as bus drivers, factory workers and air-raid wardens, thus reflecting their dual roles as workers and as mothers and wives. Products such as soap, convenience foods and household gadgets were offered as a source of help to busy women rather than as avenues to greater social status or as a means of relieving guilt feelings.

In 1945 women were urged to return to domestic life to make way for returning soldiers whose jobs they had been filling. The advertisements for commercial products in the post-war period reflected this campaign. For instance, the 'one-job' woman was a popular theme in advertisements. One for Milk of Magnesia showed a woman looking cheerfully at the viewer and saying 'I'm clocking in at home'. 'Glamour is returning', warbled an ad for handcream. There was a return to ads depicting women in their domestic role usually looking directly out at the consumer from the picture; the ads during wartime had invariably shown women concentrating on their work and unconcerned about the spectator's gaze. Perhaps the transition from peace to wartime stereotype and back again can best be seen in a series of ads for Macleans' toothpaste. Before the war the image of the woman in Macleans' ads showed her as a docile secretary; during the war she was represented as a munitions worker (replying to the question 'Did you Maclean your teeth today?' with 'Yes, and I always shell!'); after the war she was shown looking contented and glamorous, baking a cake.

If wartime brought a check to the rapidly expanding industry of advertising, the post-war period changed all that, for the 1950s brought a spectacular extension of advertising, the mass media and the commodity market generally. It is with some irony that we can look at a statement made in a book published during the war by a critic of advertising, Denys Thompson:

> advertising as we know it may be dispensed with after the war. We are getting on very well with a greatly diminished volume of advertising in wartime, and it is difficult to envisage a return to the 1919–39 conditions in which publicity proliferated. (in Williams, 1980)

Contrary to Thompson's assertion, advertising has in fact proliferated since the war. Consumer goods flooded onto the market with the arrival of the post-war 'affluent' society and the mass-media channels expanded accordingly in order to cope with the demands of the advertisers. Although we should not glorify the austerities of war nor be particularly nostalgic for the days when there were genuine hardships, it is hard not to be alarmed at the expansion of advertising in recent years and the degree to which we have grown to accept it without question. We ought, perhaps, to consider if it is possible to get on 'with a greatly diminished volume of advertising'.

Note

1. See Baran and Sweezey (1968) for a detailed explanation of this term.

Suggestions for further work

1. In what way could advertising be said to have changed the structure and function of the British press since the turn of the century? (There are quite a few books on the history of the press which are worth consulting: J. Curran (1981), *Power and Responsibility*, or Golding (1974), *The Mass Media*, are two easily available works.)
2. Do you consider the First World War poster mentioned in chapter 2 to be unreasonable? Are the same appeals used today to attract volunteers to the armed services? Look at the visual and verbal imagery of today's ads for the army, navy and airforce. What are the underlying messages of these ads? You might also look at ads for nursing.
3. Can you spot any psychological tactics in the ads of today? Do ads play on our insecurities and our desire to be accepted and popular? Do they undermine our own sense of self and self-

confidence like the American ads of the 1920s mentioned in this chapter? In this respect you could try to get hold of some American magazines and compare their ads with those for similar products in British magazines. Are the lines of appeal broadly similar?

4. Can you spot any tactics used in advertisements today that relate to or are indicative of the general economic climate? (The Sunday newspaper colour supplements might be a good source of material.)

5. Make a glossary of terms used in advertisements of today similar to the glossary mentioned in this chapter. Ads for cars or beauty products might be a good place to start. List the words or phrases on one side of a piece of paper and what you think they really mean on the other.

6. During the Second World War, the stereotypical image of women in ads changed from one which depicted the woman as a 'passive object' to one showing her in different, more industrial roles. What kind of stereotyped women do you find in ads today? How do you think they differ from those in wartime ads? What accounts for differing images of women in different historical periods?

3 THE NEW MEDIA

After the Second World War, advertising expanded rapidly alongside the media of mass communication. New methods of persuasion emerged and the field extended to embrace more market and motivational research, organized publicity of all kinds, various applications of computer software and hardware and a variety of non-media techniques of promotion. It has been estimated that by the end of the 1980s, advertising's total world billings could exceed 300 billion dollars. And in a special feature in the *Financial Times* (15 October 1980), one advertiser declared that for the most part, face-to-face selling has disappeared.

Post-war developments

From 1940 to 1956 there was statutory newsprint rationing in Britain due to a shortage of paper. When this rationing was at its most severe, national newspapers shrank to less than a quarter of their pre-war size, which meant a considerable cut-back in advertising in the national newspapers; regional newspapers and magazines escaped the worst of the controls. During the affluence of the post-Second-World-War boom, the consumer market expanded, new agencies were founded and scores of new products, particularly domestic durables (like washing machines) and non-durable products (like convenience foods), were launched. One of the most popular if notorious weapons in the ad man's arsenal during the 1950s was motivational, or depth, analysis.

Among the promotional methods established during this period and still much used by advertisers was the product jingle — an often irritating if effective catch-phrase or piece of verse set to a catchy tune, such as the immortal: 'Murray Mints, Murray Mints/Too good to hurry mints.' The jingle was first used in commercial sound broadcasting during the 1930s in the US and was quickly adopted by television advertisers on both sides of the Atlantic after the war. Famous pieces of music are often used to back jingles and well established musicians and lyric writers often write (anonymously) for advertising. Writing verse for publicity has a noble ancestry for it is claimed that the poet Byron wrote verse for Warren's shoe blacking in the nineteenth century. And today many authors (including the winner of the 1981 Booker Prize for fiction) write or have written copy for ads.

Advertising has become an international enterprise over the past thirty years. Today the mecca of the advertising industry is Madison Avenue in New York, and its agencies, or empire, stretch all over the world. Many ads originate in the US and are then exported to other countries where they may be slightly modified to suit local circumstances. The twelve biggest agencies in America are the same which make up the world's top twelve agencies. In Britain, France, West Germany, Canada and Australia over half of the ad agencies are owned by or are subsidiaries of one of the large American agencies. In many European, Asian and South-American countries, the top agency is a branch of an American one.

During the 1950s and 1960s there was a boom in women's periodicals; this paralleled the boom in domestic consumption and the vast amount of advertising which accompanied it. The focus of attention in these magazines and their ads has been the domestic role of women and home values. A further area of expansion and diversification of consumption which opened up during this time was clothes and make-up and in the 1960s came the growth of the teenage market and the emergence of many teenage and 'young set' glossy magazines.

However, perhaps the most significant aspect of post-war advertising was caused by the coming of television.

Television

Two major changes in British broadcasting occurred after the war. First, television replaced radio as the major broadcasting medium, and second, an alternative commercial network was born and has since expanded rapidly. Advertisers were not slow to recognize the potential of broadcasting as an advertising medium. In most developed countries of the west, radio and television are as widespread and available as any other public utility such as water, gas or electricity. They offer advertisers access to a vast audience of potential consumers, and in the case of television, the combination of sound and vision ensures the message great force and impact.

In Britain radio and television were set up as public-service systems, similar to nationalized industries. The concept of public-service broadcasting was extended from radio (set up under Royal Charter in 1927) to television, which started a regular service in 1936. The first Director-general of the BBC—John Reith—was anxious that broadcasting in Britain be founded on a tradition of public service rather than public exploitation, arguing that 'the serving of public interest and the serving of financial interest are not normally fully compatible'.

The BBC's monopoly of broadcast frequencies lasted until 1955 in the case of television, and until the 1970s in the case of radio, when several independent local radio stations financed by commercial interests were developed to broadcast alongside the BBC national and regional services. The BBC's monopoly of television was broken after a fierce campaign by financial, commercial and political interests, in and outside parliament. The campaign against the BBC was helped by what was generally considered to be the BBC stuffiness, aloofness and resentment of any criticism of its established role as 'voice of the nation' — an image which gave rise to the nickname 'Aunty'. After much debate and heart-searching, the forces of commerce and 'enterprise' won and the Independent Television Authority (ITA) (later to become the Independent Broadcasting Authority (IBA)) was set up in 1954 by Act of Parliament, 'to provide television broadcasting services additional to those of the BBC and of high quality'. Its network of production companies, or programme contractors, went into operation the following year.

Commercial television

The adjective 'independent' in the ITA's title was resented by many people at the BBC who regarded themselves as truly independent since they did not depend on commercial interests for revenue. Commercial television's programmes are not provided by the IBA, whose function is to manage the transmitters and exercise overall control of the statute. Programme-making franchises are allocated to consortia who bid for the licence to broadcast. (In the words of the late Lord Thomson, a former owner of *The Times* and chairman of Scottish Television, such a commercial television franchise is 'a licence to print money'.) For this right, the programme companies pay the IBA a fee for the rental of transmission facilities.

The contractors draw their income (including profits) from commercial advertising. In order to attract advertisers, the companies must attract audiences, the programmes (with different degrees of success) acting as the bait. Advertisers buy slots of air time for their 'spot' messages which go out in the programmes' 'natural breaks'. The more people that are attracted to programmes and thus delivered to advertisers, the more the contractors and the advertisers like it. The cost of air time on television (see Appendix II) depends on the time of programme transmission, the type of programme and the potential volume of viewers. And this is where audience research comes in, for if it can be proven that there is a substantial audience for a particular programme, then the advertiser considers it money well spent to reach its members. To buy the attention of each thousand viewers, the advertiser has to pay 'the cost per thousand'. This notion is central to the running of commercial television. The TV company tries to attract the largest possible audience for which it can charge the advertiser a high cost per thousand. This can sometimes mean that programmes more likely to attract a 'mass' audience get produced more often than programmes of a more specialized or 'difficult' nature, which are consequently either less frequently produced or banished to an unfavourable spot in the schedule, such as Sunday morning. So although pressure from advertising is by no means overt, it *is* a factor in commerical programming and scheduling policy. However, the situation is much more cut-throat in American television than in the British or European systems of broadcasting.

Aware of the excesses of American television advertising, western

European countries have laid down controls which limit the amount and type of advertising. For instance, advertisements are not allowed to occupy more than six minutes per programme hour on the British commercial networks. (Advertisements are not allowed during religious or royal ceremonies and are not meant to deal with political or religious issues.) The American model allows much greater freedom to advertisers. Competition for advertising is particularly intense between the three main TV networks in the US and there is a consequent drive for the maximum audience at all times.

Safeguards were built into the British 1954 Television Act which forbids any form of advertising sponsorship other than 'spot' announcements. One clause in the Act says: 'nothing shall be included in any programme broadcast by the Authority . . . which states, suggests or implies . . . that any part of any programme . . . has been supplied or suggested by any advertiser'. The dangers of American-style sponsorship lie in the fact that having paid for a TV programme or series the sponsor might also wish to influence editorial matters or aspects of programme content. Sponsors could insist that they and their products are favourably treated or at least immune from criticism in a programme. They might also bring pressure to bear on producers not to alienate any potential customers. In any country as socially, culturally, racially and religiously mixed as the US, this is almost − but not quite − impossible, which explains why the kind of television that has emerged in the US is by and large of the blandest and most superficial nature. It aims not to upset any group or sectional interest, particularly not the sponsor. No wonder then that Americans call their television the 'boob (meaning a simpleton or fool) tube'. Networks and stations which are constantly chasing dollars are anxious to avoid upsetting anyone who might demand the right to 'reply time', which has to be donated 'free' to the complainant.

Direct intervention and instructions to producers and writers is not unknown in the American broadcasting system and guidelines have been issued by sponsoring companies to broadcasters in order that their product or service be seen in a positive light. However, over the years sponsors have rarely found it necessary to exercise a veto, ask for changes or withdraw sponsorship from programmes or series. The producers and writers involved have become attuned to a sponsor's wishes and are well aware of what is acceptable or uncontroversial. As Erik Barnouw (1978) has commented in his book on broadcasting sponsorship, 'The tamed artist was perhaps

59

as ominous a phenomenon as the vetoing sponsor' (p. 54).[1]

Not only do advertisers on British and American television want large audience figures or ratings, but the audience that TV provides must be of the right age and socio-economic group. In a word, advertisers want audiences with purchasing power. Sometimes programmes have been taken off the screen because the audience, although large, was not the kind which was in a financial position to buy the products advertised. Some programmes, probably quite important ones, never even reach TV screens in America because of lack of sponsorship.

Commercials appear much more frequently on American TV than on the commercial channels in Britain. Often the dividing line between normal programme material and commercial messages from programme sponsors is extremely thin. For instance, on some programmes the host/interviewer/master of ceremonies will 'plug' products as if it was part of his act. Such direct plugs by programme personnel are not allowed on British TV, where commercials have to be, in the words of the Television Act, 'clearly distinguishable as such and recognizably separate from the rest of the programme'. The one case of a programme which blurred the distinction between programme and advertising matter by mixing plugs with supposedly disinterested consumer advice ('Jim's Inn'), was removed from British TV screens following criticism of the format in the Pilkington Report on broadcasting published in 1962.

The current system of 'spot' commercial messages on British TV insulates the programme makers from direct influence by advertisers on programme content. Advertisers do know in advance what the programme schedules are going to be and are able to select space for their commercials next to specific programmes. Programmes can therefore be chosen on the basis that their content might complement a particular advertising campaign. In practice this does not happen very often. Where commercials and programmes do harmonize (an ad for a perfume with a romantic drama for example, or one for pet food with a documentary on animals) this is more likely to be the exception rather than the rule.

Commercial television and the BBC

After a hesitant start in the 1950s, commercial TV in Britain went from strength to strength. The programme companies have made huge

60

profits from advertising and have succeeded in attracting a sizeable, and growing, share of the TV audience. At one period in the late 1950s the BBC was only capturing a third or less of the available viewers. Since then they have managed to win back viewers so that on occasion they have about a 50 per cent share of the audience, although it is uncertain if this will continue. The reason why a public service has over the years become so interested in its ratings is partly a political matter. The BBC's income comes from the public's licence fee, an amount fixed by parliament or, more accurately, the government of the day. If the BBC's share of the audience falls too low, it could be argued that it is not 'popular' with audiences. If the BBC is providing a service which is not popular, it has, in the eyes of some people, less justification for claiming an increase in the licence fee, or even for receiving a licence fee at all. In response to pressure from certain politicians and from the commercial networks, the BBC has tried to make itself more lively and attractive to audiences. The competition for high-audience ratings pressurizes the public-service BBC channels into acting more like commercial ones.

When competitiveness overshadows decisions about what programmes should be produced, the audiences tend to get viewed and treated as an homogenous mass. In other words, programmes are produced which appeal to the widest possible cross-section of people, and minority interests or 'experimental' material, although not ignored, are hived off into unpopular times in the schedule. Many critics view the output of the television services with growing alarm since it is rapidly becoming more bland, superficial and undemanding as a result of commercial pressures and shows a tendency towards 'catch-all' broadcasting — quality, they argue, too often gives way to quantity.

Diversification

It is worth mentioning in passing that commercial television companies make enormous profits from advertising and have diversified their wealth into other leisure, communication and culture industries and indeed into other types of business as well. For example:

Thames Television has interests in a computing firm and in a film company;
Granada Television has interests in television rentals, bingo halls, motorway services, paperback books, cinemas and property;

Yorkshire Television has interests in Windsor Safari Park, commercial radio and Scarborough Zoo.

Most of the newspaper companies are financially involved in commercial TV because much of their advertising has been lost to the small screen and this kind of investment partially protects them against losses. For example:

Trafalgar House owns Express Newspapers and has a large financial stake in Associated Television (Midlands);

News International which owns the *Sun*, the *News of the World* and Times Newspapers has a large interest in London Weekend Television, as does the *Daily Telegraph* and the *Observer*.

The number of interconnections, such as interlocking directorships and financial investments, that commercial TV has with other industries almost defies description, and it indicates the extent to which the communications industries, as a direct and indirect result of advertising, have come today to direct or control powerful social institutions. Concentrated ownership of the communication channels also means that commercial interests are in a position to exert possibly unwarranted influence on editorial and programming decisions in the media themselves.

The pattern for the future

Television is a very attractive medium for advertisers. Advertisers have to a great extent shifted their business from the national press to television where they can reach millions of viewers with any one commercial. In 1980 television attracted a 22 per cent share of a total advertising media expenditure of £2.53 billion, whereas the national press received only 16.3 per cent.

The pattern of television advertising has changed in its twenty-five year history. In 1955 most commercials were for branded grocery products – soaps, detergents and patent foods like cereals, soups and margarine. From the late 1960s to the end of the 1970s, manufacturers' consumer advertising, which was mainly for packaged groceries, declined from half the total advertising in 1968 to less than 40 per cent in 1979. (See Appendix II for a table of types of advertising as a percentage of total UK advertising for this period.) During the 1970s, television advertising revenue rose from £177 million to £347 million, but the medium's reliance on packaged goods fell. The sectors which gained most from this decline were the retail and durable-goods outlets, the leisure and holidays industries, building societies and other financial and industrial services.

The increase in this type of advertising, as I have said, has been at the expense of the national newspapers. When retail and financial advertising moved to television, the pressure on available air time was greater, and as a result the TV companies' advertising rates went up. Some advertisers moved back to the press, but a pattern had been set. New types of advertisers became interested in TV and wanted to use the medium to a greater extent if more air time could be made available. It seems likely that the advertiser's desire for more broadcasting time will be met in the 1980s with increased use of satellites, cable television and possibly pay TV.

Television is about to embark on a decade of upheaval which will change domestic TV out of all recognition. A second commercial channel (Channel 4) will start operating in 1982, and breakfast television in 1983. Both these developments will provide advertisers with more opportunities to reach audiences. Indeed, they could change the face of mass communications in general. Channel 4 is planned as an 'upmarket' station and will possibly take audiences from the BBC, and advertising away from the already struggling quality press like *The Times* and *The Guardian*. It is quite likely that a quality newspaper will have to fold as a result because there will not be enough 'quality' advertising to go around all the possible 'quality' channels.

Narrowcasting is also going through a period of expansion and is likely to become more available to the general public, which will probably please the advertising industry. Pay TV, cable TV, videotape and videodisc systems, teletext and viewdata are revolutionizing patterns of viewing and storing information generally. Nor do possibilities opened up by intercontinental satellite broadcasting dismay the advertisers, since this will increase the size of potential audiences.

On the whole the future points to even greater penetration of the media by advertisers and the possibility both of more advertising at home and that satellites will beam in advertising from abroad as well.

The press

No general review of advertising in our society can ignore its relationship to the newspaper industry. The two are inextricably entwined. Advertising shapes the tone and style of newspapers (you have only to look at the Sunday colour supplements to notice this), and it ultimately decides their viability.

Today's newspapers are the products of two factors: industrialization and concentration. As I mentioned in the previous chapter, Lord Northcliffe's recognition of the importance of advertising to his papers had a profound and lasting influence on the financial structure of all newspapers. The 'Northcliffe Revolution' marked an important stage in the industrialization of the press. When advertisers started to contribute to newspaper production costs, they not only changed the economic base of the press, they also began a period of press concentration. This meant a growth in newspaper circulation, the arrival of circulation wars, a decline in the number of titles and the concentration of titles into fewer and fewer hands. Consequently the range and diversity of viewpoints and opinions has also decreased. Financiers entered the picture in the 1920s; by 1929 four leading businessmen owned half the daily circulation of national newpapers. Competition for readers became fierce, with the result that the number of titles reduced from twelve in 1921 to nine in 1937.

The post-war period has been one of recurrent crises for the press. The concentration of titles into a few, rich and powerful hands has continued. Production costs have forced up the cover price of newspapers, many readers have defected to television, as have advertisers, and sales have dropped. Fleet Street has seen the closure of a number of major national newspapers since the war, notably the *News Chronicle*, the *Daily Herald* and the *Daily Sketch*.

The pursuit of advertising is a major preoccupation in Fleet Street and is intensified by the fact that there is a decreasing amount of advertising to be distributed among the papers. The quality press derive about three-quarters of their revenue from advertising, which is therefore critical to their survival. Classified advertising contributes to this income, but there are signs that this too is diminishing in volume as jobs disappear and unemployment rises. Media watchers predict that the addition of Channel 4 to the commercial network will mean that 'quality' advertising will be diverted from the quality press to the new channel. The popular press derive about one-third of their revenue from advertising; for the rest they are dependent on circulation, which, according to some accounts, is going down. In this financial maelstrom, very few national newspapers make profits.

64

This is hardly surprising if, as is sometimes the case, the cost of gathering and producing advertisements costs a newspaper more than the ads actually earn them in revenue.

Newspapers have responded to the financial crisis by combining into protective groupings either with other newspapers (e.g. the *News Chronicle* merged with the *Daily Mail* in the 1960s), with provincial newspaper chains, or with other publishing, cultural and leisure industries. In 1981 two groups (the International Publishing Corporation, a subsidiary of Reed International, a multinational paper group, and Rupert Murdoch's News International) controlled over 75 per cent of the circulation of nine national dailies. The same two also controlled over 85 per cent of Sunday newspaper circulation. The major national daily newspaper companies account for over half the circulation of provincial dailies and nearly half the circulation of provincial evenings.

Another significant trend in the newspaper world, which took place during the 1970s, was the entry of industrial giants into Fleet Street. For instance, Trafalgar House (a property, finance and shipping conglomerate) bought the Express Group from Beaverbrook Newspapers, and Atlantic Richfield (an American Oil company) acquired the *Observer* in 1977, which was then sold to Lonrho, the international trading group, in 1981. Mergers, conglomerations and interlocking directorships are a feature of other media industries, as we have noted in the previous section.

Advertising sponsorship in the press

In a general sense, advertising lies at the heart of these changes in media ownership and structure. In a more direct way advertising influences what we read in newspapers. Although we often hear the phrase 'freedom of the press', there is, I think, some question about this freedom. The 'free-market' approach which gives the advertiser access to newspaper readers does not guarantee a neutral source of support nor an independent press. Successive Royal Commissions on the press have looked at advertising and questioned whether the press is influenced by it. The McGregor Commission of 1977 decided, like its forerunners, that while it was difficult to demonstrate advertising influence on editorial matters, it was probably negligible and harmless. Of course, on the face of it, advertisements look different from the news in newspapers, so no direct crossing of the boundaries

65

between advertising and editorial material can be detected. Indeed, advertisers rarely attempt to persuade journalists to give them favourable reports in the editorial pages.

But advertising influence is subtle. If there *is* advertising pressure on journalists and editors, it is indirect. One could say that editors and newspaper managements have 'internalized' the advertisers' demands just as TV producers in America have become attuned to sponsors' wishes. Editors and management have to keep their newspapers viable and the necessity to attract advertising is such that they will go out of their way to make their newspaper attractive to sponsors.

If we are looking for overt pressure it is more likely to be found in specialized magazines such as music papers, where, for example, the record companies are often the source of news and topics, and have to be treated favourably. In the local press, influence could exist because local advertisers and newspaper executives have more opportunities for social contact than in a large metropolitan area like London. An extreme and fairly rare case of advertising pressure on editorial matters occurred recently in North Wales. The local newspaper supported villagers in their protest against the building of a gas-storage depot close to their homes, whereupon the Gas Board withdrew its advertising from the paper.

However, in response to financial pressures, newspaper publishers have accommodated advertisers by developing their papers along lines which appeal to advertisers; for instance, introducing special pages and features which allow advertisers to place their messages in specific sections of a paper. These sections organize readers into 'market lots' for sale to advertisers, who are thus assured of reaching their 'targets'. Special features include those for home-buyers, film-goers, holiday-makers, motorists, gardeners, *et al*. These sections have not been introduced with the over-riding aim of attracting advertisers but their appearance does indicate a degree of influence by advertising considerations.

Advertising's increasing influence on editorial features in the national press can be seen in the results of a study by James Curran (1978), which shows that there has been a growth in advertising-related editorial features (defined as editorial items covering the same product or service as advertisements on the same or facing page) during the post-war period. This increase is most significant among the quality newspapers which derive over half their revenue from advertising, and least among the populars which are not so dependent on advertising. In the period of the study (1946–76) Curran also found that a growing proportion of ads were placed on the same or facing pages as features covering the same topic. He remarks: 'This growing convergence between editorial and advertising content reflects the increasing accommodation of national newspaper managements to the selective needs of advertisers' (p. 235).

Sponsored features not only organize readers into market categories, they provide the advertiser with an 'editorial ambiance' which increases their ad's effectiveness. Advertisers will look for the right editorial environment as well as the right readers when they buy space. From this we might conclude that any criticism of an advertiser's business activities will be avoided in the editorial sections of newspapers.

But there is also a wider question to be considered. In a subtle way advertising sponsorship 'dictates' what material is covered by the press and also indirectly influences the way that it is covered. In short, advertising has come to distort 'reality'.

This process of distortion can be seen most clearly in the financial and business sections. In his study, Curran found that these sections gave priority to investment guidance, market prices and tips for the individual investor, whereas general economic and financial matters such as inflation and unemployment were largely ignored. Business news mainly consisted of company gossip to the neglect of serious investigative journalism of firms and financial issues. Women's pages exhibit similarly narrow preoccupations. In them women are defined as consumers of fashion, cosmetics and domestic goods, and feature articles are biased towards this aspect of women's lives. While there might be no direct endorsement of these consumer commodities, the fact that feature articles are product-related tends to reinforce a stereotypical view of women as mothers, fashion objects and home-makers.

Advertising as a publishing authority

Because advertising money is what keeps so many papers alive, it operates as a kind of licence to print in a way analogous to the operation of the BBC's licence fee which allows it to broadcast. If advertisers are not disposed for one reason or another to pay the 'licence' to the newspaper, then the paper will either have to accommodate itself to the advertiser or it will cease to be able to publish.

So when you hear someone talk about the 'freedom of the press' you ought to consider whose freedom they are talking about. 'Freedom' is in fact part of the basic ideology of advertising; it is a word used to justify advertising and claims to give the press its 'independence'. What it really means is that the freedom to publish rests in the hands of the advertisers; they are free to compete, and free to take their advertisements elsewhere, if the editorial matter, the ambience or the audience is not to their liking.

As in commercial television, the audience/readers have to be delivered to the advertisers in large numbers and they have to be of the right kind. It is of no use to advertisers to reach millions of readers who cannot, or who are unlikely to, buy their goods. For instance, the popular press likes readers who are not too old and not too young, and who include a high proportion of women, since it is women who usually spend the family income and have been historically defined as consumers. The quality press only survive with their comparatively low circulation — less than 20 per cent of national newspaper circulation — because their readership has higher status, greater influence and higher spending power than the readership of popular newspapers, and consequently advertisers are prepared to pay high rates to the newspaper for the privilege of reaching these readers.

A brief example of the power of advertising can be found in the case of demise of the *Daily Herald* in the 1950s. Although this newspaper had a high circulation and was considered 'popular' with its readers, it appealed to the wrong kind of people. Its readership consisted of more men than women, older rather than younger, and it was predominantly working-class as opposed to middle-class. *Daily Herald* readers were not useful to advertisers because they were not wealthy, did not drive cars, were not young and had not been defined as 'consumers' at that time.

The significance of the forced closure of the *Daily Herald* lies in the fact that a large readership lost a serious newspaper and now have to be content with tabloid entertainment sheets like the *Daily Mirror* or the *Sun*. These papers do not devote much editorial space to political, economic or social matters.

What happened to the *Daily Herald* has happened to similar, mass-circulation newspapers in the post-war period. They have been left high and dry by advertisers, who have trickled away to television. They have had to rely increasingly on mass sales and have tried to maximize sales by appealing to a balanced profile of readers. This profile has shown less interest in news as such, so the mass-circulation popular papers have downgraded news in favour of sensational crime stories, celebrity gossip, sport and the inevitable pin-ups.

The crisis

Advertising affects the viability of vulnerable newspapers, as I have tried to indicate. It has also contributed to the precarious position of the national press as a whole. Some people have even warned of the death of Fleet Street, others of another sharp reduction in the number of national dailies. Newspapers are in cut-throat competition for readers and advertisers. Production costs have risen and advertisers have taken their patronage to the provincial press or to television. Newspapers have responded by paring down their advertising rates to suicidally low prices. In some cases the returns from advertisements have barely covered their production costs. In 1960 the national popular dailies obtained roughly 40 per cent surplus on advertising; in 1973 they obtained 15 per cent on adverts published; in 1975 they received no surplus at all. National quality dailies suffered a decline in advertising profit from 60 per cent in 1960 to 35 per cent in 1975. In 1975 only four dailies and one Sunday paper out of a total of seventeen national papers made a profit.

The commercial media's dependence on advertising has meant that important forms of public communication have become increasingly subject to the competitive needs of giant corporations such as those who produce cigarettes, detergents, soap, beer, cornflakes and so on. Advertising no longer constitutes a marginal pressure group of 'quacks' nor a manageable form of subsidy. It is a highly developed and sophisticated institution which touches the centre of cultural as well as economic life and organizes newspapers and the broadcast media so that they are not truly independent but fall in with the demands of the dominant economic institutions. Advertising's influence on the media is exerted invisibly without acknowledgement. (Note also the amount of 'free' advertising companies get even on the public-service network by sponsoring cultural and sporting events.) The press in general professes to be the watchdog of the man or woman in the street; but such a claim fits uncomfortably with the hidden economic power of the advertiser and the large, diversified conglomerate. Can the press really serve two masters with such different interests?

69

Note

1. See also Fred Friendly's book (1968) *Due to Circumstances Beyond Our Control* for an account of the influence of advertisers on editorial matters in American broadcasting.

Suggestions for further work

1. Examine the regular programme material on commercial TV and compare this with the advertising material which appears during the 'natural breaks'. Are there links made through the kind of language used, the situation or people described, the kinds of ideas expressed or the type of music used? If there are any links why do you think this might be so and what would you consider their effect to be?

2. How much will it cost an advertiser to have a commercial placed in a sports programme and an arts/culture programme? Consult the *TV Times* to find out when these programmes are on, and how often, and also look up the advertising rates in BRAD (British Rate and Data) which can probably be found at your local public library. Is there a difference in cost?

3. Look for any links between the editorial matter and any advertisements in the following publications:
   (a) the *Guardian*;
   (b) the *Daily Mirror*;
   (c) a teenage comic;
   (d) a woman's magazine.
   Examine the paper page by page. Are there any ads for washing powder on the sports pages?

4. Looking at the large display ads, what kind of people do you think read:
   (a) the *Daily Telegraph*;
   (b) the *Sun*;
   (c) the *Sunday Express*;
   (d) the *News of the World*;
   (e) the *Observer* ?

5. How much space is given over to advertising in the following newspapers:
   (a) the *Financial Times*;
   (b) the *Daily Telegraph*;
   (c) the *Daily Mirror*;

(d) the *Morning Star*;

(e) the *Sunday Times* colour supplement;

(f) *Oh Boy, Patches, Blue Jeans* ?

What are the reasons for any variation? How much does it cost to advertise in the different newspapers? Consult BRAD.

Draw a diagram of the pages of the *Sun* and the *Daily Telegraph* shading in the area which is an ad thus:

Measure the percentage of the total paper/page area that the ads occupy. Why is there a difference in the amount of space occupied by ads in the different newspapers?

6. What does Curran (1978) mean by the term 'advertising ambiance'? How can advertising influence the media system? (See Curran, 1981.)

4 THE EFFECTS OF ADVERTISING

In the previous chapter I discussed the influence of advertising on the decision-making and the output of broadcasting and the press. In fact, the whole question of the influence of advertising, particularly on us as individuals, is one of continuing debate. It is an issue which concerns a number of people, not least the advertisers who want to know or be sure that people buy advertised goods and therefore that their messages are effective.

In some respects the impact of advertising is all too obvious — children chant jingles instead of nursery rhymes at a very early age, and we can probably all remember occasions when we have bought something because we have been attracted by the advertiser's claims. In other respects the effects of advertising on society over a long period of time are hard to assess. Many people would deny that they are influenced by advertisements and regard them at worst as lies, at best as idiot triviality. It is probably true to say that most people are consciously sceptical of advertising. However, although they might not believe the claims made for a product by an advertiser (such as 'Persil washes whiter'), they might find it more difficult to resist the more general social image or message presented along with the overt sales pitch — for example, that we can make friends by drinking the right kind of beer, get a boyfriend by using the right kind of shampoo, become a supermum to an adoring family by buying the right tin of baked beans, or avoid being a social outcast and guilt feelings if we buy life assurance.

In addition to influencing some of the general values and beliefs of society, advertising interacts with and affects other forms of communication — literature, art, and even language itself. Some of this influence is not particularly sinister or detrimental to the original form, or to us, but it does mean that in many areas of modern life, we can find the central values of a consumer society — conspicuous consumption, wealth, sexual attractiveness and sexual power, competitive one-up-manship and so on. In this chapter I want to examine both the specific and general 'effects' of advertising and the problems associated with research into 'effects'.

Effects research

The problem of the influence or effects of advertising is multi-faceted and can be approached from a number of perspectives. We could examine the influence of ads on the individual and look for evidence of the ability of the advertising media to shape and sometimes change a person's behaviour, opinions and attitudes. Another angle to take would be to consider the effects of advertising on the society as a whole and the extent to which consumer advertising promotes general ideas and beliefs. For instance, it could be argued that because advertising stresses the private accumulation of goods, and almost hedonistic lifestyles, it encourages people to think in terms of escape from the real world, although they might not actually buy the specific products advertised. It could also be said that the utopian imagery of advertisements encourages passivity and makes people unaware of the extent to which they are controlled by consumerism and unable to determine the terms of their own existence.

These kinds of questions have generated a variety of answers and there is a vast literature on the subject of advertising's effects, coming from both the industry itself and from academic social and behavioural scientists. Mass-communication research in general indicates that over a wide range of media, any direct effects are limited or exceptional although the media are to some extent 'socializers' of young children and powerful in terms of the definitions of reality they provide.

At this stage it might be useful to distinguish between two kinds of 'effects' study. Williams (1981) suggests the following kinds:

(a) *Operational*, which study effects as indicators of policy and marketing decisions, e.g. 'attitude' surveys or testing for 'post-

73

exposure consumption patterns'; studies of responses to programmes in broadcasting research; private political polling on 'issues' like government policy. These studies, particularly market research conducted by agencies for clients, are not generally published.

(b) *Critical*, which look at the media's presentation of, say, violence or at political broadcasting or other distinguishable kinds of production (like advertisements) which are assessed for both specific (immediate) and general (long-term) social effect, often in response to an expressed public concern.

Neither type of research is methodologically or conceptually neutral, but the latter is perhaps more aware of the difficulties of investigating something like televised violence or political broadcasting.

Market research

The advertiser is involved, through an agency, in researching the effects or likely effectiveness of a campaign. The advertising agent usually provides a market-research service for clients as well as designing and producing ads, and buying space in the media. When an agency has accepted an account from an advertiser, one of the first things to do is to survey the market to find out something about the possible customers, what they need and want from a particular product, if they will buy what will eventually go on sale, and what are the best ways of influencing them via an advertising campaign. Questionnaires are given to a cross-section of people, sometimes picked randomly from a telephone directory or stopped in the streets and asked to answer some questions. Sometimes prospective consumers are interviewed by psychologists trained to analyse deep, or psychological, motivations and attitudes. Research might even be conducted for hypothetical products so that a producer or manufacturer can design an actual product with the benefit of the research.

Clients and agents are also concerned to know that people have bought the goods after a campaign. This can be done by looking at sales figures and estimating if the campaign had the desired effect among a certain group of people or in a specific area. Or again, questionnaires can be administered after the launching of a campaign and people asked if an advertisement influenced their purchasing decisions.

Market research of this type is not designed to pick up complex, long-term issues concerning consumer choice or social needs, but to provide quick 'post-exposure' results to determine if a 'stimulus' (the ad) has achieved a 'response' (a purchase). The methods used by market researchers to test and discover consumer behaviour and attitudes have become very sophisticated over the years and they include a battery of research techniques, computerized data analysis, demographic statistics and so on. But their notion of effects is defined quite narrowly and the assumption that lies behind much of this type of research is that anybody can be persuaded if the right techniques are used.

Sociological research

The 'hypodermic' model

The question of whether advertisements influence people is also of concern to the general public, to teachers, politicians and policy makers. Professional sociologists and psychologists often take up the concerns initially expressed by lay groups of people and work on questions about the 'effects' of the media and advertising using the concepts and methods of research of their disciplines. A vast amount of research has been conducted into the influence of advertising. There have been studies which have tried to detect any difference in impact on different age groups, on the different sexes or between the different media. Some of the research into advertising's effects has investigated the change in people's attitudes, values or behaviour brought about as a result of exposure to advertisements. Children are a favourite subject of social and psychological researchers because they are considered to be particularly vulnerable to persuasion and propaganda. And on the more positive side, some of the effects research has looked at any possible functions that advertisements might have for audiences: whether they are considered to be informative, fulfil any needs and give satisfaction to audiences.

As a matter of fact, when sociologists and psychologists first turned their attention to problems associated with the commercial media much of their research was influenced by the concepts and methods of market research and was quite often financed by the mass media and by advertisers who wanted precise data on their target population — such as an audience breakdown according to age, sex, economic status, tastes, habits and so on. Early 'effects' research, especially of the market-research type, and some contemporary research concentrates on finding evidence of the short-term impact

75

of a media message (e.g. investigations of a person's change in brand choice as a direct result of an advertising campaign), rather than evidence of longer-term shifts or changes in attitudes and values. Implicit in many of the short-term, behavioural studies is a view or model of media influence which is like a hypodermic needle that 'injects' a message into the mind of the audience. Much of the research based on the idea of a hypodermic needle has made heavy use of concepts like attitude change, learning, imitation and emotional arousal, has been conducted under experimental conditions in laboratories, and it has come in for some criticism. It is argued, for instance, that 'experimental' social and social-psychological research leads to a distorted and artificial view of the role that the media play in society. Research that looks for immediate responses to a single stimulus like an advertisement is probably over-simplified (although 'scientifically' controllable) and inadequately conceptualized. Not all effects can be observed in the short term or in laboratories under experimental conditions. In fact there is some evidence that advertising's effects on people are complicated by a number of factors, and that people themselves do not always reveal their responses to advertisements under interrogation from a sociologist nor under laboratory conditions.

The 'socially-mediated' model

We should remember that the media and its audiences are part of a complex social structure and are not stimulus–response mechanisms. Advertisements are part of a flow or pattern of culture and are certainly not the only influences in people's lives. The 'audience' is not a homogenous mass; different audience members belong to different social and class groups. Factors such as a person's class or family relationships act like filtering mechanisms or protective screens around an individual, and any potential influence of much of the output of the media is therefore somewhat limited. Some of the research on the media–audience relationship suggests that the audience is much less passive than might be thought and that people actively or purposefully 'use' media products according to their circumstances. The media's effects can thus be thought of as being dependent on the functions that they perform for individual audience members, whether they are used as sources of information, entertainment or escape. A member of the audience, some research has shown, cannot be affected by the media if they do not fulfil or gratify a need. For instance, if a person leads an active, varied life and is secure and stable, no amount of advertising which appeals to fears of loneliness or of being a social outcast, or to social snobbery will succeed.[1] In general the optimistic research argues that the media reinforce rather than change a person's prior dispositions and are capable of satisfying a plurality of needs. In addition, audience members are held to be active and involved in their understanding/interpretation of the media and are not, as has been thought, totally passive.

This view of the effects of the media is quite reassuring. It means that the audience is not a bunch of gullible dupes waiting for messages to be imprinted on their brains, and is capable of being critical of the products of the media. And no doubt the advertisers themselves are also relieved to hear from the researchers that people are capable of resisting messages according to their individual and social circumstances, since this draws criticism away from their activities and puts the onus on the audience. Many advertisers will even argue in justification of some of their more exaggerated ads by suggesting that they are providing wanted and needed fantasies to some of their audiences.

Clearly there is room in the interpretation of ads and other media messages for individual responses according to our personal perceptions or experiences. There is no law that says we must receive an ad's meaning in a uniform manner or in precisely the way intended by its producer. People can respond differently to different ads according to their language, imagery and modes of address (or terms on which ads identify and communicate) — and anyway, as I have said before, many people take advertisements with a pinch of salt.

The 'cultural values' model
However, I would argue that although we should not look for effects that aren't there (or are not proven), nor claim for advertising a decisive influence upon the way we see the world, neither would we be justified in underestimating the contribution that the world of commerce makes to the cultural climate of their societies. It is more than likely that an advertisement's effects are diffuse and long-term, and there is some evidence that advertising plays a part in defining 'reality' in a general or anthropological sense. It projects the goals and values that are consistent with and conducive to the consumer economy and socializes us into thinking that we can buy a way of life as well as goods. For instance, the sex-role stereotyping common

77

to many advertisements—the 'little woman' as household functionary thrilling to her newly polished table or whiter-than-white sheets, or the masterful, adventurous male — act, many social scientists argue, as agents of socialization and lead many people, young and old, to believe in traditional and discriminatory sex roles.

Any commonsense view of advertising should take into account the very central role that advertising and its associated institutions play in the economy. Advertising must have more power to persuade than the average individual, or for that matter organized labour, both in terms of available resources and access to the channels of mass communication. Our ability to withstand the constant stream of compelling and repetitive messages must be seen in the light of the institutional power of advertising which provides, according to Galbraith, 'a relentless propaganda on behalf of goods in general' (1968, p. 213). The idyllic and alluring ads with their witty catch-phrases, vivid imagery and stereotypes work on an aggregate level. They are not read 'transparently', word-for-word as it were, by the audience, but they do offer a 'preferred reading', characters with whom to identify, and general meanings about what should be admired and desired. They do not mirror or reflect social meanings and conditions, but teach us ways of thinking and feeling, generally through fantasy and dreaming. It is, of course, still possible to argue that the effects of advertisements are not harmful to people or society. To the degree that they manipulate rather than inform, distort rather than reflect the quality of life in our society and are the products of decisions taken by an unrepresentative, unelected group of powerful businessmen, I would argue that they are harmful. The sad fact is that many people, while recognizing the frustrations of their daily lives, are caught up in the fantasies offered by ads and are unable to see through them and their false utopias.

Advertising's effectiveness

Although it is hard to pin down the social effects of advertising in any precise numerical sense, it might be possible to measure the effectiveness of single messages. There is a vast amount of market research conducted every year although most of it is devoted to 'pre-sell' research. 'Post-sell' research is limited by certain methodological weaknesses — much of the research relying on transitory street corner or door-step interviews, which are no guarantees of truth.

Nevertheless, it seems to be the case that advertising is generally successful in the sense that one can normally chart a growth in the sales of a product after a corresponding increase in advertising. This, however, is not always true for all categories of product. Some products are bought in volume independently of advertising. For example, it is possible that the purchase of washing machines is directly attributable to mass advertising; it is equally likely that people buy washing machines despite advertising because they prefer them to the alternatives — laborious scrubbing, boiling, wringing, etc. In other words an alternative causal explanation for a rise in washing-machine sales may be that people have come to the rational decision that they are useful things to have in the home. Similarly we could argue that the huge sales of some mass products like instant foods can be attributed to the dominance of the market monopolists as much as to advertising in any direct sense — the food giants like Nestlés, General Foods and Kraft can carve up the market between them so that the effectiveness of promotion can often be attributed to lack of alternative provision of goods as much as to the power of advertising.

So when considering 'effectiveness', it is difficult to prove any short-term and one-to-one effects of advertising, and it is probably unnecessary to argue over detailed findings. The economic and institutional power of advertising goes beyond the strictly empirical and registers across the whole movement of a society, in social and economic institutions and in the styles and values of popular culture and art.

Cultural effects

Many critics of modern consumer/popular culture argue that the real impact of advertising is on the cultural climate of society. For instance, there are indications that the language and values of advertising suffuse a variety of communication forms in modern society; that 'sales talk' and genuine communication have become intertwined in such media as the commercial cinema, in TV programmes and in popular literature. The prose in many fictional stories in popular magazines for example, adopts the tricks and style of advertising copy and imagery, and is very similar to that in the more developed ads which prop up the product with a fictional situation. Whether it describes a product or a romantic adventure, the prose is bland, superficial if persuasive, and relies upon the use of romantic clichés and images. Certain values such as love, friendship, neighbourliness, pleasure, happiness and sexual attraction are the staple diet of advertisements and are often confused with or transferred to the possession of things: 'Gold is for lovers', 'A diamond is forever', 'I love my new Hygiene kitchen', 'I'd love a Babycham'. The love for someone and for something is, of course, not the same thing, although there is often not much distinction made between the two in ads. (Look at the ads not only for jewellery but also for banks, airlines, cigarettes, etc.) The drift if not the impact of the use of these values in selling means that genuine feelings are devalued or corrupted, and previously acceptable words become false and used loosely. The shift of meanings and values and the debasement of ordinary language has brought about what Fred Inglis calls 'a distortion in symbols and established meanings like love or warmth or friendship or indeed success and possession' (1972, p. 114). And Williams (1974) argues that there has been a 'mutual transfer' between the formulae of commercials and those of separate programmes. Items in television and radio news bulletins feature a kind of encapsulated information which has also become a mode of recommending cat food in commercials; the domestic serial interacts with the headache tablet commercial which also uses the instructional device reminiscent of educational television. 'In these ways' says Williams 'and in their essential combination, there is the flow of meanings and values of a specific culture' (1981, p. 19).

Discussion of advertising's cultural effects is not a new phenomenon. As early as the 1930s, the literary critic F. R. Leavis accused the popular media, particularly advertising, of evoking cheap, almost mechanical emotional responses, and inculcating 'the choosing of the most immediate pleasures got with the least effort' (1933, p. 3). He warned that advertisements corrupted feelings, debased language, exploited people's emotional needs and fears and encouraged greed, snobbery and social conformity. Leavis's writings on culture and society, it must be admitted, are faintly puritanical and steeped in nostalgia for pre-industrial folk (thus organic) culture. He also argued heavily in favour of the uplifting values of great works of literature whose appreciation can function as an antidote to modern mass culture. Nevertheless, his criticisms of advertising have some force and relevance even today, and he did draw attention to what he considered to be the numbing effect that advertisements have on people's critical responses to their environment.

A more stringent, more radical and less nostalgic response to advertising can be found in the work of a group of writers and academics known collectively as the Frankfurt School. Although this group no longer exists, their thesis has had a great deal of influence on critical and non-empirical sociology and on consideration of the long-term impact of mass culture. One of their conclusions was that the commodity culture, while offering a better material standard of living and certain comforts and gratifications, in fact encouraged social and political apathy. One of the writers of the Frankfurt School was Herbert Marcuse, who claimed that the manipulation of false needs is repressive and leads to 'one-dimensional thought'. It blocks people's ability to recognize that they are being controlled. He wrote 'Free choice among a wide variety of these goods and services does not signify freedom if these goods sustain social controls over a life of toil and fear — that is they sustain alienation' (1968, p. 23). Alienation is a concept which is used to refer to the mental and physical separation of people from each other and from real involvement with their work and society. The modern social world dehumanizes and alienates people while modern mass culture, including advertising, attempts to conceal or compensate for the deficiencies in a person's real social and personal life.

Marcuse, borrowing from the critical semiotics of Roland Barthes (see chapter 6), argued that the conventions of mass communication are founded on faulty or abridged grammar. The mass media use an abridged or condensed language (of which Marcuse gives several examples in chapter 4 of *One Dimensional Man* (1968)) which short-circuits thinking and suppresses cognitive evaluation. Advertising in particular uses hypnotic and intimidatory language and imagery. Its propositions assume the form of suggestive commands, and at the same time the language is tinged with false familiarity which, according to Marcuse, is the result of skilfully managed popular directness and constant repetition. Marcuse contends that the media define the terms in which we think and that their influence has to be assessed not in the strict sense of their impact on what we think about but in terms of the way in which they condition our entire intellectual outlook. This means that the media inhibit or confuse conceptual thought by encouraging us to live in a world of hypnotic definitions which deny any effective cognitive evaluation on our part.

81

Images

In some respects the influence of advertising can be attributed to recent technological improvements and innovations in the production and distribution of pictorial or visual representations of reality. What the historian Daniel Boorstin (1963) calls the 'graphic revolution' has been helped by advanced techniques of pictorial reproduction (in printing, broadcasting, etc.) and has also changed the significance of the character of the 'image'. We may want to agree with Marshall McLuhan's aphorism 'the medium is the message' (that the influence of the media is a result of their technology), but we must recognize that the images conveyed by the media have, over the past thirty years, become so sophisticated and persuasive that they now organize our experiences and understanding in a crucially significant way. If you look at any pre-war or immediately post-war advertisement, you will see that the visual imagery tends to be crude, simplistic and generally much less important than the words. Today the situation is reversed. We live in a world of spectacular and exciting images. And the word 'image' now also refers to a fabricated or shaped public impression created with the help of visual techniques. An image can sell soap, toilet paper, whisky, a corporation, a celebrity, a politician or a political party. According to Boorstin, images have become more interesting than the original and in fact have become the original: 'the shadow becomes the substance'. Advertisements, he argues, encourage extravagant expectations because they are more dramatic and vivid than the reality — reality cannot match up to the image. Ads present us with images and then make them seem true. As a result they befuddle our experience and mystify our perceptions and experiences of the real world by offering spectacular illusions which ultimately don't satisfy.

The consumers

Advertising is capable of real if limited success. Some people might think the better of you for buying a certain product such as an expensive car or fashionable dress. But its success is tempered by a general air of unreality. And advertisers are caught up in the general confusion which they foster. As it is now constituted, industrial society allows no collaboration and little mutual communication between producers and consumers. Consumers are set apart from the

82

arena of production and treated as private individuals, making private decisions about the commodities in their private, family lives. Decision-making about production is left to the producers. Because people are treated as markets, no arena exists where arguments about alternative products or the provision of goods and services for social needs can take place.

The language used by advertisers shows that they think of people as targets on which they wish to make an impact, rather than as human beings. In advertisements, they use a language which is subtle and cajoling, but when they speak to each other (for instance in trade or professional journals) their words reveal a certain hostility and aggression; marketing is called a 'weapon', advertising is 'doing battle on the sales front', advertisers' skills are those of 'unarmed combat' and consumers are 'forces of sales resistance'.

The use of 'psychological warfare', and its effects on consumers, can be seen in its most horrifying extension in the use of *motivational research* (MR) by many advertising agencies (though currently it is less in vogue). MR was developed to probe people's unconscious sales resistance, and its methods and applications are exposed by Vance Packard in his book *The Hidden Persuaders* (1970). Depth interviews, projective tests and 'living laboratories' were techniques developed to uncover a person's hidden anxieties and insecurities, guilt feelings or secret desires. Armed with such knowledge, the advertisers have transposed MR revelations into deceptively simple or outrageous advertisements. One classic advertising campaign based on this type of research was a series of advertisements for a make of car which presented the sports car as the personification of a man's mistress and the saloon car as his wife.

Women have traditionally been targets for this kind of research since they are the people who make most of the purchases in our society. Packard cites several examples of housewives who have been persuaded to buy such items as cake mixes which allow them a degree of creativity in order to give them a sense of achievement, or household gadgets which don't make them feel guilty for not working as hard as their grandmothers. According to Packard, advertisements which flatter consumers and which disguise the emptiness and drudgery of much household work and glorify the role of housewife are guaranteed a certain amount of success. Eventually, however, we must always come back to the question of whether soft toilet paper *will* make a woman a better wife and mother, whether a new shampoo *will* prevent her ageing or an aspirin give her a new identity, and consider that such promises can keep people from knowing what the root causes of social and personal problems are and from knowing what they really want.

Notes

1. See Fiske's (1982) *Introduction to Communication Studies*, a companion volume to this book, in which the 'uses and gratification' theory is discussed in more detail.

Suggestions for further work

1. What would you consider to be the general and the specific effects of advertising?
2. Have you recently spent money because of an ad? Give details of the ad. Was there anything about it that was particularly memorable/effective? Did you want or need the product before you saw or heard the ad? Discuss with your friends what kind of ads they like or dislike.
3. What other factors beside possibly ads themselves influence our purchasing decisions?
4. If you were the marketing manager of a confectionary company and you wanted to launch a new chocolate bar onto the market, how would you go about it? What kind of promotional campaign would you use? How would you ensure that your advertising was successful?
5. Do you think there is a link between advertising and people's general outlook and behaviour? Would you consider advertising to have harmful effects on children? Is there a relationship between anti-social behaviour and advertising? Can advertising contribute to people's feelings of unhappiness and frustration or does it provide valid incentives and desires? Is it possible to answer these sorts of questions by interviewing people and asking them directly if they think advertising affects their attitudes, behaviour, etc?
6. What are the differences between 'effects' research which is based on the 'hypodermic' model and that based on the 'socially-mediated' or 'cultural-effects' models? What view of the audience

is implicit in each of these models? Which do you think is the most accurate view?

5 WHAT DO ADVERTISEMENTS MEAN?

What advertisements mean is obviously dependent on what is apparently observable on the TV or cinema screen or in the pages of magazines and newspapers. It is important to establish what is there, even though in the normal run of events we don't pay much attention to advertisements as we walk along the streets or flip through the pages of magazines. Having scrutinized what ads consist of we can then make more reliable judgements about what they mean beneath the surface gloss and witty catch-phrase. By adopting more thoughtful and critical approaches we can check our fleeting, more personal observations against some general survey-type information. In this chapter I want to suggest some possible approaches to the analysis and interpretation of advertisements and present the results of some studies which have looked at the content of ads.

Analysing the content of ads involves looking at both verbal and visual aspects of an advertising text, and regarding the pictures to be as, if not more, important than the written or spoken material. Pictures are 'easier' to understand and have more impact than words, and they generally offer greater opportunity for the communication of excitement, mood and imagination. A picture is used to lead the eye to the written copy in magazine ads and in commercials; language is often used merely to reinforce a photograph or filmed sequence. Although we usually think of images, particularly photographs, as 'life-like' and thus real, we should be aware that the meaning of an image is not 'transparent' but like other aspects of ads, constructed and manipulated.

86

Approaches to the study of meaning

Non-textual analysis

One way to identify the meaning of a text is to ask the *producer/author* what he or she meant. This, of course, is not always possible (he or she might be dead, live a long way away, be inaccessible for other reasons or might in fact not be one person but a collective or organization). The 'producer's-meaning' approach assumes that the 'correct' interpretation of a text is the one intended by the author. But the intentions of an author cannot always be precisely stated and this is especially true if the sender or author of a message is more than one person.

It would be dangerous to base the analysis of a text solely on the intentions expressed by the sender. He or she may not remember, may lie or try to deceive, or may not even have had any clear intentions. At any rate 'intentions' ·are rarely available for analysis. A sender's subjective comments on the text can be informative and indicative but must be supplemented by precise, objective and systematic research.

Another 'non-textual' approach to the question of what a text means can be the identification of meaning with the *consumer/receiver*'s experience of it. Different people 'read' and interpret texts in different ways, and it is possible to ask different groups of consumers how they interpret or understand a specific text. Audience research — as we saw in the last chapter — is an important branch of both marketing and the social and behavioural sciences. It is, of course, not without its methodological problems, but some sort of empirical investigation of what and how media audiences understand, or the conditions of reception and consumption of texts, is not only useful but necessary.[1]

However, the focus of this chapter is on the text itself: that is, we will try to identify the meaning of a text with the text itself.

Textual analysis

Textual analysis of one sort or another is based on the meaning ascribed to a text by an *analyst/interpreter*. This person is of course a consumer or audience member, but for the purposes of serious investigation he or she is not a lay member but someone who has particular expertise in analytic methods.

There are a number of ways of approaching textual analysis via the text. 'Qualified' analysts can explain what a text means by observing it closely and describing what it says or by making a simple paraphrase of it. They would try to clarify any ambiguities in the text, and bring out hidden meanings. How this reading is accomplished is largely up to the individual, relying on his or her sensitivity and acquaintance with the material, and is largely based on the value-judgements and individual skill of the 'reader'. The problem with this approach is that it tends to be subjective and is unable to deal with large quantities of material. In order to be more objective, especially where the analyst is dealing with mass-produced artefacts, the criteria on which the analysis is based need to be explicitly formulated and a systematic approach adopted.

One of the first tasks of the analyst is to devise a system whereby a large amount of apparently unordered material can be broken down into more manageable size and *classified*. A classification system provides a basic tool for the analysis and interpretation of a varied corpus of material. It can be used to uncover any prevalent or recurring pattern in the material, and eventually to discover its possible meanings and messages. A preliminary classification will help to sort out just what is being investigated; what types of advertisements, for what products, in what media and so on. Once the analyst–researcher has decided on a particular focus of attention, the ads can be examined in terms of their constituent features.

Classifications of ads
One way of classifying ads, both in the press (static) and on TV (dynamic), is to look at their functions and techniques ranging along an axis from the purely informational to those that exhort or command.

Classified ads might be regarded as *informational* ads: they contain few superfluous words (redundancy) because they are usually brief and small, and the people who consult the classified columns in the press usually have in mind what they are looking for so there is no need for sales 'patter'. Some classifieds, however, contain both facts and patter.

> TV interviewer's family house, Kensington. Superbly elegant living-room, 4 bedrooms. Modern kitchen, secluded garden. Rent . . .

The number of bedrooms is a fact, modern kitchen is possibly factual, but 'superbly elegant' is not — the advertiser has included it as a piece of persuasion. The words 'TV interviewer' are of course a blatant appeal to snobbery — the supposed desire to live in a house once owned by a famous person.

Another category of advertisement found in posters, magazines, newspapers and even on TV, is the *simple*. The ad in plate 9 for instance gives specific functional information such as the price, the ingredients of the product and where it can be bought. The ad itself is quite small in relation to the rest of the page and contains a small black and white line drawing of the product. There is no slogan, although there is repetition in the signature line at the bottom of the ad. Advertisements of this type are generally unobjectionable. They contain a certain amount of 'hard' information like the advantages of a product, its convenience, cost, etc. If a background setting is used it might be somewhere unremarkable like a kitchen, although this would probably be newer, tidier and better equipped than in real life.

'Simple' advertisements are often found in hobby or special-interest magazines where the relationship between supplier and consumer is straightforward; the hobbyist is an untypical consumer in that he is able to make a reasoned judgement on an advertiser's claims about cost, need, value, use and so on. TV commercials on local and regional TV are often examples of simple format and appeal. A simple picture might accompany some relevant information about a product and there might be some modest encouragement coming from the announcer/voice-over.

Other categories of advertisements are suggested by Hall and Whannel (1964). These include *compound, complex* and *sophisticated* ads.

In *compound* advertisements what is mild encouragement in simple ads becomes subtle association and persuasion. This type of ad still contains information, but it relies on pictures to do the persuading, while the facts are left to the copy. In some fashion ads in women's magazines the name of the store, the address, the telephone number, the brand name of a garment might be listed alongside a drawing or photo of it. If there is a headline or a caption it is of a semi-technical nature: for example 'Terylene', 'made from pure new wool', 'Liberty -style', 'New spring collection from Travona', although in the last example 'new' might be regarded as persuasive rather than informative. The real persuasion comes in the picture, which is usually

89

Mackenzie
Decongestant Tablets
WITH ANTI-HISTAMINE

Specially formulated to bring fast relief from the pain and discomfort caused by nasal, sinus and bronchial congestion. The analgesic content quickly relieves the pain while the other ingredients reduce the congestion in the affected areas.

You will find them at your chemist for just 39p - A small price to pay for breathe-easy days and restful nights, free from that 'stuffed-up' feeling!

**MACKENZIE
DECONGESTANT
TABLETS
WITH ANTI-HISTAMINE**

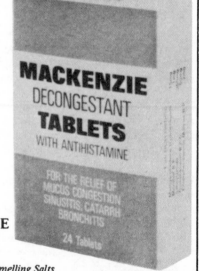

*Another product
from the makers of Mackenzie Smelling Salts*

Plate 9 The simple ad

glossy featuring attractive-looking models or an 'artistic' modernist line drawing of a pencil slim and elegant woman. In a compound ad for a product such as a gas fire, a hi-fi system or a car, the setting or background in which the object is placed is readily identifiable if unattainable. The advertiser is obviously hoping that the reader will associate the *product* with the *total impression* — garment with model and object with setting. In other words, the feelings aroused by the atmosphere are subtly transferred to the product and some amount of information is linked to more general and alluring promises.

The ads in the Sunday newspaper colour supplements are usually of the compound type; The photography is realistic but vivid; the product is projected into the foreground, usually in crisp, clear magnification while the background is visible enough to hint at the pleasures the commodity can bring. Cars, for instance, are usually set against some elegant mansion, an approved public building like a bank or a cathedral, or possibly a race-course, an alpine ski resort or an exotic tropical beach. The copy tries to limit itself to some technical data about the performance of the car but the language of mechanics and electronics is often no more than the familiar encouragement to power, prestige and excitement.

Complex advertisements usually concentrate on the presentation of luxury and status; the background takes over, the product merges into it. The visual and verbal imagery evoke the status feelings associated with money, wealth, elegance, luxury and the public display of these things. In most advertising for expensive consumer durables — kitchen equipment, furniture, carpets, bedroom suites, etc. — it is the 'image' created by the combination of commentary and photography that is the selling point, not the specific carpet or suite. At first glance, it is sometimes hard to see what precisely is on offer in complex advertisements because the product is buried in the total image created. Similarly, ads and commercials for airlines, cruises and big companies like Esso, IBM or banks work through context or setting plus the technical sophistication of the photography or camera work. These 'prestige' ads exude confidence, success, responsibility and power. Some bank ads even communicate a benign and sentimental intimacy — from a superior position.

Sophisticated ads are extensions of the complex. They usually explore hidden or subconscious feelings; subtle associations are made between product and situation, and dream-like fantasies are acted out. The visual imagery might be blurred to suggest a dream- or trance-like state and the colours and lighting are those usually associated with dreams and fantasies. Sexuality may be exaggerated and sexual symbolism exploited. Self-indulgence and violence lurk beneath the surface. Women become the imagined fetishes of men — passive, narcissistic, exhibitionist — inviting male voyeurism. As John Berger has argued in relation to the portrayal of women in publicity, 'men act and women appear. Men look at women, women watch themselves being looked at' (1972, p. 47). Elements of Freudian symbolism are often present in sophisticated ads — animal furs, feathers, mirrors. The advertisements for Dormeuil menswear, Colmans mustard and commercials for jeans often exploit these psychological areas of experience.

Lines of appeal

Another way of analysing ads is to classify them according to their themes or the attitudes and feelings they are meant to appeal to or mobilize. Although advertisers will try hard to make each ad special and different, when you look at a large number of ads you realize that most are variations on a few basic ideas. Feelings and attitudes can be aroused by associating a product with, for example:

Happy families
Rich luxurious life styles
Dreams and fantasy
Successful romance and love
Important people, celebrities or experts
Glamorous places
Success in career or job
Art, culture and history
Nature and the natural world
Beautiful women
Self-importance and pride
Comedy and humour
Childhood

Not a few advertisements are based on appeals made to scientific 'fact' and on the technique of 'before-and-after' using the product. And another powerful technique of persuasion is to play on guilt feelings and worry, the fear of being lonely or socially ostracized or of old age. Sheer repetition is also a powerful advertising instrument of persuasion, and of course devices such as slogans ('Drinka Pinta Milka Day') and jingles ('Only Oxo can, like only Oxo does') are good examples of repetition. Normally any single commercial will use a combination of association, recommendation, repetition, jingle, fear and before-and-after.

Approaches to form and content

Iconographic analysis

When trying to understand the meaning of an advertisement we must consider not only the elements of which it is made up, but also the overall impression that it creates and the techniques it uses to create it.

If we concentrate first on the visual, illustrative material of ads, we need to list the items present in the picture (such as products, props, settings and actors) and then to move beyond this simple level to try to perceive links and relationships to other elements and other layers of the picture. Description and interpretation are inevitably linked.

The art critic Panofsky studied the iconography (imagery and symbols) of paintings, and proposed a simple model for the analysis of the subject matter of visual communication (see Panofsky, 1970, chapter 1). He suggested that there are three levels of meanings in an image. By unpeeling the first and second you can get at the third.

1. The first level is that of primary or natural subject matter consisting of lights, colour, shape and movement and the elementary understanding of representation, whether of people, objects, gestures, poses or expressions, and the interrelations which comprise events.
2. The second level is that of secondary or conventional subject matter which relates to the wider culture. At this level, motifs and combinations of motifs are linked to themes and concepts. According to Panofsky, certain motifs (which carry secondary meanings) may be called images, and combinations of images may be called stories or allegories.
3. At the third level we come to intrinsic meaning or content, which is discovered by 'ascertaining those underlying principles which reveal the basic attitudes of a nation, a period, a class, a religious or philosophic persuasion — unconsciously qualified by one personality and condensed into one work' (Panofsky was referring here to paintings).

Panofsky's approach is useful because it suggests this breakdown of

93

levels of meaning and a fairly systematic way of identifying the constituents of a picture and relating these to themes and concepts and wider cultural meanings.

Let us take the ad for Jøtul stoves (plate 10) and analyse it icono-graphically. At *level one* we need to list the contents included by the advertiser — books, paintings, antique furniture, whisky decanter, labrador (gun-) dog, horse brasses, copper log basket and two people of a certain age, class and implied relationship. We also need to note the basic colours and tones — warm, orangey browns. At *level two* we observe how these objects relate to our culture, that is, what they 'mean'. We recognize that they are images of an upper-middle-class, traditional, country lifestyle. The gun dog and the horse paintings are motifs of the hunting/shooting/fishing set, the books and antiques are motifs of education, high culture and taste. At this level, too, the ad tells a story in which the woman 'manages' the household economy (hence the little picture, top right) while the man is out at work earning a living. He has returned, it is early evening, and he is toasting his wife's good decision in buying the stove and thus fulfilling her role as household economist/manager and comfort provider. *Level three* is where we explain how the ad means all this. It can only mean what it does because it condenses into the one work a whole range of the underlying principles and attitudes of one particular class in one particular period. These principles and attitudes are the ones concerned with the appropriate roles of the two sexes, with the desirable status within our culture of certain objects and their meanings (books, paintings, etc.), and with the belief that muted harmonious colours are a sign of 'good taste' for a particular class. We could well say that level one is the denotative, level two the connotative and level three the ideological. These terms are explained in chapter 6 (but see also Fiske, 1982).

Visual perception
Even at Panofsky's hypothesized first level of meaning, our under-standing of the objects before us is not completely natural, innocent or intuitive. Although we take for granted the process of seeing and observing the people, things or events in our environment, visual perception is not altogether straightforward. To start with, our vision is unlike that of a camera; it is not a passive operation. We actively explore, select and organize sensory stimuli in the visual field. Our eyes usually see only the essentials of an object and what

"I don't care what the experts are predicting for the economy this winter...

...now we've got our JØTUL"

Just to look at a JØTUL woodstove is enough to reassure you that the future needn't be too bleak. Beautifully built JØTUL woodstoves give an immediate impression of reliability and robustness, and you can be certain appearances don't lie. JØTUL Norwegian woodstove technology is solidly founded on 127 years of accumulated craftsmanship.

But of course this is only the beginning of the good cheer that JØTUL is bound to bring to your hearth, home and bank balance. The highly efficient JØTUL woodstoves are designed to deliver the maximum warmth with minimum wastage from one of the lowest priced fuels available. And the good name of JØTUL ensures they will continue to do so for generations to come.

The magnificent JØTUL No. 6
The compact, impressively styled No. 6 is a classic illustration of how to save fuel costs handsomely with JØTUL. The precision-built JØTUL No. 6 is certain to give you magnificent warmth combined with economic fuel consumption.

For the full picture of the JØTUL woodstove range and the name of your nearest main dealer write to Dept. C, Norcem UK Limited, Old Bath Road, Twyford, Berks. RG10 9PQ.

JØTUL

A cast-iron promise of warmth since 1853

Plate 10 Analyse the iconography

we see is rarely determined merely by the look of an object in front of us. We know this because it has been found that even the simplest images are interpreted and reproduced differently in different cultures. Seeing has more to do with learning and knowledge than with the unambiguous transfer of images to the brain. When we see things we know what is there partly because of knowledge gained from previous experience. When we observe an image we 'read' it rather than just absorb it, and it is therefore accurate to talk of visual 'literacy'. Although children can recognize objects in a picture long before they can read, they are eight to ten years old before they can understand still or moving pictures in the same way that adults can. There are several perceptual exercises such as visual illusions and puzzles and unfamiliar diagrammatic representations which demonstrate the general way in which our brains deal with the information it receives; how we are selective about what we see and how our previous learning and experience constrains our perception.[2]

Non-verbal communication

Whilst we are on the subject of visual communication, we ought to touch on the question of non-verbal and para-linguistic meaning. There is a body of thought and material on this subject, mostly stemming from social psychologists and anthropologists, some of which can help us construct a system for the analysis of advertisements.

Let us start by considering the obvious. An advertiser's aim is to capture our attention and favourably dispose us to a product or service. This means that by and large the product will be shown in a desirable context so that some transference is made from the latter to the former. If you buy the product you are likely to attain the glamour and prestige of the situation depicted. One of the most successful ways of gaining the consumer's attention and getting him or her to infer the right message in a limited amount of space and time, is to use proxy advertisers or typical consumers — actors or actresses who will act out and typify favourable persons and dramatize the value of the product. By using characters and scenes which can be stereotypically identified, the spectator is drawn into the ad and invited to identify or empathize with what is said and done. This is a clever technique because when we look at an ad our attention is usually drawn immediately to its human aspect.

In any analysis of ads we ought, therefore, to pay some attention to the way human actors communicate feelings, social meanings and values like power, authority, subordination, sexuality and so on. Facial expressions are of course very important, as are gestures, poses, body movement, size and the way people group themselves in particular situations. All these ways of communicating meaning non-verbally seem to be natural and spontaneous. But with the possible exception of size and some basic expressive movement of the face and body which might have a physiological or biological origin, expressive displays are conveyed and received according to learnt cultural traditions. Some expressions can be read and understood cross-culturally, but to understand fully the function and meaning of affective displays we need to refer to a particular context or social situation *within* a culture. In ads, because they need to communicate swiftly, unambiguously and economically, you will find that devices like facial expressions, poses and movement tend toward stylization and generalization, or what the social anthropologist Erving Goffmann has called 'hyper-ritualization' (1979, p. 84) — tendencies which contribute towards the stereotyping of people (particularly with regard to their gender), activities and situations.

Equally important as conveyors of meaning in ads are the clothes, hairstyles and accessories used by the actors; quite precise meanings can be attached to someone's overall appearance. For instance, the labels 'punk', 'chic', 'county-set', 'mod', 'rocker', etc. conjure up certain specific appearances and styles.

In order to understand the meanings of ads featuring human subjects we need to delineate the principle non-verbal means by which people communicate. We can divide these means into appearance, manner and activity.

Appearance

1. *Age*. The age of the people in ads is a crucial focus of identification and an important factor in how we view the product. Research indicates that the age range of people in ads is typically narrow—the preferred age of the models/actors is between 18 and 35. Particularly where women are the subjects of ads, the emphasis is on youth.

2. *Gender*. This again is a most important source of identification. The display of a character's gender refers to conventionalized portrayals of culturally established correlates of sex. Analysis of ads suggests that gender is routinely portrayed according to traditional cultural stereotypes: women are shown as very feminine, as 'sex objects', as housewives, mothers, homemakers; and men in situations

of authority and dominance over women. Femininity and masculinity are prototypes of an essential expression which, according to Goffmann, can be 'conveyed fleetingly in any social situation and yet [is] something which strikes at the most basic characterisation of the individual' (1979, p. 7).

3. *National and racial.* These characteristics are usually related to stereotypical views of 'other' people and are frequently used as sources of humour.

4. *Hair.* This is one of the most potent symbols in cultural communication. Female hair in particular is considered to be seductive and narcissistic, meaning an object of love or self-admiration. The colour, length, texture and style of a person's hair are important qualifiers of their overall appearance. Sometimes young women in ads are shown with their hair mysteriously hiding their face or their eyes.

5. *Body.* This can be thin, fat, short, tall, clothed or partially clothed. The naked body is, of course, not value-free, carrying meanings according to a particular society's norms. Advertising has been quick to exploit the potential meaning of human, particularly female bodies. The body may be presented in such a way as to convey exhibitionism, narcissism, incongruity or daring. In some ads it is pictorially dissected or presented in a fragmented way, or as Trevor Millum describes it, photographically 'cropped' (1975, p. 83). Lips, eyes, legs, finger nails or hands are shown divorced from the body. Men are less often dismembered in this way, although the Flora margarine ads, which show only a man's torso, are an exception.

6. *Size.* Size is an important signifier of meaning. Relative size can convey social weight and superior status, power, authority, rank, etc. Men usually take precedence over women in this respect, although as Goffmann notes there are a few exceptions that prove the rule — women are sometimes pictured taller than men when the men are inferior in social class and 'thoroughly costumed as craft-bound servitors' (1975, p. 28).

7. *Looks.* Looks are related to the overall class, age, style and impression created by a character. Looks, needless to say, are conventionally 'good looks' — handsome men, beautiful women, cherubic children, kindly old folk. Ads generally confirm conventions of 'ideal type'. Although sophistication is a prevalent 'look' in ads, the plain, straightforward kind of person also appears — there is some

98

advantage to be gained in a studied naturalness or simplicity. In recent years and particularly on television, some ads have tried to capture a type of 'ordinary' person in everyday surroundings. The 'normal', 'average' people in Players Number 6 ads are an example of this. The captions read 'People like you are changing to No. 6', directly addressing the smoker so that he or she becomes a part of the message.

Manner

Manner indicates behaviour or emotion at any one time, and is manifest in three main codes of non-verbal communication.

1. *Expression*. The face and facial expression are a particular focus of attention in ads. Most expressions are based on socially learned, conventionalized cultural codes, which vary from culture to culture. The expression is meant to underwrite the appeal of a product and arouse our emotions. Normally the expression of the 'actor' will be positive, contented, purposeful, delighted, happy, gleeful, etc. There is considerable empirical evidence to suggest that in our society women smile more than men — both in reality and in commercial scenes. Women are often depicted in a childlike state of expectation and pleasure. They frequently seem to be too easily pleased in ads, as Goffmann suggests:

> If television commercials are to be believed, most American women go into uncontrollable ecstacies at the sight and smell of tablets and cabinets that have been lovingly caressed with long-lasting, satin-finish, lemon-scented, spray-on furniture polish. Or they glow with rapture at the blinding whiteness of their wash — and the green-eyed envy of their neighbours . . . (1979, p. 68).

In cosmetic ads in glossy fashion magazines the model's look might be cool and haughty as she looks the reader in the eye. Other typical expressions in ads may be seductive, alluring, coy, kittenish, inward-looking, thoughtful, pensive, carefree, out-going, comic, maternal or mature.

2. *Eye contact*. The attention of the actor in an ad is significant whether it be directed towards audience/camera (person to viewer eye contact), at an object (product), towards other people in the ad or to the middle-distance (detached, distant). Goffmann discusses the ritual of withdrawing one's gaze, mental drifting and social

dissociation under the general description *licensed withdrawal*. He remarks that

> Women more than men . . . are pictured engaged in involvements which remove them psychologically from the social situation at large leaving them unoriented in it and to it, and presumably, therefore, dependent on the protectiveness and good will of others who are (or might come to be) present. (1979, p. 57)

Covering the face or mouth with the hands is one way of hiding an emotion like remorse, fear, shyness or laughter. The aversion of the eyes and lowering of the head can indicate withdrawal from a scene and symbolize dependency and submissiveness. In many advertisements women are shown mentally drifting while in close physical contact with a male as if his mental and physical alertness were enough for both of them. Women may focus their attention on the middle distance, on some object (like the product) or on a piece of the man's clothing. Women are sometimes seen with a dreamy luxuriating look in their eyes (see plate 11). Eyes may be covered up or shaded by hair, hats, hands, dark glasses. Similarly, blinking or winking have great cultural significance. However, an equally important feature in ads is the shielding of everything but the eyes so that the person can observe an event without actually participating in it; some ads show women coyly peeping from behind fans, curtains, objects or products.

3. *Pose.* This can be static or active and sometimes corresponds to expression. Poses can be composed, relaxed, leisurely, passive, leaning, seductive, snuggling. Bodies can be vertical or horizontal. An individual can use another to act as a shield or as an object to lean against, or rest hands or legs on. Pose is also related to social position and status, hence women are often seen in a lower position than the man, for instance sitting at their feet.

4. *Clothes.* These are obviously extremely important carriers of meaning in ads, even when they are not the object being sold. They can range from the formal (regimental or work costume), to the informal (leisure, relaxation, sports wear), and can be smart, sophisticated, glamorous, elegant, trendy or comfortable and casual. They can of course sum up a 'look', e.g. the 'twenties' look.

Activity

Body gestures, movement and posture can be related to what the actor is doing.

1. *Touch*. The finger brought to the mouth or face can signify thoughtfulness but of a dissociated kind; women and children are often shown with the tips of their fingers in the mouth. Finger to finger touching similarly implies dissociation. Women more than men are pictured touching, or delicately fingering objects, tracing their outline, caressing their surfaces. This ritualistic touching is different from functional touching like grasping or holding.[3] Hand-holding can be a significant gesture in ads and often is used to allow the man to protect or direct the woman. Self-touching is again something that women do more than men; it conveys the impression of narcissism, admiring one's own body and displaying it to others, so that everyone can share the admiration of this delicate and precious thing. Sometimes the act of touching is displaced onto things — sun, wind or water on the naked body when sunbathing or swimming. The feel of clothes against the skin — satins, silks, furs — is conveyed as a pleasurable thing.

2. *Body movement*. This might be quite functional, i.e. simply related to what the actor is doing — cleaning the kitchen floor, making beds, filling up the car with petrol, playing football, gardening. These movements may be exaggerated, ridiculous or child-like, calling into question the competence of the performer. Bodies, particularly women's, are often not treated seriously, either through what Goffmann calls 'ritual subordination' (that is lowering the body in front of others more superior, lying or sitting down, ritually bending the knee or lowering the head) *or* through puckishness and clowning. An example of body movement is where two people are engaged in 'mock assault' and this is sometimes seen in advertisements, men usually playing these games on women.

3. *Positional communication*. The relationships between actors and actors, actors and objects are extremely significant, and are shown by their position within the frame of a picture. Superiority, inferiority, equality, intimacy and rank can be signified by people's position, size, activity and their relationship to the space around them, the furniture and to the viewer/consumer. Close-up shots, for instance, are meant to signify more intimacy and identification than long-shots.

101

Plate 11 The submissive woman

102

What to consider
when buying
fine jewelry.

Exotic mingling of fine jade
and gold-filled beads
creates extraordinary moods.

Danecraft

Affordable jewelry designed
to look expensive. Gold filled,
sterling silver, and sterling silver vermeil.

Millum has suggested four categories to deal with the relationships that occur in ads (1975, p. 96):

(a) Reciprocal — a two-way relationship in which each person is the centre of the other's attention.
(b) Divergent — each person's attention is directed towards something different.
(c) Object — the attention of each person is directed towards the same object.
(d) Semi-reciprocal — one person's attention is concentrated on the other, whose attention is elsewhere.

Props and settings

Non-verbal communication is associated mainly with 'actors', but we must not forget that there are other visual elements in ads: stage *props* and other objects (like grass), the *setting* (including weather), and of course the *product*. You might think that the meaning of an inanimate object or place is fairly straightforward. But physical objects can convey meanings to us in both literal or objective ways and also more subtly by suggestion and association. Objects are cultural as well as physical. Their appearance, shape, size and colour are the intentional result of a series of conscious choices and decisions made by human beings. The look of things is rarely accidental. The furniture we use, the rooms we live in, the meals we eat, our activities and everyday household objects implicitly or explicitly embody meanings. The best example of the analysis of everyday cultural objects can be found in Roland Barthes's book *Mythologies* (1973), in which the author 'decodes' such unlikely but totally accepted things as a wrestling match, a plate of steak and chips, an ad for margarine, the Citroën car, a travel guidebook and hairstyles. He shows how these objects function as cultural communication and reveals their underlying social values.

Props

Props are often used in ads and can be as prominent as the product or relatively insignificant. Props can be selected because they help demonstrate the product's use (e.g. a paint brush in a paint commercial, a cup and saucer in an instant coffee commercial) or results of usage (a damp cloth can be shown rubbing over a newly painted wall). They are more likely to appear, however, with a signifying as well as

104

a functional role to play. An ad for a food product might show it on a plate or in a bowl (functional), but if this piece of crockery is high quality Spode rather than mass-produced Woolworth's, we can see that the prop is intended to convey a special meaning: good taste and superior quality. In this example the prop has both a functional and a symbolic meaning. If coffee is shown in a coffee cup, the prop is there for functional reasons; if a bunch of freshly-cut daisies is placed next to it, it suggests that the coffee is as fresh as a daisy: the flowers are used as a metaphor.

Some props occur so frequently in ads that they have gained a conventionalized or symbolic value; they stand for what is regarded as being desirable — wealth, love, power, luxury, security. A Rolls Royce used as a prop in an ad signifies wealth and power. Country houses appear frequently, as do certain breeds of dog and thorough-bred horses. Dogs usually signify loyalty and devotion, cats and French poodles are used as symbols of (particularly feminine) fastidiousness and luxury. Drinks such as brandy or champagne are symbols of extravagance and good taste. Beer has strong connotations of masculinity, and might be used in ads for mens's clothes or accessories or to assure the reader that a brand of after-shave is adequately 'masculine'. Books, especially if accompanied by bowls of flowers, symbolize sound educational taste, while spectacles are meant to suggest cleverness.

Settings

Advertisements do not always contain settings; even those with actors sometimes have non-specific backgrounds. Like objects, settings are carriers of meaning and are rarely value-free. They act as a context which qualifies the foreground. Sometimes, of course, the setting is the advertised product itself, as in travel/holiday ads. In such instances, people and objects personalize the picture. The more defined, obtrusive or cluttered the background, the more it will affect the main action or purpose of the ad. The setting of an ad can be quite vague and hazy or it can be a collection of specific props, but as far as impact goes the whole may be greater than the sum of the parts. Panofsky's iconographic analysis is particularly useful here, for it demonstrates how a 'level-three' meaning can carry far more significance than an analysis on levels one and two alone might suggest. In some ads several backgrounds/settings are shown in order to show off the product's versatility or to provide some kind of juxtaposition of meanings — the mundane versus the exotic.

One way of categorizing settings is to decide whether they have been staged or are meant to give the impression of a 'slice of life' like a documentary. The two are not mutually exclusive. *Outdoor settings* generally look 'real' (although the desert-island setting for a Bird's Eye fish-fingers ad was designed to look artificial and cartoon-like). *Indoor settings* can vary from looking extremely natural to highly contrived or even surreal. A series of ads for Dulux paint show an interior setting without walls, which reveals the outdoors: here the setting is both realistic and surrealistic. Needless to say, indoor, realistic settings are actually unrealistic: they are tidier, more expensively equipped and better planned than in real life, and thus are idealized versions of reality, not reflections of it.

Millum suggests a useful categorization of interiors:

1. The familiar, known, real, that which we can experience or have experienced for ourselves.
2. The wishful, slightly unusual, imaginative, at one remove from direct experience: a wishful-thinking interpretation of reality.
3. The fantastic, exotic, very strange, improbable, dreamlike: far from daily, conscious experience.

To look at them in a slightly different way: a fantastic setting is one which the reader would never rationally expect to inhabit, a familiar one he or she would expect to inhabit, and a wishful one he or she might hope to inhabit. (1975, p. 93)

Analysing photographs

The advertising image and the way we see it are of course crucially dependent on the actual techniques of production and reproduction and on photographic or filmic techniques such as focus, film stock, lenses, close-up, cropping, editing (special electronic effects), camera movement, lighting, etc. Advertising and TV images are so eye-catching and persuasive largely because the advertisers use some of the most technically sophisticated equipment available and constantly experiment with new techniques, often the same which are used in feature films like '2001: A Space Odyssey' or 'Star Wars'.

Focus and depth of vision can make things appear clear and crisp or fuzzy and misty, and may be used to emphasize some parts of a picture and fade others away.

Close-ups are used frequently in advertisements to show objects in all their appealing detail or to give them a larger-than-life appearance. Blow-ups are also used to exaggerate the sensuousness of their physical characteristics.

Lighting and colour can be used in non-naturalistic ways, to give a dramatic or mysterious atmosphere. Colours can be soft and muted or impart a dream-like or nostalgic quality.

Cropping is the device of cutting up a picture, often to draw attention to certain parts of the body — isolated legs, eyes, lips or hands. Women are more frequently represented in this fragmented way than men, as if their bodies were made up of spare parts.

Camera angle does not usually draw attention to itself; we rarely notice that a scene or person is shot from an eye-line 'angle', but it can be altered to produce dramatic or unusual effects, or to control connotation.

Special effects, or *montage* are some of the devices which give moving film greater opportunities for special technical effects. Scenes and shots can be spliced together, and although we don't usually notice 'realistic' editing or 'montage', it can be used to great effect, e.g. to give the impression of dynamism and excitement. For instance, Welch *et al.* (1979) have shown that TV ads for boys' toys have far more 'edits' per 30 seconds than do ads for girls' toys. They conclude that this style of editing reinforces society's belief that boys are more active than girls. Images can be superimposed one on top of another in both still and moving photography, and trick effects are now widely used in TV commercials.

Many insights into the technical and 'creative' dimension of ads can be gathered from photography manuals and advertising primers. These kinds of books generally attempt to define guidelines and rules for 'good' pictures and good advertising campaigns. They provide useful pointers for analysis but in themselves are not concerned with analysis or interpretation but rather with professional practice and expertise.

In relation to visual techniques, we can also note the overall impact and impression created by an ad. Although the standard elements in a press ad are the product, a person, props, setting, headline, body copy, slogan, signature line, price reference, etc., the overall impression of an ad will depend on how many of these elements appear in an ad and on how large they are. The more elements that appear in an ad and the more space that is used up, the more crowded it will appear, although it will not necessarily lose impact as a result.

Content analysis

Having outlined a possible approach to the study of advertisements based on the observation and classification of their component parts, I shall now discuss an analytical approach which is based on the quantifications of textual elements. This approach is called *content analysis* and is a well-established research procedure in the social sciences. The basic assumption of content analysis is that there is a relation between the frequency with which a certain item appears in a text/ad and the 'interest' or intentions of the producer on the one hand and on the other, the responses of the audience. What the text is all about or what the producer means by the text is 'hidden' in it and can be revealed by identifying and counting significant textual features. Content analysis is usually confined to large-scale, objective and systematic surveys of manifest content using the counting of content items as the basis for later interpretation (see Fiske, 1982).

A study based on content analysis published by T. Manstead and C. McCullogh (1981) surveyed 170 different commercials broadcast on Granada TV. The researchers found that 66 per cent of the central figures in financial ads (for banks, credit cards, insurance companies, etc.) were men or 'voiced-over' by men. In all ads men were depicted as independent, whereas women were shown as dependent. Men were typically portrayed as 'having expertise and authority', as being objective and knowledgeable about the product; females were typically shown as consumers of products. Of the central figures shown in the home, 73 per cent were women and of the people who voiced no argument about the product, 63 per cent were women.

Although men were less likely to appear in commercials for body, home and food products, male voice-overs were used in 94 per cent of the sample of ads for body products, 83 per cent of home products and 80 per cent of food products. These figures confirm similar content analyses of ads on American TV, where for instance all-male ads appear more frequently than all-female ones (though these appear less frequently than mixed sex ads). In one American study 946 ads with voice-overs were analysed — 6 per cent used a female voice and 86 per cent a male voice (the remainder used both). In summary:

Women were seven times more likely to appear in ads for personal hygiene products.

75 per cent of all ads using females were for products found in the kitchen or bathroom.

Men were significantly more likely to be shown outdoors or in business settings than were women.

Twice as many women as men were shown with children.

56 per cent of the women in ads were judged to be only housewives.

43 different occupations were coded for men, 18 for women.

TV commercials clearly portray sex-role stereotypes, and according to some researchers repeated exposure to such stereotypes must influence the learning of sex-role stereotypes. The British research suggests that advertisements are not even approximately accurate in reflecting the real nature of sex roles. In 1978, for instance, 41 per cent of all employees in the UK were women. In the sample of British ads women comprised a mere 13 per cent of central characters portrayed in paid employment.

This treatment of women in ads amounts to what an American researcher has called the 'symbolic annihilation' of women. In other words, ads reflect the dominant social values: women are not important, except in the home, and even there men know best, as the male voice-over for female products suggests.

Not all examples of content analysis strictly adhere to the principle that significance is synonymous with frequency and in some cases latent content is considered to be as worthy of analysis as is manifest content. It is doubtful after all if the counting of isolated content items alone will indicate what a text means or how meaning is produced, nor how the audience interprets it.

In one recent study of ads in American magazines, the authors tried to get round some of the serious limitations of traditional content analysis by studying the rhetorical and persuasive devices of a sample of 300 ads. They also examined the ads for their ideological values and evaluations, and their norms and concepts of reality. In other words they tried to assess how an ad persuades and attempted to uncover more latent messages.

In the first part of their study, Andren and his colleagues (1978) discovered that in their sample of 300 magazine advertisements there were 576 instances of the different rhetorical means for non-rational persuasion that they had hypothesized and for which they had developed categories. Twenty of the sample contained rational argumentation only, with no persuasive devices.

The authors of the research used the following criteria to judge whether a part of an advertisement is persuasive or rationally argumentative:

1. An argumentative part of an advertisement deals with the product advertised and does not include statements that obviously lack relevance for the ad-thesis.
2. It does not contain emotionally coloured language when more neutral expressions can be used that have the same cognitive content.
3. When possible it contains precise and easily interpreted language.
4. It does not contain obvious untruths and exaggerations.
5. It does not invoke themes which are psychologically or socially loaded in the society in which it is published.

They concluded that ads do not act as objective guides to the audience to any significant degree and that if an ad is filled with persuasion (as occurred in 93 per cent of the ads in their sample) then it has a tendency to block or disturb rational examination and critical examination.

The authors also found that although the ads that they analysed were not overtly political, they did carry a number of latent messages that could have been regarded as ideological. For instance, the vast majority of ads stressed youth and leisure activities at the expense of older age groups and working environments. The portrayal of working life was found only infrequently in the ads, and where it was referred to, the jobs depicted were of high status and reward. The ads generally supported an individualized consumer mentality and one that was compatible with the aims of the consumer/capitalist economy. They presented images of a world and society devoid of conflict of interest such as those between nations, classes, racial and sexual groupings. Any expressed discontent with a situation or person was channelled into dreams about a better past or future or into self-criticism or self-contempt. It was a general tenet of all ads that any social or personal problems could be dealt with and overcome through the use of more and more commodities, gadgets, etc. The people in the ads were first and foremost consumers, and rarely workers, especially workers involved in collective work or in routine conveyor-belt work. The world depicted was a world of hedonistic, individual pleasure. How the rest of society fared seemed to be irrelevant.

110

Content analysis, a procedure which relies on the identification and counting of significant categories of content, can tell us a great deal about ads that we would not normally discover by impressionistic or cursory readings. But sometimes the counting or quantification of isolated elements in a piece of content cannot tell us everything about how meaning is produced in the text nor how the audience understand what is after all a complex piece of signification — the whole is often more than the sum of the parts. Advertisements are experienced as part of a flow of many sorts of cultural communication and their significance cannot always be reduced to their manifest, objective content. In the next chapter I want to look at an approach to the analysis of content which treats messages as complexly structured texts composed of signs combined into codes which allow meaning to be produced.

Notes

1. For a useful discussion of the problems associated with developing an adequate methodology for the investigation of audience 'readings' see Morley (1980), especially chapter 4.
2. See R. L. Gregory (1966), E. H. Gombrich (1962) and R. Arnheim (1967).
3. See Winship (1981) for a discussion of women's and men's hands in advertisements.

Suggestions for further work

1. Why do ads in magazines and newspapers and commercials on TV use the following techniques or formulae?
   — dramatized sequences,
   — song and dance routines/jingles,
   — sophisticated photographic/cinematic techniques,
   — experts and celebrities and scientific tests,
   — slogans and repetition.
   Can you think of any other standard advertising devices?
2. Why do many advertisements show products in a family setting? Are real families like the ones in the ads? Can the purchase of a product help towards an ideal family?
3. What impression of young people do advertisements seem to give? How is this impression put over? What language is used in ads

111

featuring teenagers and what images are presented?

4. How is 'love' portrayed in ads? Collect a range of ads that feature people in love or products that will help their love life and make them attractive to the opposite sex.

5. Try to construct/design an ad showing how extreme some ads are.

6. Collect a series of ads featuring women in a principal position. Group them according to age, 'looks', clothes, hairstyles, relationship to men/children, posture, setting etc. Do any consistencies emerge? What does Goffmann (1979) mean by 'licensed withdrawal' in relation to the way women are posed in ads? Collect some ads where women are shown in apparent ecstasy over a product. Are men shown 'transported' like this? Can these images have any possible effect on society's attitudes towards women and on women themselves?

7. Using a set of categories such as sex, occupation, status, facial expression, clothing, do a content analysis of ads in a teenage magazine and/or a hobby or specialist magazine. Break down the ads into these categories and indicate how many ads feature certain occupations or lifestyles, men, women, etc. Alternatively, construct a category system for analysis on the lines suggested by Andren *et al.* in *Rhetoric and Ideology in Advertising* (1978); base your analysis on the following categories:

Eye catcher	Picture or graphic occupies more than 50 per cent of space of ad.
Sex appeal	Sexually stimulating as opposed to informational.
Slogan	Phonetic or prosodic qualities designed to catch the eye.
Paradox	Syntactical or semantical peculiarities.
Value transference	Some quality, person or phenomenon is made to seem obtainable through use of product.
Pop method	Suggestion that product is in great demand, fashionable, etc.
Nature method	Product is natural; contains no artificial ingredients.
Flattery	Ad flatters viewer/recipient of ad in some way.
Temptation	Ad asserts that the owner of the product can achieve some generally desirable state of affairs or process.

Testimonial	Some identifiable person or institution recommends the product.
Entertainment	Ad contains a joke, a pun, a funny figure.

Take a sample of ads and identify the categories appearing in the ads. (For a fuller explanation of the content analysis method see Fiske and Hartley (1979), chapter 2, and Fiske (1982), chapter 7.)

6 SEMIOTICS AND IDEOLOGY

When we talk about advertisements or attempt to analyse them, most of us tend to assume that they are vehicles for the communication of usually somewhat distorted or exaggerated publicity; and that they are 'transparent' or invisible carriers at that. We tend to take for granted that what is on the screen or page is what the ad means and we 'measure' ads against some assumed reality which could replace the 'unreal' images which constitute most ads. The images of men and women in ads, for example, are usually considered to be mythic rather than real, and also stereotyped. This kind of criticism usually gets bogged down in arguments about the extent to which such images are true or false and seeks to replace distorted images with representations of people and situations as they really are. It assumes that there is a simple and better reality with which to replace the stereotypes and myths and ignores the fact that ads are in themselves a kind of reality which have an effect. In this sense ads are not secondary to 'real life' nor copied or derived from it. Ads are what some critics call 'specific representational practices' and produce meanings which cannot be found in reality. There is no simple reality with which to replace the falseness of ads, and there are no simple alternatives to stereotypes. In order to gain better understanding of the role that advertising plays in our society, we need to ask how advertising organizes and constructs reality, how ideology and meanings are produced within the ad discourse and why some images are the way they are, or how they could have been constructed.

In order to approach these questions we need to consider a framework for analysis established by semiotics, described by its founder Ferdinand de Saussure as 'a science that studies the life of signs within society'. It is an approach which has adopted some concepts and tools of analysis from structural linguistics, which attempts to uncover the internal relationships which give different languages their form and function. Although language is a basic model, semiotics has cast its net wider, and looks at any *system of signs* whether the substance is verbal, visual or a complex mixture of both. Thus speech, myth, folktales, novels, drama, comedy, mime, paintings, cinema, comics, news items and advertisements can be analysed semiotically as systems of signification similar to languages.

This approach involves a critical shift from the simple interpretation of objects and forms of communication to investigations of the organization and structure of cultural artefacts and, in particular, to enquiry into how they produce meaning. It is argued that the meaning of an advertisement is not something there, statically inside an ad, waiting to be revealed by a 'correct' interpretation. What an ad means depends on how it operates, how signs and its 'ideological' effect are organized *internally* (within the text) and *externally* (in relation to its production, circulation and consumption and in relation to technological, economic, legal and social relations). Implicit in this approach is a rejection of much impressionistic criticism and 'scientific' content analysis which assumes that the meaning of an ad is evident in its overt, manifest content and ignores the form that the content takes. As I said at the beginning of this chapter, ads are not invisible conveyors of messages or transparent reflections of reality, they are specific discourses or structures of signs. As such we do not passively absorb them but actively participate in their production of signification, according to the way they 'speak' to or 'ensnare' us. We come to advertisements as social readers. According to Janice Winship 'We all, so to speak, bring our social positions with us to the reading of any discourse; and we are not automatically "interpellated" as the subject(s) which the discourse constructs' (1981, p. 28). She cites the example of a poster for a car which proclaimed: 'If it were a lady it would get its bottom pinched', and which was defaced with this rejoinder: 'If this lady were a car she'd run you down'. This challenge is effective because it uses the same means of representation as the ad. It also highlights the fact that the original ad was clearly addressed to a male and that

115

the social reader objecting was a female. It matters, then, who an ad is implicitly addressed to, which may or may not include you.

Most semiotic/structural studies of advertising texts distinguish between their outward manifestation and inner mechanisms — the codes and conventions which organize and release the meanings of a text in the process of viewing or reading. Such codes are what makes meaning possible. Texts result from the dynamic interplay of various semiotic, aesthetic, social and ideological processes within them which also operate in the culture outside them. The audience member is involved in the work of the text and the production of its meaning; his or her own knowledge, social position and ideological perspective is brought to bear on the process of the construction of meaning. As Judith Williamson argues:

> Advertisements must take into account not only the inherent qualities and attributes of the products they are trying to sell, but also the way in which they can make those properties mean something to us ... Advertisements are selling us something besides consumer goods; in providing us with a structure in which we, and those goods are interchangeable, they are selling us ourselves. (1978, p. 13)

Advertisements do not simply manipulate us, inoculate us or reduce us to the status of objects; they create structures of meaning which sell commodities not for themselves as useful objects but in terms of ourselves as social beings in our different social relationships. Products are given 'exchange-value': ads translate statements about objects into statements about types of consumer and human relationships. Williamson gives the example of the ad for diamonds ('A diamond is forever') in which they are likened to eternal love: the diamond means something not in its own terms as a rock or mineral but in human terms as a sign. A diamond cannot buy love, but in the ad it is the diamond which is made to generate love and comes to mean love. And once this initial connection has been made we almost automatically accept the object for the feeling. People and objects can become interchangeable as in, for example, the slogans 'The Pepsi generation', 'The Martini set'.

It is in this sense that advertisements should be seen as structures which function by transforming an object into something which is given meaning in terms of people. The meaning of one *thing* is transferred to or made interchangeable with another *quality*, whose value

116

attaches itself to the *product*. In the simplest of cases, we can see how something (someone or some place) which we like or value transfers its qualities to the product. Two things are made interchangeable or equal in value — 'Happiness is a cigar called Hamlet'. Williamson calls this transfer of meaning between signs in an ad 'currency'. The cigar represents or replaces the feeling of happiness: 'Currency is something which represents a value and in its interchangeability with other things gives them value too' (1978, p. 20).

Feminists have pointed out that ads addressed to women define women in terms of the commodity. Goods like convenience foods, domestic appliances, toilet products and fashions are sold not as commodities but in terms of what they can do for relationships (with men, with the family, with neighbours). Women are made to identify themselves with what they consume — 'You, Daz and your Hotpoint automatic', 'You and Heinz together make a perfect team'. Success with the family and friends can be purchased for the price of a packet of detergent, a bottle of cough syrup or a jar of moisturizing cream. Of course, it is women who usually do the washing and cook the meals, but they are made to feel inadequate without the commodities which help them perform the tasks which constitute their family and social relationships.

So in order to understand the image of a woman in an ad, it is important to identify how she is signified and positioned in the ad as a female person, and to remember that any representation is also partially defined in relation to the material position of women 'outside' the ad, within what feminists call 'patriarchal relations' — their economic, political and ideological position in society.

Semiotics — concepts and methods

In order to clarify the contribution that semiotics/structuralism can make to the analysis of ads as signs and sign systems, I will describe some of the basic features and concepts of the structuralist model and apply them to different advertisements.

Structuralism (and I am taking this word to be more or less synonymous with semiotics) usually makes a distinction between the systematic and social part of *signifying practices/structural systems* — the material, conditioning and determining aspects of culture — and the resulting *individual signifying practice*. The former is usually referred to as *langue* (language) and it consists of structural rules and conventions, which are independent of the individual use of them. The individual use is called *parole* (speech), and is the manifestation of the selected, combined and articulated elements of *langue*. In language itself, the distinction between *langue* and *parole* is perhaps more clear-cut than in a system like advertising. Nevertheless it could be argued that an advertisement is the *parole* — the ordered combination of verbal and visual signs into messages — and that *langue* is the means (codes) which allow the messages to function. *Langue* conditions and is conditioned by *parole* and consists of a diverse set of social constraints, references and discourses, images, formal techniques and rhetorical figures which advertisers draw upon to create the publicity message.

A second distinction, which is important for understanding how sign systems work, is that made between the two parts which make up the sign, be it visual or verbal. A sign is made up of the *signifier*, a material vehicle, and the *signified*, a mental concept or reference. A signifier has potential but not actual meaning whereas the signified is the concept or meaning which the signifier refers to. The two are materially inseparable, although it is useful to distinguish between them for the purpose of analysis in order to see how the sign works. A simple example will illustrate the two aspects of the sign.

The ad for gold (plate 12) consists of the photographic image of two people in profile. They can be identified as a woman and a man, although only part of their faces are showing and the 'eye-line' of the photo is their shoulders (naked). We assume they are about to kiss. She has her hand on his shoulder and this reveals a gold wedding ring and a gold bracelet on her wrist. A linguistic caption, strategically placed between them, proclaims: 'The strongest links are forged in gold'. At one level this message can only mean that the links in her bracelet are made of gold and that they are strong and durable. This is more or less a rational/objective statement about the properties of the metal. Thus one of the *signifiers* of this ad is the gold bracelet; its *signified* is that this piece of jewellery is long lasting and a sound investment. But there is an assumed narrative in the ad which works beneath the surface. We need to delve deeper into the ad's rhetoric. He has given her a gift, she is rewarding him with a kiss. Their relationship is founded on this transaction: gold is the basis of their 'link'. Their (and by implication your) relationship will therefore be strong and durable. Much of this ad then, works at an unconscious level where a connection is being made between a gold bracelet

118

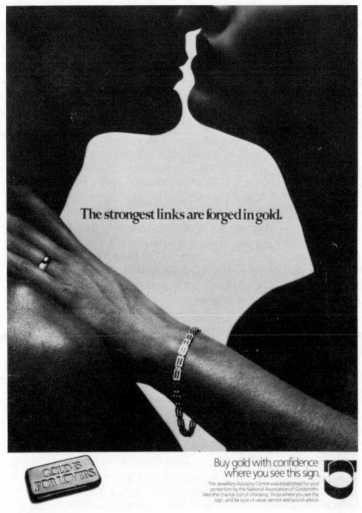

The strongest links are forged in gold.

GOLD IS FOR LOVERS

Buy gold with confidence
where you see this sign.

The Jewellery Advisory Centre was established for your
protection by the National Association of Goldsmiths.
Take the chance out of choosing. Shop where you see the
sign, and be sure of value, service and sound advice.

Plate 12 Signifier and signified

(signifier) and an intimate (sexual) relationship between two people
(signified). The significance of the message lies in its implicit narrative,
the world it creates (which denies questions about the object's

119

production — who made it, where does it come from, for whom is it intended) and the relationship it coins between the significance of love and its transference to gold. We have to make the connection. It is only implied by the visual message, although somewhat helped by the punning linguistic message. Gold is a precious and valued (expensive) metal; its currency is recognized outside the ad. This meaning is incorporated into the ad and carried by it. Romantic love is similarly an ideal in our society. The two are made interchangeable. The value of each is attached to the product — a gift of jewellery.

A further point can be made about this ad and that is the way in which colour is used. It is obviously no accident that the two unclothed bodies appear to have golden tans. The background is a simple, neutral colour. Again a connection is being made between the couple in the ad and the commodity, gold. Many ads use colour as an 'objective correlative', where the colours of the product, a packet of cigarettes, a cosmetic range, etc. are echoed by its surroundings: the décor in a room or a natural setting, by the clothes a model is wearing or by an object placed next to the product. The assumption is that the qualities and style of one will enhance the other through this visual link. The people or the world they inhabit in the ad become accessories of the product.

The colour technique is also used in TV commercials. The Kellogg's cornflakes advertisements, for instance, rely on the connection between the golden colour of the flakes and fine sunny skies, golden beaches, etc. In one commercial for this product, the image on the screen of cornflakes cascading out of a packet is spliced in with an image of a person jumping on a trampoline with the same abundant exuberance. The movement of flakes and person is almost continuous although the subjects of the two juxtaposed images are different. Here the formal techniques of cinematic editing act, like the colours, as signifiers of an implicit signified: energy, youthfulness, happiness, etc.

An ad for Renault cars (plate 13) sets up a correspondence between the car and a woman through the content and form of the signifiers. The woman is made synonymous with the car through the shiny dress she is wearing and through its colours, and in addition through the formal techniques of cinematic dissolves and the montage of images. The silk-clad, slinky, fashionable model lies in a sensuous horizontal position in the first frame of the commercial. Her image dissolves slowly into the image of a car in the next few frames, the curves of her body forming the outline of the car. Subsequent frames show

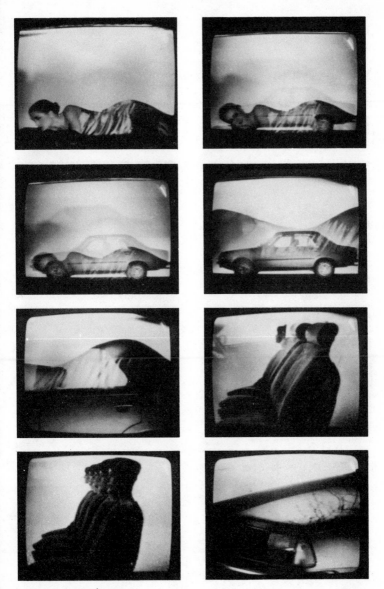

Plate 13 Renault cars

121

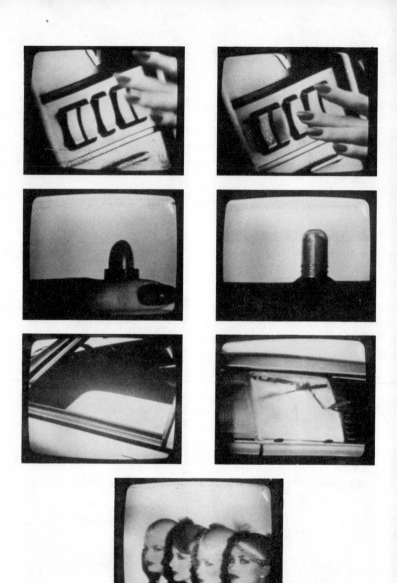

the fragmented parts of a woman; her hands, head, torso, etc. are juxtaposed with, dissolved into or made to stand instead of the car's instruments, headlights and reclining seats. Elongated fingers and manicured, painted nails sensuously touch and caress the control panel and the car's phallic-looking locking mechanism. Woman as a sign, shaped and moulded like a car, displays herself to be looked at by men. She is made into a decorative, passive object available and controllable like the car. She is moulded in the form that men desire; she is controlled by the gaze of the absent man and is represented by the imagined fetishes which men are supposed to respond to. She adorns and caresses the car and men are invited to caress their cars/women. The images are misty and the music throbs. This kind of ad expresses women's sexuality in men's terms; it invites the signified voyeurism and sexual power and control through the forms of the signifiers.

The important thing to remember about signs is that their meaning can only be assessed in relation to their structure and their structural relationships with other signs. A sign not only means in and for itself but also through its place in other signifying systems, for instance the individual ad within advertising. The signified does not exist except as a function of a particular signifying system. Meanings are organized in 'chains' of signification and signifieds can become signifiers for further chains of signification (see denotation and connotation below, p. 127).

Advertising, like language, is a system consisting of distinct signs. It is a system of differences and oppositions which are crucial in the transfer of meaning. In the commodity market there are many products such as soap, detergent, cosmetics, breakfast cereal, margarine, beer and cigarettes which are essentially the same. Ads for these products have therefore to create differences and distinctions through the use of signs arranged in structures. The most obvious way of creating a distinction between products and to make one stand out from the rest is to give it a distinctive image. Perfume ads, for instance, try to create an image of the product because of the lack of any 'hard' information that can be given about its properties. And cigarette ads use brand images extensively. For instance, the series of ads for Marlboro cigarettes trade on the well-established image of cowboys, cattle round-ups, wild horses, wide-open prairies, etc., drawn from the mythic world of cowboy films. These images of the old wild west transferred to the world of cigarettes act as signifiers for the signifieds:

adventure, masculinity, freedom, etc. The product substitutes for the scene and is meant to signify these attributes too. Virginia Slim's cigarettes also appropriate a referent system, this time women's history: their exploitation and oppression, and also their 'quaint old-fashioned' ways. This image is juxtaposed with one of today's women – free, swinging, carefree, sophisticated – a contemporary system of reference to the liberated woman. Hence the slogan 'You've come a long way baby'.

Ads continually move between systems of meaning like this, transferring from one meaning we are already aware of to create a new meaning.

Iconic, indexical and symbolic signs

It is worth digressing here to explain in a bit more detail the nature and form of signs, since they are the bedrock of communication. It is easy to be misled by advertisements, which consist mainly of photographic representations.

Photographic images look like the thing, place or person being represented. This makes them *iconic* signs, and the signifier-signified relationship one of resemblance or likeness. A portrait of a person is an obvious example of an iconic sign, because the picture resembles that person. Some signs go beyond the mere depiction of a person or thing and are used *indexically* to indicate a further or additional meaning to the one immediately and obviously signified. For example, the idea of Paris or Parisian holidays can be indicated by a picture of the Eiffel Tower, a landmark in the city which is frequently associated with it. The costume a person is wearing may denote iconically the mode of dress worn by a person or character in an ad, but at the same time stand *indexically* for a social position or profession. A character's movements may simultaneously represent some (dramatic) piece of action and indicate his or her frame of mind, habits or livelihood. For example a man who walks with a rolling gait is probably a sailor and one who has a swagger might be a cowboy. A woman in ads is often represented indexically by bits of her body – hips, eyes, head, hands or legs – which signify not only in themselves but also her whole being. They can also signify a commodity – lipstick, eye make-up, shampoo, nail polish, tights, etc. – thus suggesting that women are commodities also.

If an advertiser wants to convey the idea of heat he or she could

124

show a picture of a thermometer rising, beads of sweat on a person's brow, hot, shimmering colours, etc. As with all indexical signs, there is a sequential or causal connection between signifier and signified — the mercury in a thermometer rising, sweat, or shimmer, and the idea, concept or feeling of heat.

The relationship between signifier and signified in some signs is arbitary based neither on resemblance nor on any existential link. In other words, the signifier does not resemble or cause the signified, but is related to it only by convention or 'contract'. This kind of sign is called a symbol. A rose is a symbol of love or passion not because a rose looks like love or passion or even because the flower causes it. It is just that members of some cultures have over the years used the rose in certain circumstances to mean love; just as in the ad campaign for gold we are invited to connect gold with love; and in cigarette ads, cool, refreshing things like mountain streams or fresh-looking and tasting foods, are made to symbolize (very unhealthy) cigarettes. In some ads, people like judges, policemen or nurses are used to mobilize feelings associated with the job or profession. In many cases the symbols used to convey meanings or ideas are not entirely arbitrary: the symbol for justice, a pair of scales, for instance, could not be replaced by any other symbol. In other words there are the rudiments of a 'natural' bond between signifier and signified in many symbols. An example of a pure symbol, with no such bond, would be that of the white horse used by White Horse Whisky, where the horse standing in a bar or on top of a mountain or at a building site stands for the bottle of whisky itself, although there is no 'logical' connection between the bottle and the sign horse. The sign and its referent co-exist in the brand name. The function of presenting a horse in these ads is to make more real the meaning the brand name gives the drink and is backed up by the slogan 'You can take a White Horse anywhere'. Brand images generally act as symbols for their products, but it is perhaps important to note that in most ad campaigns iconic, indexical and symbolic signs invariably overlap and are co-present.

Advertisements may look 'real' and 'natural' and the connections they make between dissimilar things may have the appearance of a system that is 'logical', and belongs to a 'real' or 'natural' order, but such connections are not inevitable. Even in the incongruous and illogical case of placing a white horse in a bar or living room or an enormous bottle of whisky on top of a mountain, the 'system' of

125

the ad makes more 'real' the natural signification that the brand name gives to the drink, which is never out of place in a bar, as a horse never is on a mountain side, and vice versa. The whisky becomes a natural object through the white horse. In the end we come to accept the 'logic' of the system without question. The signs of other meaning systems, which have certain images, feelings or ideas attached to them, are transferred to the products rather than springing from them and are given the status of 'facts'. We are of course meant to see the meaning of the product as already there in its image on the screen as it unfolds. We rarely notice the inherent dissimilarity of objects and products placed together. As Judith Williamson has pointed out, 'a product and image/emotion become linked in our minds, while the process of this linking is unconscious' (1978, p. 30).

This linking of thoughts, emotions or feelings with something 'objective' and external is not a new phenomenon; it forms the basis of much art and many myths and rituals. However, advertising has a particular function in evoking emotions and feelings through promises of pleasure connected to the purchase or possession of a product. A product can even go from being the signified of a correlating thing, person or lifestyle which acts as a signifier, to generating or being that feeling, e.g. 'Happiness is a cigar called Hamlet', 'Bacardi and friends'. The act of consuming the product sign releases or creates the feelings it represents. As Williamson reminds us, when the product precedes the feeling we can end up not only speaking but feeling in clichés: 'The connection of a "thing" and an abstraction can lead them to seem the same, in real life' (p. 37).

Syntagmatic and paradigmatic sign relations

Before discussing the coding of photographic signs in more detail, I need to introduce another pair of semiotic concepts. De Saussure proposed a distinction between the *syntagmatic* relation between elements in a language, and *paradigmatic* relations. Syntagmatic relations are the permissible ways in which elements succeed each other or combine together in a chain of discourse. These elements have nothing in common and are brought together by virtue of 'combinatory (syntactic) rules'. A syntagm is defined by its opposition to that which follows or precedes it.

In advertising the syntagm is the advertisement or series of advertisements as they appear on the screen or page — a 'chain' of

126

visual, verbal and aural signs. In order to discover the paradigm and eventually the rules of an ad's signification we have to break up the syntagmatic chain and isolate (for the purposes of analysis) a distinctive unit, in order to find the roots of its meaning. A unit or sign thus identified, for example a stallion in a Marlboro ad, can then be (theoretically) classified according to its paradigmatic (*vertical*) relations, which in this case consist of all other functionally similar objects: ponies, donkeys, mules, dray horses, foals, mares, etc. Obviously the stallion was chosen to appear in the Marlboro ads because of its particular associations. It recalls a system of meaning beyond the immediacy of the syntagmatic (*horizontal*) text. Paradigmatic structures facilitate the associative and connotative use of terms: they assume a code or coding. A stallion is understood by virtue of its relation and opposition to mules, asses, cows, etc. but it is connotative due to a 'deeper' paradigmatic relation. Connotation relies on the reader's cultural knowledge of a system which can relate 'stallion' to feelings of freedom, wide open prairies, masculinity, virility, wildness, individuality, etc.

Paradigmatic relations are those which belong to the same associative set by virtue of the function they share. So a sign is in a paradigmatic relation with all the signs which can also occur in the same context but not at the same time. An example from Barthes's *Systeme de la Mode* (1967b) might help to clarify these concepts: In the garment/fashion semiotic system, the paradigmatic order is 'A set of pieces; parts or details which cannot be worn at the same time on the same part of the body, and whose variation corresponds to a change in meaning of the clothing: toque–bonnet–hood, etc.' (p. 63). The syntagm consists of the 'juxtaposition in the same type of dress of different elements: skirt–blouse–jacket' (ibid.). A linguist, Roman Jakobson, extended the idea of paradigm and syntagm to the notions of metaphor and metonymy: metaphors belong to a paradigmatic order and metonymy to a syntagmatic order. Metaphor is a matter of the selection of elements from an associative plane; metonymy is concerned with combination at a horizontal level (see Jakobson, 1971, p. 67).[1]

Denotation and connotation

The concepts denotation and connotation are two of the most important in semiotic analysis (although they are not exclusive to semiotics). Roughly speaking, denotation and connotation refer to first and second levels of meaning in a sign. The term denotation refers to the literal meaning of a sign; to what is 'objectively' present and easily recognized or identified. Connotation is a term used to refer to meanings which lie beyond denotation but are dependent on it. Connotative readings of signs are introduced by an audience/viewer/reader beyond the literal meaning of a sign and are activated by the means of conventions or codes. Roland Barthes elaborates these concepts in *Elements of Semiology*, where he says 'the first system (denotation) becomes the plane of expression or signifier of the second system (connotation) ... the signifiers of connotation ... are made up of signs (signifiers and signifieds united) of the denoted system' (1967a, p. 91). We the spectators can only join up or make sense of these two systems by our knowledge of cultural codes and associative meanings without which the second system, connotation, is not possible. A rose, for example, means on the denotative level, a flower. This signified can become the signifier (vehicle) of another signified at another level. Depending on the context, the rose can connote love or passion. In the context of a historical film like *Richard III*, the images of a red or white rose would connote the houses of Lancaster or York. In the context of an ad for beauty preparations or perfume, a well-known film star signified by a photo can in turn become the signifier of the connoted meaning glamour, beauty, sophistication, fame, etc.

Readers or spectators have actively to introduce cultural codes in order to interpret a sign by uniting signifier and signified. In an important essay on semiotics and publicity images, Barthes draws attention to the levels of meaning in ads. He calls the denotative, first level of meaning of an advertising image, a non-coded iconic message and the second level, a coded iconic, or symbolic, message. The latter is based on pre-existing bodies of knowledge of a practical, cultural, national, historic or aesthetic nature. According to Barthes, interpretation at the iconic, denoted level is relatively unproblematic and even suggests that the photographic image is a 'message without a code'.

In the essay 'Rhetoric of the image' (1977) Barthes lists the component (discontinuous) signs of an ad for Panzani pasta products. These are some packets of pasta, a tin of spaghetti sauce, a sachet of parmesan cheese, some tomatoes, onions, peppers, and a mushroom all in or emerging from a string shopping bag placed on a surface (table). The colours are predominantly greens and yellows on a red

128

background. Barthes analyses the ad at the connotative level in terms of a narrative or story:

> the idea that we have in the scene represented is a return from market. A signified which itself implies two euphoric values: that of the freshness of the products and that of the essentially domestic preparation for which they are destined. (1977, p. 34)

Further signs are present; the vegetables and the colours of the picture signify Italy or Italianness just as the connoted sign of the linguistic message, Panzani (the product's brand name and the ad's caption) itself signifies Italianness. The collection of different objects falling out of the bag also communicates the idea of a 'total culinary service', and the composition of foods (and container) in the image evokes the memory of innumerable still-life paintings.[2]

Barthes's analysis of the Panzani ad demonstrates how the ad's meaning is constructed not just by the discrete signs but by the ordering of events or the 'world' it implies. It is a 'frozen moment', but with a before and after created by the advertisers. In a critique of photographs, Manuel Alvarado argues that photos, including those for ads, have possibly more than one level of narrativity — the order of events implied by the photograph and an implicit or second level of narrativity:

> The second would question the actual history of the production, circulation and consumption of the photograph within particular institutions and under the regulation of technological, economic, legal and discursive relations and practices. (1980, p. 8)

Alvarado suggests that the second level is invariably repressed in favour of the first, but that this line of analysis suggests some further questions: namely that it challenges the authority (verisimilitude) of the photograph and suggests that 'How it could have been is politically a more interesting question' (ibid.).

The world of the advertising photograph or what Barthes calls 'the common domain of the signifieds of connotation' is ideological, and 'cannot but be single for a given society and history no matter what signifiers of connotation it may use' (1967a, p. 49). Ads as a means of representation and meaning construct ideology within themselves through the intervention of external codes which are located in society. The ad will use images, notions, concepts, myths, etc. already available in the culture. An ad does not simply reflect ideology; it reworks it, thus producing new meanings. It uses objects which are signifieds of ideological systems and thought that already exist and then makes them signifiers of another structure (the ad). Its connotational process depends on our knowledge of the forms of ideology that advertisements employ.

In advertising there is almost no denotative communication. Although it is useful to distinguish between denotation and connotation for analytical purposes, denotation is not neutral or untouched by ideology. It may seem to be more fixed and taken for granted but it is still dependent upon a context of meaning and association. The supposed absence of a code at the iconic, denotative level merely reinforces the myth of photographic naturalness. According to Barthes, 'it innocents the semantic artifice of connotation, which is extremely dense in advertising' (1977, p. 45). And in *S/Z* (1975) he expands on his earlier 'innocent' definition of connotation:

> denotation is not the first meaning, but pretends to be so. Under this illusion, it is ultimately no more than the last of the connotations ... the superior myth by which the text pretends to return the nature of language to language as nature. (1975, p. 9)

This is why the ideology of advertisements is so powerful; it is naturalized by the image, the neutral realm of the signifier.

We should not forget that ideology also works through the linguistic message — Barthes's third level of meaning in an ad. This level 'fixes the floating chain of signifieds in such a way as to counter the terror of uncertain signs' (1964, p. 37). All images are made up a number of 'floating' signs and subject to a variety of interpretations. The function of the linguistic message — caption, headline, copy, etc. — is to 'anchor' the variety of possible meanings, inviting some interpretations rather than others and resolving ambiguity or contradictions in the image. As I mentioned the linguistic message of the Panzani ad aids identification and also connotes, backs up or secures the meaning intended — 'Italianness'.

The linguistic message can also function as 'relay'. This is rare in fixed images, but important in moving images such as TV commercials, where dialogue, for instance, elucidates the image and advances the action or narrative, spelling out what cannot be found in the images. Sometimes it is the linguistic message and not the image which predominates, and the image is used to 'anchor' an eye-catching but unspecific or puzzling caption.

130

Photographic and filmic images have their own connotative abilities in addition to those drawn from the wider 'maps of meaning' in a culture. For instance, a scene can be shot from different angles, the camera can be moving or static and the film stock can be colour or black and white. The stills in plate 14 illustrate some of these connotations.

(a) The mother and young daughter in the 'Comfort' commercial are shot in soft, fuzzy focus and the lighting gives a golden, warm hue to the scene. The characters are lit from behind to emphasize softness and the scene exudes caring, warmth, mother love, etc.

(b) The 'Ladyshave' commercial is similarly shot in soft focus but the hues are bland and white, suggesting a sophisticated coolness without detracting from the implied femininity of the scene. (Notice the model's narcissistic interest in her own body, with the implication of a male's attention and gaze.)

(c) The 'Krona' commercial is crisply focused to give the impression of 'objective' reality. The main character poses in the stance of a news reporter and the distance between him and the camera lens/screen also indicates objectivity and factual reporting unlike the close-ups in the previous two examples.

We derive meanings from kinds of shots and other filmic techniques because we have learned the codes and conventions of TV and film practice. We unconsciously compare high-angle with low-angle shots and know how to distinguish between the two and what they both indicate. The fact that a certain shot conveys a meaning depends not only on our ability to relate it to other potential shots in a paradigm of shots but also to actual shots that precede or follow it in the syntagmatic discourse. Thus an isolated shot might mean something different from the same shot in the context of a sequence or chain of shots/events.

Codes

The concept of code is central to semiotic analysis. The formation and understanding of messages (encoding and decoding) is made possible by codes — a set of rules or an interpretative device known to both transmitter and receiver, which assigns a certain meaning or content to a certain sign. We recognize the signifier,

(a)

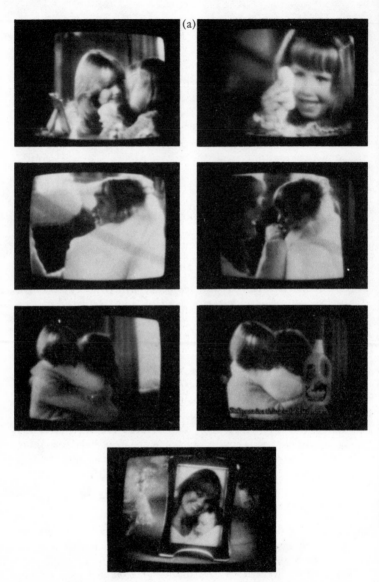

Plate 14 TV commercials: (a) Comfort (b) Ladyshave (c) Krona

132

(b)

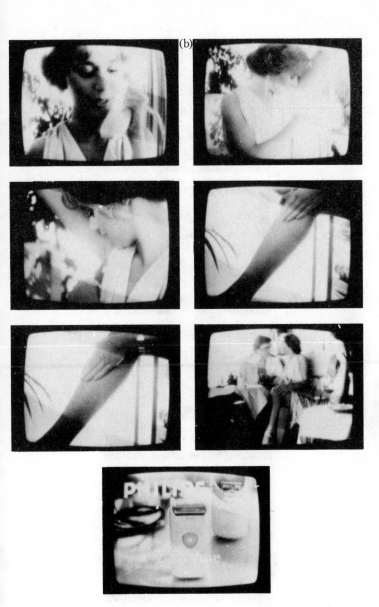

long blonde hair for example, as a sign of femininity when we interpret it through the code of femininity as the signifier of a certain signified, woman. Within that code there is a sub-code which assigns this long-blonde-haired woman a particular meaning — a particular kind of 'healthy sexuality'. Codes are forms of social knowledge which are derived from social practices and beliefs although they are not laid down in any statute. Codes organize our understanding of the world in terms of 'dominant meaning patterns', patterns which vary from culture to culture and from time to time but which we largely take for granted and which are uppermost in our minds when we interpret things or think about them.

There are a number of codes at work in both press and TV commercials. Before the ad reaches the page or screen it undergoes a complex coding process involving a large number of people, including at the outset an account executive/team, a copywriter, an art director and possibly a graphic artist or photographer. These people make decisions about the finished advertisement and have a determining influence on what it will look like. At a further stage in the encoding process, decisions have to be made about what kind of transmitter will be used (photographic stills, drawings, film, actors, voice-over, etc.). The lighting technician, set designer, costume designer, composer, camera operator and actors in their capacities as performers and creators are also involved in the 'coding' of the ad and they draw on their own general knowledge, social, professional and technical skills and aptitudes. Actors in ads are themselves multiple coders: their bodies, voices and metonymic accessories like costumes and props act as transmitters of signs.

In effect, ads consist of many messages; several channels are used simultaneously although in synthesis. The viewer interprets this complex of messages — images, speech, gesture, costume, setting — as an integrated text according to the media/cultural codes at his or her disposal. In addition to the multi-levelled nature of an advertisement, there is the question of the mediation of the ad as a whole. We are, as Goffmann points out, willing and ready 'to switch at any moment from dealing with the real world to participating in make-believe ones' (1979, p. 23). Commercial realism like other forms of fiction requires that we frame it off from the rest of life; indeed it has advantages over real life, probably being richer and fuller and less ambiguous than glimpses of real life. We are normally perfectly aware that ads are ads however much we might believe in them, and this is due to our ability to bracket off and to accept the 'factitious' in advertising texts.

An advertisement could be said to be 'semiotically thick': it comprises a heterogeneity of signals and is characterized by its spatial as well as temporal dimensions. Each image or frame operates spatially, whilst linguistic messages and the unfolding of the text/message is temporal. Movement, however, is both spatial and temporal.

We can begin to understand how an advertisement works if we look at the complex of codes which permit a range of messages to be brought together in a text. Not every ad will contain every possible code available to it. Most ads contain a broad type or class of code — a linguistic code and an 'iconic' code. These enable us at a minimum level to understand them as pieces of communication. Further, there is an advertisement or framing code, which probably comes into operation and allows us to apprehend it in its own terms. Similarly, we bring to an ad our knowledge of generic and stylistic rules relating to ads and the more general cultural, behavioural, ideological and ethical principles which we apply in our everyday social activities.[3]

Notes

1. See also chapter 8 for a discussion of advertising's use of metaphor and metonymy.

2. See also Berger (1972), chapter 7, for a discussion of the way publicity appropriates art to lend allure or authority to its own message.

3. See Appendix IV for a taxonomy of advertising codes.

Suggestions for further work

1. What are the main advantages of analysing advertisements as sign systems like language? What would the equivalents of words and sentences be in advertisements? (See Barthes, 1968, and Williamson, 1978.)

2. Analyse the ad for Philips Ladyshave (14b) in terms of its codes and conventions. What is the relationship between the way this ad is organized (coded) and social experience? How important is our experience of other texts and discourses to the understanding of this ad?

3. Why is there little iconicity in ads? Collect some ads in which a photo image of an everyday object is meant to signify more than itself. Have these images become indexical signs or symbols of

Plate 15 Paradigmatic dimension

another, additional meaning? Collect some examples of brand images (e.g. Marlboro cigarettes). What are their meanings? How are these conveyed?

4. What use are the concepts syntagm (or metonymic pole) and paradigm (metaphoric pole) to the analysis of ads? (See Barthes, 1968, Jakobson, 1971 and Fiske, 1982). Discuss the Colman's mustard ad (plate 15) in terms of its paradigmatic dimension. Break down the syntagmatic chain into its relevant constituent units (i.e. woman, fur rug, fire, etc.) and then group them into paradigmatic classes (colours/tones, lighting, body language, decor, etc.). How do these paradigmatic structures facilitate the connotative meanings of an ad?

5. What codes and sub-codes are at work in the famous series of ads for Benson and Hedges cigarettes or Guinness? Cut them out of magazines, and paste them on a sheet of cardboard in order to help you in your analysis.

6. What binary oppositions like nature/culture can you observe at work in television commercials? Are there other fundamental kinds of binary oppositions which underly many commercials?

7 THE LANGUAGE
OF ADVERTISING

I have discussed the changes that have taken place in the appearance of ads over the past thirty years and the contemporary emphasis on the visual aspects and image-making of promotion and publicity. It would be wrong to suggest, however, that advertising language is unimportant. In fact the language of ads is sometimes more important than the visual aspect.

Advertising language is of course loaded language. Its primary aim is to attract our attention and dispose us favourably towards the product or service on offer. Advertisers use language quite distinctively: there are certainly advantages in making bizarre and controversial statements in unusual ways as well as communicating with people using simple, straightforward language. Copy-writers are well known for playing with words and manipulating or distorting their everyday meanings; they break the rules of language for effect, use words out of context and even make up new ones. Plain and direct language and modes of address can, however, still be used to attract attention and add emphasis to a picture. The use of the imperative mode is of course very common in advertising: 'Buy this', 'Try some today', 'Don't forget . . .', 'Treat yourself', as are plays on words or puns: 'Short, Black and Sides', 'Black hander', 'Black on the map', etc., have appeared in a recent campaign for John Player cigarettes. Of course some ads are completely devoid of language or speech, relying on the visual image of the product to speak for itself.

Catching our attention and imagination and aiding memory are

139

perhaps the primary functions of advertising language: unusual or stylish words and short, crisp sentences are easy to repeat and remember. And our memories are also served by brand names, slogans and catch-phrases, rhythm and rhyme, alliteration, snatches of song or verse and of course endless repetition. In addition to conveying meanings and feelings through the judicious and experimental use of vocabulary and syntax, language can function not just as a sign system but also as a sign itself. For instance, some ads rely more on the style of language than its actual content. In ads for, say, a foreign product like French cheese, wine or cigarettes, the speech or writing might be in the French language. We are not really expected to understand the literal meaning of the words used nor to decipher the details of the sales message but merely to recognize that it is French — a sign in itself that signifies 'Frenchness'. Similarly, colloquial language can be used to indicate everyday life, and childish language to connote childishness. Different typographical and calligraphic techniques can also be used as signifiers so that language can signify the product directly by uniting language and product. I will examine some of these aspects of advertising language in the following pages.

Words have feelings

When we choose a word we do more than name an object, person or situation, we also convey feelings about what we are describing. What you feel or your attitude towards what you describe is an important part of meaning. Words can affect the beliefs and attitudes of other people. If you call a person one of the following:

obese
fat
chubby
well-built

you are obviously giving your opinion, and it might be the case that the person would prefer to be called the last of these four adjectives. The advertising copy-writer is well aware that words can work like this, and indeed the fact that they can adds a richness to our communication. The copy-writer will use words to project the product he or she is bringing to people's attention in the most attractive way.

Words not only describe things, then, they communicate feelings, associations and attitudes—they bring ideas to our minds. For instance,

140

the names of these lipsticks bring certain ideas to mind: sleek peach, hanky pinky, quiet flame, warm coral. When products like carpets, paints or make-up come in a number of shades, colours or patterns, the advertisers choose attractive names for them which are designed to do more than just separate and distinguish one from another.

Brand names
Brand names communicate denotatively and connotatively. When it comes to naming the product in the first place, there is considerable scope to invest it with particular meanings and associations. The manufacturer has to give a product a distinctive name in a mass market. The name should do more than just label or identify the product; it should also bring flattering associations to mind, associations which will help sell it. The names given to cosmetics and other beauty products frequently recall images of beauty, cleanliness, sophistication and naturalness: Moondrops, Natural Wonder, Rainflower, Sunsilk, Skin Dew. Sometimes the names of products convey scientific authority: Eterna 27, Clinique, Endocil, Equalia. Men's toiletries (not 'beauty products', you notice) also have evocative names: Brut, Cossak, Denim, Aramis, Devin. And it doesn't take much imagination to work out why cigarette brands are called by such names as Piccadilly, Embassy Sovereign, Consulate, State Express, Lambert and Butler, nor why there are cars called Jaguar, Mustang, Triumph, Princess.

A popular identifying technique is the deliberate misspelling of words in brandnaming to give a product uniqueness while at the same time allowing it to retain some recognizable elements. In the names Rice Krispies, Ryvita and Brylcreem, the elements 'Krisp', 'Ry' and 'creem' are still meaningful although they are not spelled correctly.

The tone of voice
It is not only words that attract attention to an advertiser's product. Usually we are more inclined to listen to a speaker if the voice sounds pleasant or friendly. Television and radio have a considerable advantage here because the advertiser can use actual voices to create the right impression. Some advertisements try to stimulate interest in their products by using a bright and breezy or efficient sounding voice, others use a warm and cosy voice or a seductive and intimate one. Some voices are insistant, pushing and aggressive. Even press

and magazine ads attempt to suggest a tone of voice by the style of language used:

Earl Grey [Tea]
Reminiscent of the warm natural
scents of a far-away summer evening
with a tantalizing taste and delicately
scented in a secret way described
by a Chinese mandarin many years ago.
Much to the satisfaction of its many
admirers Twinings share the secret.
At its most refreshing served
straight with only a sliver of lemon.

To keep your grip, you need more than the
latest in tyre technology — we're talking
about the Cavalier's suspension.
It is designed to complement the most
recent thinking in the tyre world.
And it produces a ride that Starsky
and Hutch wouldn't be proud of.
No slipping and sliding.
No rocking and rolling.
No shaking all over.
Independent, computer-tuned
suspension with coil springs at the front,
live axle with coil springs at the rear,
plus anti-roll bars at both ends — those
are the reasons.
Not that you need anything as
unexciting as a reason to drive a Cavalier.

In the first example a sensuous, quite high-class tone of voice is suggested by the use of such words as 'tantalizing' and 'delicately', and it also sounds as though the message is coming from a knowledgeable person. In the second example (from a car ad) the tone is more conversational, jocular and breezy. A tone of brisk efficiency is suggested by this copy:

Its sleek, sporty styling shows a careful attention to aerodynamics:
Low-slanting hood. Sharp high-tipped rear end. Air-clam front

spoiler. And a wedge shape that slices air cleanly — all of which adds up to better fuel economy.

Notice the short clipped sentences, sometimes with no verb, and also the 'shape' words like slanting, high, wedge. In the following example of copy from an American magazine, the imagery and tone are intensely patriotic: it almost reads more like a national anthem than an advertisement:

America the Beautiful.
From the prairies. To the cities. To the oceans
    bright with foam, America shows its true colors.
Colors with a strong constitution. Proud colors.
    Young colors.
Colors destined for greatness. Sand soft, plum deep
    and mauvy.
Some of these new colors are: North-West Rose,
    Prairie Mauve, City Lights, Gold Coast Red.
For your eyes, your lips, your cheeks, your nails.
    Ultima II.

The 'tone of voice' of an advertisement as well as the words used and the rhythm of the copy will sometimes try to recreate the experience of having and enjoying the product:

    'M' is for moments you'll never forget
    For days marvellous with flowers and laughter
    For nights magical with moons and old promises
    'M' Fragrance by Henry C. Miner.
    It's Magic.

Here the mood is pitched towards fantasy and dreaming. In the following copy for a type of fire, the language is cosy, intimate and domestic (and, incidentally, sexist):

Having a quiet night at home for once — and very nice too. You'll browse through magazines, he'll try to read his paper, and you'll both enjoy the sheer comfort of your new fire.

The language for fashions is often tactile and caressing and uses adjectives of touch, shape and physical comfort. The intention is to invest the product with meaning by tone, rhythm and association.

The role of advertising language

Advertising language is generally informal and colloquial. Sentences are usually simply constructed and short. Imperative clauses are frequent. The prospective customer is continually exhorted: 'Buy X', 'Discover Y', 'Find out about . . .', 'Try it today', 'You'll feel better for it', 'Don't ask a man to drink and drive', 'Don't be vague. Ask for Haig'. As an example of direct and colloquial speech consider this copy:

> Let's face it, isn't it worth considering? Of course it is and there's no time like the present — so get that pen right away and fill in the coupon in this week's *TV Times*. Or call in at your nearest branch and talk things over with the branch manager.

This mode of address would be unthinkable and even rude in private English. (Some people would argue that it is also 'rude' in advertising language and that the advertiser is not only invading a person's privacy but also assuming that he or she is of pretty mediocre intelligence.) Nevertheless it does illustrate some typical features of advertising language. The tone is jocular, even disingenuous, the grammar is abbreviated and disjointed.

In TV commercials there is an even greater tendency towards the abbreviated or disjunctive mode of discourse. Time is short (some commercials are only seven or fifteen seconds long), and the spoken word often plays a relatively minor role because of the combined power and impact of visual and auditory material. There are even commercials with no speech at all or just an end-line of slogan: 'X, the name you can trust' or 'Big on convenience. Smaller in size. New all around.' The following ad for an insurance company illustrates the disjunctive mode:

> If you're a married man.
> What if you died young?
> It could happen.
> And then who'd pay the bills?
> Would your wife have to go back to work?
> Who'd collect the kids from school?

Of course not all advertising consists of direct exhortation or direct address where the advertiser seems to be communicating directly with the audience. Often an advertisement will have a presenter who does a monologue on behalf of the advertiser or there might be a dialogue, where two secondary participants (actors) talk to each other. The most common type of advertising dialogue is the domestic playlet, where the *dramatis personae* are ordinary men, women and children — mothers, fathers, neighbours and shopkeepers — and the 'plot' is an unremarkable happening in everyday life, the theme being the excellent qualities of the product. This situation gives the viewer the position of eavesdropper; it has often been argued that people enjoy watching other people, preferably ordinary people, going about their day-to-day business.

Another common form of advertising is the dialogue interview with an 'ordinary' customer:

Q Mrs Facet, do you ever get a headache?
A Yes, I do.
Q And do you take a pain reliever?
A Yes, I do.
Q Is it possibly this, the number 3 best seller?
A No.
Q Or this, the number 2?
A No, not that one.
Q Or this, the number 1 best seller?
A Ah yes, Anadin, that's the one I take.
Q Can you tell me why?
A Nothing works better than Anadin for me.

Try Anadin for headaches. For tense nervous headaches. Anadin is the number 1 best seller.

Interviews which act as testimonials for products can be very effective, particularly when the interviewer is an experienced broadcaster or celebrity and is able to elicit what look like spontaneous remarks from the 'man-in-the-street'. But some interviews can involve fictional participants or even be jokes or parodies of 'real' interview styles. Another familiar type of commercial is the monologue testimonial by a celebrity, showing him or her in suitably expensive or luxurious surroundings. A caption might identify the celebrity, for example 'David Niven at home'.

Sometimes advertisers use the interior monologue technique which conveys the inner thoughts of the person seen in the ad using the product. The viewer is invited to identify herself or himself with a secondary participant and see the product through her or his eyes. This technique is more suggestive than overtly persuasive. The speech style is usually impressionistic and like a stream of half-formed thoughts rather than a connected line of argument. It may be used in advertising which uses appeals associated with dreaming and fantasy, where rational judgement is suspended in favour of indulgent instincts.

Advertising also borrows the styles and idioms of other types of discourse, such as scientific or legal language. In other words, an ad might use particular linguistic features which are more appropriate in a different context. In private conversation we might borrow someone else's language for sarcastic reasons. In literature, language is borrowed for artistic purposes; in comedy, language-borrowing is a form of parody. There are many advertisements which use features strictly appropriate to another role. Both TV commercials and magazine display ads sometimes use the format of an official form, a medical record card or a medical interview. Here is part of a full-page ad from a teenage magazine:

Period Problem No. 5
Name: Angie
Age: 15
Problem: Angie believes her Mum knows best, but her info's not up to date.

At the bottom of the page, after a series of photographs, the same copy is repeated but this time printed on a piece of paper, which looks as though it has been torn from a note book. Next to the copy is a passport-style photograph of a smiling young girl and 'stamped' over the top of copy and photo is the word 'solved' in official-looking lettering. The rhetorical effect of this type of advertisement lies in its seeming objectivity and terseness and also in the way that it mingles formality with emotive images. The language of science would, of course, not be appropriate in advertising because few people would understand it. But copy-writers like to use scientific-sounding terms because they impress the audience. The word science itself and related terms are no less popular and are probably less baffling: 'laboratory tests show . . .', 'scientifically clean', 'science tells us . . .'.

Role-borrowing often disguises the sales message and persuades the public into thinking that the message is a disinterested and not a 'loaded' piece of writing. Some commercials, for instance, have all the trappings of a TV documentary using neutral-sounding but earnest voice-over commentary, and 'objective' film techniques which one might expect to find in 'factual' news or current-affairs programmes. In magazines it is not difficult to make an ad look like a feature article, because some publications have tended to adopt the visual and linguistic techniques of ads for all kinds of material. Another kind of disguised sales message can be found in those ads which present a piece of general knowledge. 'In 1849 Charles Dickens wrote *David Copperfield*, and it remains a classic . . .' leads to a selling proposition which is linked only tenuously to the body copy: 'Today the art of fine writing lives on in . . . pens'. In the advertisement for Birds Eye orange juice (plate 16), the language and style appropriate to the wine waiter in an expensive restaurant has been 'borrowed' or parodied for comic effect. This also allows the highly-valued qualities of wine to be transposed to orange juice.

Language and the law

Before discussing some more examples of advertising language and rhetoric I should briefly raise the question of legality. The associations that words have can mislead people into thinking that they are buying something other than what the product actually is or contains. For instance, orange squash is sometimes called orange crush which might make people think that the drink had more real oranges in it. The Trade Descriptions Act (1968) makes it an offence to offer goods or services under descriptions that are not accurate. Descriptions can relate to a product's size or quality, to its method of manufacture (e.g. 'home-made' or 'farm-product'), to what it is made of, to what it will do, to its country of origin, etc. If a label on a tin says 'stewed steak and onions', 'produce of countries of the EEC', we can reasonably check on the former — the latter we have to take on faith. The Consumer Association has analysed the meat contents of various tinned products under terms laid down by the Canned Meat Products Regulations, and has issued a rough guide to tinned meats which includes the following points:

The more words in the name, the lower the meat content is likely to be.
Chopped usually means a higher meat content than sliced or pressed.

Birdeaux Premier Cru 1980.

Mis en boîte en Floride.

Plate 16 Parody

The sooner vegetables appear in the name, the less meat there will be.

Gravy usually means more sauce than meat.

148

As a result of complaints, advertisers are now not allowed to make the kind of excessive claims that were made, for example, in the Smirnoff vodka ad: 'I was Mr Holmes of Household Linen until I discovered Smirnoff'. It was thought that such an overt connection between alcohol and sexual/social success should not be made in an advertisement.

Nowadays you are less likely to see or hear such questionable descriptions as 'miraculous' or 'magic' for products, because of the legal sanctions.

Key words

If you listen to any commercial or glance at advertisements in magazines, you will be subjected to a liberal sprinkling of adverbs and adjectives. These are the key parts of speech for advertisers. They are the trigger words because they can stimulate envy, dreams and desires by evoking looks, touch, taste, smell and sounds without actually misrepresenting a product. Words like 'big', 'small' and 'long' are relatively easy to imagine in connection with a product, but 'elegant', 'superb', 'enchanting', 'discreet', 'sheer', 'intriguing', 'captivating', are vague, cannot easily be checked upon and are often a matter of opinion rather than of fact. A rush of adjectives often substitutes for clear and reasonable description in advertising:

> More than a peppery-potent fragrance — Aramis is a complete action-oriented master plan of more than forty grooming essentials — from shampoos to shaving needs, bath soap to muscle soaks. Aramis is the only collection of men's grooming specifics that really works with authority, speaks with eloquence and communicates success.

The most common adjectives used in advertising are good/better/best, free, fresh, delicious, full, sure, clean, wonderful, special, fine, big, great, real, easy, bright, extra, rich and golden. But 'new' is probably the favourite. It is used in connection with almost every type of product or service, from insurance to fish fingers, and applies to any number of their features: size, shape, colour, formula and so on.

You might also have noticed unfamiliar adverbs and adjectives in advertising copy. These have usually been coined for the occasion and do not have any value in standard English. For instance, advertisements often contain words like: 'tomatoful', 'teenfresh', 'temp-

149

tational', 'flavoursome', 'cookability', 'peelability', 'out-door bite-ables', 'the orangemostest drink in the world', 'Ricicles are twicicles as nicicles'. Phrases are sometimes made by joining adjective with noun or adjective with adjective as in the following example from an American magazine:

Inside this jar you'll find a *radiantly-glowing* skin, *naturally-blushed* cheeks, wondrous eyes and *color-kissed* lips. Suddenly your skin has a radiant *sun-kissed* glow.

Here are some further examples of these adjectival compounds: 'Stay-on, stay-put colour', 'elegant drop-waist swirls', 'quick drying', 'new-face hygiene', 'figure-flattering', 'the so-many-ways cheese', 'the go-anywhere blouse', 'youngshape', 'the freezer-pleazers'. These words seem to suggest that the product has a special feature, which it alone possesses. They are created to give uniqueness, vigour and impact to the advertising message. A special kind of made-up word can be seen in copy where the product's name is incorporated with other words: 'Goudanight' (cheese), 'Schweppervescence', 'Ponti-nental' (holidays), 'Lux-soft', 'Knorr-fresh', 'Afiordable' (holidays in Norway) and 'Give your feet a Scholliday'.

Another favourite device of copy-writers is to spell words wrongly in order to attract attention. Perhaps the most famous of these misspellings is the 'Beanz Meanz Heinz' slogan and variations on it like 'Supperz', 'Cornish Pastiez', 'Vol au Beanz', 'Welsh Rarebeanz'. The slogan 'Drinka Pinta Milka Day' also shows a kind of misspelling, where indefinite article and conjunction fuse with the noun and verb.

Advertisers often use verbs and nouns unusually, in emotive rather than accurate ways. To a certain extent, of couse, the emotional use of words is also favoured by poets; but if we were to make a distinction between a poet's use of language and an advertiser's, we could argue that the poet wants to create an impression, pin-point or sum up a feeling in the interests of an emotional 'truth' rather than to paint a falsely glowing picture. Here are some examples of oddly-used nouns and verbs found in a few American and English magazines.

Thirty colours. Some so spectacular they send messages. (paint)
The first bra to understand the facts of life.
Creamy soft brilliance to bloom tenderly on your lips. (lipstick)
After-shave cologne with the sharp, crisp tang of action as well as the smooth undertones of elegant charm.

. . . a raincoat that keeps its cool when the weather's not.

We use essence of almond to coax extra body into the hair and control fly-away.

It speaks freedom and friendliness.

Drink a masterpiece.

Pink goes ping in our brave new spring collection. Pink-to-ice lace frolics up from the hem . . .

In twenty-four sensational shades that wake up a morning and turn on a night. (make-up)

The shampoo that holds in health, holds out dirt.

Go footing in our new soft soft tights . . . at a low, low price.

For skin that's lit from within. Outer beauty begins with innerglow.

Enter Visible Difference . . . it performs.

Notice in the last example, and others, a typical tendency to treat intangible entities as if they were living creatures: 'pink goes ping', 'shades that wake up a morning'. Scent 'communicates', saucepans have a delicate 'touch' with food, bras 'understand', shampoo doesn't simply clean, it 'holds dirt out'. It is as if we had to be persuaded to buy things on the basis that products are more than things — almost like pets.

Although the above examples of oddly-used words of figurative language are out of context, we can see that most of them are meaningless. Sometimes meaning is sacrificed in order to introduce a rhythmic beat to advertising copy. Rhythm is very important to advertisers; it allows people to remember things more easily, and can convey and induce all sorts of emotions. A great number of advertisements read or sound like verse even though they may not rhyme. Clear examples of rhythm can be found in television jingles which are often crudely cheerful and stirring. Meaninglessness is an important technique in advertising as are loose promises that don't tie down the advertiser to anything specific. Even advertisers recognize this tendency in their work; they call meaningless copy 'resounding non-statements': 'Triumph has a bra for the way you are'.

Figurative language

Advertising language is sometimes quite standard and unobtrusive, but more often it attracts attention to itself by being highly colourful and imaginative, and it sometimes involves stretching or breaking the rules or conventions of 'normal' language. We looked at examples of the unorthodox use of language in advertising above when we discussed role-borrowing, coined or made-up words and misspellings. In addition, advertising copy sometimes breaks grammatical rules and uses words incorrectly (semantic mistakes) as for example in the slogans 'liquid engineering' (oil), 'liquid Tchaikovsky' (vodka), or in the sentence 'our dishwasher is pronounced Mièle'. This unorthodox use of language is sometimes called figurative language. There are other ways of exploiting language to create particular effects and enlarge it as a means of expression. Double meanings and puns are often used in advertisements and so are rhyme, alliteration and other types of repetition designed to attract attention and arouse emotions.

Figurative language is rhetorical language in that it tries to create effects by breaking or exploiting language rules. We use language figuratively every day; communication would be very dull if we didn't. Some figurative or rhetorical expressions have passed into daily use and as a result are less surprising and memorable. We all accept that expressions like 'musical taste', 'I'll eat my words', or 'chewing over an idea', are not to be taken too literally; we interpret them in a figurative sense. They are examples of *metaphor*, where a word acceptable in one context (e.g. 'eat' in the context of food) is transferred to another context. Eating words is an absurd proposition unless we interpret the phrase in a figurative, non-literal way. Interpreted figuratively, this metaphor suggests the right kind of association: eating — swallowing — taking in — taking back — retracting. In other words we see a symbolic identity or connection between the literal and figurative meaning of a word. In the following slogan, the copy-writer has used the word 'sizzle' inappropriately: 'Taste that sizzle — Hear it say . . .'. Taste has been joined to sizzle, which is an abstract noun and not an edible object. 'Eat a bowl of sunshine' — a slogan for a breakfast cereal — is an example of a metaphor. In fact Kelloggs, the breakfast cereal makers, have built their whole campaign around the image of cornflakes = sunshine. The cornflakes brand image is a metaphor by which the product is identified with (desirable) sunshine. Copy-writers like metaphors because they allow the right kind of emotive associations to be linked to a product. A picture or image of a product can be built up through the 'irrational' use of language. In the slogan for Malboro Cigarettes, 'Come to where the flavour is . . . Marlboro Country', cigarettes are associated with a place, and an ideal one at that. You can't literally visit a flavour in the same way that you can visit Kansas or Wyoming, and by the same token you can't go to Marlboro Country because it is a fiction and doesn't exist on the map. In the Consulate cigarette ads we can see another kind of figurative meaning at work, this time a simile. In 'Cool as a mountain stream . . . cool fresh Consulate', the properties of the stream are directly compared to the cigarettes and incidentally given as the reason for buying them. Figurative language like this which, at least initially, catches the eye is very useful for slogans and headlines.

The examples on p. 150 illustrate figurative meanings. In the first we can see a case of *personification*: colours are invested with the human faculty of communication; likewise in the second a bra is given human abilities. An example of the rhetorical figure *synechdoche* can be found in the slogan 'Bring a touch of Paris into your life'. Here a very specific meaning, Paris, stands for general concepts — fashion, sophistication, good taste. 'Clarks bid to get Britain back on its feet' is another example where Britain stands for the British people. The slogans 'Go to work on an egg' and 'Wash the big city out of your hair' fit into the category of *metonymy*: 'egg' and 'big city' could be said to stand for the more general 'a good nourishing meal of eggs' or 'breakfast', and 'the dirt of the big city'. 'Egg' substitutes for a whole thing (breakfast) of which eggs form a part, and a part of big cities, their 'dirt', is substituted for the whole 'big city'.

Copy-writers also explore the ambiguous properties of language. Ambiguity can either be used for humorous reasons or to provoke interest in the ad. A statement could be said to be ambiguous if different meanings can be expressed by using the same word or if different meanings are expressed by words that are alike in spelling and pronunciation. A famous example of the latter, which linguists call *homonymy*, is the 'Players Please' slogan. It can be read as either 'Please give me some Players' or 'Players are pleasing'. Puns or plays on brand names are particularly popular. In the advertisement for More Cigarettes (plate 17), the name of the product is linked to a quality or idea. 'More' the product is made synonymous with 'more' the measure of quantity. The ambiguity in the word does not allow us to separate the product from the 'fact' that these cigarettes are longer, slimmer, milder. (American brands of cigarettes seem to go in for punnable brand names. There are brands called Real, Target, Vantage and City Lights.) The slogan 'Spoil yourself and not your figure' for weight-watchers' ice-cream is a common type of play on

Announcing More.

A new style of cigarette.

It's longer.

It's slimmer.

It's surprisingly mild.

More is the first filter cigarette that's 120mm long.

How long is 120mm? To give you an idea, the average king-size cigarette is only 84mm.

More is slimmer. The very first time you hold one you'll appreciate the way this new cigarette fits in your hand.

More's long, slim shape burns slower and draws easy.

Flavour?

More tastes mild, surprisingly mild. Because it's made from specially selected, mild cigarette tobacco.

More—long, slim and brown. Definitely a new style of cigarette.

One day this week, instead of buying your usual brand of cigarettes, try something new.

Try a pack of More.

50p FOR TWENTY.

*RECOMMENDED RETAIL PRICE CORRECT AT TIME OF GOING TO PRESS

The tar yield of this brand is designed to be **MIDDLE TAR** Manufacturer's estimate, December 1975, of group as defined in H. M. Government Tables

EVERY PACKET CARRIES A GOVERNMENT HEALTH WARNING

Plate 17 More cigarettes — a pun

ambiguity in advertising. It involves interpreting 'spoil' in 'spoil yourself' as an idiom or well-known phrase and as a word in its own right. 'Population down 30 per cent' is a headline of an ad for Kellogg's 30 per cent Bran Flakes. It involves our interpreting it as a

154

statistical statement about population which catches our eye because it is plainly not true and anyway is out of context next to a picture of the packet. We then have to look further into the statement and see that 'down' here means 'eat' or 'swallow', as in the expression 'down the hatch'.

An important class of rhetorical effects depends not so much on breaking rules or exploiting semantic ambiguity as on repetition of linguistic patterns. *Parallelism* is the repetition of formal patterns and *alliteration* is the repetition of initial consonants or consonant features. In the 'Beanz Meanz Heinz' slogan we have an example of both parallelism and alliteration. A sort of parallel scheme is at work in the More advertisement:

> It's longer
> It's slimmer
> It's surprisingly mild.

And there is a cheese advertisement which says: 'Grate it, grill it, spear it, stuff it, bake it, break it, toast it, roast it, post it' (a coupon). If this were a television commercial, the clauses would probably be accompanied by a simultaneous musical rhythmic beat and a parallel visual rhythm. In the following examples, no word is actually repeated but there is a parallelism in structure:

> Fine workmanship
> Beautiful design
> Real compactness
> Wonderful value.

> More Chic. Less Cheek.

Alliteration is also very common: it is not hard to find examples:

> The Superfree sensation
> It's got to be Gordons (gin)
> Pinky and Porky (pork pie)
> Guinness is good for you.

The 'absence' of language — calligraphy

Language is of course a primary reference system in communication. Language functioning as a sign can be used in the same way as pictorial signs: it can be there to be deciphered or absent to be filled in by the

155

spectator/reader. As I mentioned at the beginning of this chapter, in some ads language is used to signify the product directly through calligraphy. This is an extension of showing the product (or sign of the product) directly without any words (as in the series of ads for Benson and Hedges cigarettes). The product of an ad can be made to be its language, e.g. when the word KITKAT is made up of pictures of the bar of chocolate wafer biscuit. This is not a new idea. I described in chapter 1 how advertisers in the nineteenth century tried to beat the newspapers' column width rule by building up the names of their products with letters in order to comply with the size of the newspaper column and also to attract attention. Ads which use calligraphy suggest that the language is absent and that the product speaks for itself; that it can signify without being named. It is a way for language to deal with absence of language; like other hermeneutic systems, the calligram tries to unite the sign and its referent and give the impression of transparent meaning.

Finally, Michel Foucault, the historian/philosopher, has offered this useful account of calligraphy:

> The calligram makes use of this double property of letters to function as linear elements which can be arranged in space and as signs which must be read according to a single chain of phonic substance. As sign, the letter permits us to establish words; as line it permits us to establish letters. Hence the calligram playfully seeks to erase the oldest oppositions of our alphabetical civilisation: to show and to name; to figure and to speak; to reproduce and articulate; to look and to read. Pursuing twice over the thing of which it speaks, it sets an ideal trap; its double access guarantees a capture of which mere discourse or pure drawing is not capable. It undermines the invincible absence over which words never quite prevail by imposing on them . . . the visible form of their reference. . . . The signs summon from elsewhere the very thing of which they speak. . . . A double trap, an inevitable snare. . . . (in Williamson, 1978, p. 91).

Suggestions for further work

1. Choose a range of products, like Jaguar (cars), Brut (aftershave), Piccadilly (cigarettes) and think of other names for them which bring opposite associations to mind than the ones intended by the advertiser.

156

2. Look at some commercials on TV and radio and try to pin down the tone of voice being used. What is the most widely used tone you have come across? What are the connotations of these tones of voice? What tone of voice would be right for the way this ad is written?

3. Why do some ads use puns, alliteration, foreign or foreign-sounding words? Pick out some examples from magazines and TV and say what their effect is likely to be.

4. What is the effect of using the interior monologue technique in ads? List some ads which use this technique and the range of products which are likely to be associated with this technique.

5. What would you say were the main differences between a poet's use of figurative language and an advertising copy-writer's? Find five different advertisements in which a verb has been used for its emotional tone rather than for straightforward descriptive accuracy. Why do you think these were chosen?

6. Find an example of a persuasive word that is currently fashionable among advertisers: try to find ads for different products. Find some examples of portmanteau or hyphened words. What conclusions about the nature of the product can you draw from the use of portmanteau words? Are these kinds of words more associated with one kind of product than another and with one medium more than another?

7. Find some examples of 'resounding non-statements' in ads.

8. What likely effects would a strong verse rhythm have in an ad?

9. Examine the language of ads in different media: a teenage magazine, the *Economist*, and a TV commercial. List the similarities and differences in the use of language, i.e. the words and grammar used and misused, the rhythm or beat of the language, the situations or images evoked.

8 THE RHETORIC OF ADVERTISING

The word 'rhetoric' comes up frequently in any analysis of advertising since it refers to those techniques, usually verbal, that are designed and employed to persuade and impress people. Rhetorical language also carries the implication of extravagance and artifice, not to mention a lack of information. In his influential essay 'The rhetoric of the image' (1964), Barthes not only discusses a semiotic of the publicity image but also suggests a rhetoric of the image or classification of the connotators of the image. Such a rhetoric, he argues, is general because rhetorical figures are never more than formal relations of elements; they vary in substance (sound, image, gesture, etc.) but not necessarily in form. This feature makes the rhetorical device a useful concept for the study of visual language as well as written/spoken language. I shall examine this argument in this chapter, although I have touched upon it in the two previous ones.

Rhetoric, the effective or artful use of speech and writing, is used to clarify or add strength and impact to persuasive oratory. Its origins can be traced back to Ancient Greece and Rome, and it was practised in institutions of learning in Europe up until the nineteenth century. Nowadays you might still come across explanations of rhetorical devices and figures of speech in school textbooks on composition. In classical times there was a very large number of these rhetorical figures, and one of the difficulties of studying them today is that the ancient names are still used to label those that survive. Since advertisers are in the business of persuasion and have developed a vast array of devices for their purposes, advertising is the most obvious place we might expect to find the practice of rhetoric today. In the first place, advertisers deliberately set out to attract and retain the attention of listeners, readers and viewers. In the second place it is obvious that every element in an ad has been carefully placed for maximum effect.

A theory of rhetoric

Roland Barthes was not the only critic to suggest the possible application of rhetorical terms to the visual field. The art historian Ernst Gombrich (1962) deals with symbols and metaphors in relation to fine art in his book *Art and Illusion*, and a psychoanalytic application of rhetoric was suggested by Giancarlo Marmori (1968) in his book *Senso e Anagramma*. The most extensive and systematic exploration of rhetoric in publicity images has been carried out by the French critic, Jacques Durand (1970). From an analysis of thousands of ads he constructed a near exhaustive inventory of figures, or modifications of figures, used in visual advertising.

Principles for the classification of figures

Durand defines rhetoric as 'the art of fake speech' (*l'art de la parole feinte*). Rhetoric brings into play two levels of language, 'language proper' and 'figurative language'. The rhetorical figure is the mechanism that allows passage from one level to the other. What is said in 'figurative' terms could, in theory, have been expressed in more direct or simple fashion. The problem, as Durand sees it, is to discover what occurs in the figurative proposition which is not expressed in the simple one. If we want to say one thing, why say another? Durand turns to the psychoanalyst Freud for some guidance on this question, and particularly to the notions of desire and censure. According to a Freudian interpretation, people will speak figuratively to satisfy a forbidden desire. Thus a statement like 'I married a bear' (Durand's example taken from a letter to a newspaper's agony advice column) violates legal, social and sexual codes of conduct. It is an improbable statement and has to be interpreted in the more plausible way 'My husband is beast-like', 'His behaviour is like a bear'. This pretend or mock transgression of rules satisfies a forbidden desire, according to Durand's interpretation of Freud, and because it is only a pretence it remains unpunished.

159

Rhetorical figures, in Durand's view, should be regarded as mock violations of a norm. These violations could be against the 'normal' use of language or the norms of logic, morality, social rules and physical reality. Advertising frequently breaks 'rules', such as those of spelling ('Beanz Meanz Heinz') or grammar ('Winston tastes good *like* a cigarette should'). It also breaks the rules of physical reality by using the devices of dreaming and fantasy to induce 'trance-like' states in the audience. The use of humour and irony could be considered as a deviation from 'straight' discourse, while some critics suggest that photographic images 'break the rules' of physical reality. Even the most life-like photo is, after all, a transposition if not a manipulation of what we generally regard as reality. The photo is two-dimensional; real scenes or objects are three-dimensional and a photograph is usually smaller than the actual size of that which is being photographed.

In order to understand how rhetoric works, Barthes proposed that rhetorical figures be classified into two types: *metabolas*, based on the *substitution* of one expression for another (e.g. metaphors, metonyms and puns); and *parataxes*, based on the *relationship* between elements in a discourse (such as a sentence), that is, on the modification of 'normally' existing relationships between successive elements (e.g. elipses, parallelisms, alliterations). Durand's definition of rhetorical figures goes further:

> The figure of rhetoric being defined as an operation which, starting from a simple proposition, modifies certain elements of that proposition:
> (a) on the one hand, the nature of the operation
> (b) on the other, the nature of the relation which unites the variable elements. (1970, p. 72)

The former is situated mainly at the level of syntagm, the latter at the level of paradigm.

(a) *The nature of the operation*
According to Durand, there are two fundamental *operations* in rhetorical figures:

> *Addition*: where one or more elements are added to a word, a sentence or an image. (Repetition is a special case of addition as it consists of the adding of identical elements.)

Suppression: one or more elements in, for example, a sentence are suppressed, excluded, or concealed.

There are two operations which derive from these:

Substitution: a 'suppression' followed by an addition; an element is suppressed or concealed and replaced by another.

Exchange consists of two reciprocal substitutions. Two elements of a sentence can be permutated, as for example in the saying 'I eat to live not live to eat' or 'I cannot beg, to beg I am ashamed'; the second phrase inverts the order of elements in the first phrase.

(b) *The nature of the relation*

The *relation* or connection between the figurative use of language and the 'proper' use of language can be based on:

identity (uniquely 'same' relations)
similarity (at least one 'same')
difference (uniquely 'other' relations)
opposition (at least one 'opposed' relation)
false similarity (as in paradox and ambiguity).

This breakdown of the structure of the different rhetorical figures may seem abstract, but the theory will become clearer when we look at actual examples of advertising rhetoric. Meanwhile, here are two very well-known lines from poems; both use the figure *simile*. 'I wandered lonely as a cloud', and 'O, my love's like a red red rose'. In the first example, cloud is *added* to lonely, so the rhetorical *operation* is addition. In the second, rose is added to love. The *relation* between cloud and lonely, love and rose is one of similarity. One thing is compared to another, although the form of the things compared is actually different.

All figures of rhetoric can be classified according to the two dimensions defined above and can be tabulated as shown in table 1.

We will now look at some examples of visual rhetoric in advertising according to table 1.

Visual rhetoric

Figures of addition

1. *Repetition*. In classical rhetoric this is the repetition of the same sound, the same word or the same group of words. In advertising,

Table 1 *Classification of rhetorical figures (from Durand, 1970)*

Relation between elements	Rhetorical operation			
	Addition	*Suppression*	*Substitution*	*Exchange*
Identity	Repetition	Ellipsis	Hyperbole	Inversion
Similarity				
— of form	Rhyme		Allusion	Hendiadys
— of content	Simile	Circumlocution	Metaphor	Homology
Difference	Accumulation	Suspension	Metonymy	Asyndeton
Opposition				
— of form	Zeugma	Dubitation	Periphrasis	Anacoluthon
— of content	Antithesis	Reticence	Euphemism	Chiasmus
False homologies				
— Ambiguity	Antanaclasis	Tautology	Pun	Antimetabole
— Paradox	Paradox	Preterition	Antiphrasis	Antilogy

verbal and visual repetition is a well-used device. The After Eight mint ad shown in plate 18 is an example of visual repetition.

The white spaces that separate the identical images are in themselves not insignificant and in some cases indicate temporal change. Durand has suggested that if the spaces are narrow, the everyday use of a product is signified, while if the spaces are larger, a more widely spaced activity (e.g. the seasonal or occasional use of a product) is indicated; if the images are fused together, the continuous use of a product is indicated. He also implies that a large border of white around an image of a product connotes high class. In the advertisement for Evette cosmetics (plate 19) there is a multiple image of the same lips and finger nail. The form of the image is the same throughout its twelve separate versions. It is the content of the image that changes. Each one shows a different colour in the range of lipstick and nail polish colours. There is no space between the images; they almost fuse together as in a dream movement. (Notice also the alliteration in the headline, an example of sound repetition). Some ads consist of a repeated visual image in order to show how the same product works over a time period. An ad for a hair-setting lotion consisted of seven different pictures of the same woman in the same position with seven different hair styles to demonstrate how the product can be used to style hair for every day of the week.

Petit Fours

Plate 18 The device of repetition

2. *Similarity.* In classical rhetoric, a figure can be based on similarity of *form* as in rhyme, or on similarity of *content* as in comparisons (simile) and pleonasm, and of course it can also be found in visual rhetoric. There are many advertisements which are based on the idea

163

Plate 19 Multiple repetition

of similarity of 'formal' features. An ad for a biscuit had a picture of a raised finger next to a picture of the biscuit. It was trying to compare the two by indicating how similar they were in form. The caption said 'It's like a finger' (should there be any doubt). An ad for a baby-chair showed the product next to a picture of a woman's

164

encircling arms, and the caption read 'The security of a mother's arms'. These two examples show how an idea can be expressed 'formally' both in the image and in the content of the written text.

Durand (1970) defines a figure of similarity as 'an ensemble of elements of which some are carriers of similitude and others of difference' (p. 70). There is a great variety of advertising images based on constructions of similarity. For example, if an advertiser wished to show a range of nightdresses, the advertisement might consist of a number of pictures of the *same* model against the *same* background in a similar pose. However, the nightdress would be *different* in each photo. In this structure the user/person is the consistent feature. Conversely, an ad for a carpet or range of kitchen furniture might show several *identical* pictures of the product, each one containing *different* people showing off its *various* features — durability, good looks, etc.

3. *Accumulation*. When a message contains a number of different elements it is a figure of 'accumulation' and can convey the idea of abundance and quantity or disorder and chaos. Objects or people can be seen in a state of confusion, heaped up or crowded together as opposed to neatly and judiciously arranged or posed. Durand observes that 'relations of identity and opposition are not only absent, they are denied. Expressing profusion, accumulation is a romantic figure.' In the advertisement for TU cosmetics (plate 20), we can see objects scattered in disorder around the room. The slightly neater arrangement of the products below (which acts as the ad's signature) shows the figure of *epitrochasm* (a figure of accumulation), which in classical rhetoric is a hurried summary of points. There is also *ellipsis* in this ad because people are unseen or absent (suppressed) although their presence is implied. We can see their and by implication our tastes and habits 'written in' to their possessions — the champagne, the evening gown, the carpet, etc.

4. *Opposition*. Opposition can exist at the level of form or content. For example, the same scene in an ad can be presented in the same style but set in two different countries or centuries (formal opposition). On the other hand a single image can bring together elements which are in opposition to each other. An ad for a detergent showed a man dressed in white sitting on top of a heap of coal, and one for a deodorant consisted of a person who looked as though he smelled placed next to an image of a delicate nostril. The clash or juxtaposition of opposites is a certain way of gaining a spectator's attention.

Plate 20 A figure of accumulation (and ellipsis)

5. *Double meaning (ambiguity) and paradox.* These figures play on the opposition between appearance and reality. In double meaning an apparent similarity conceals a real difference (a similarity of form

hides a difference of content). In paradox an apparent difference conceals a real identity or sameness (a difference in form hides a similar content).

(a) In classical rhetoric *double meaning* is essentially the repetition of the same sounds with different meanings (antanaclasis): 'Learn a *craft* in your youth so that in your old age you can earn your living without *craft*'. In an advertisement this figure is present if the difference between identical-looking objects or people is pointed out in the text or caption. In the advertisement for Kraft margarine (plate 21) the caption offers an explanation of an image which contains what appear to be identical roses.

Kit-e-Kat cat food ran a press and TV advertising campaign for some years which consisted of a picture or film of two identical cats with the caption (or voice-over commentary): 'Of these two cats which one is the Grandmother? Difficult to tell'. Of course it was supposed to be the product which kept the older cat young. An ad for a home perm showed a pair of identical twins and the question to the audience was 'Which one is the Toni twin?' Over the caption 'One of these pullovers is new. Which? — impossible to see', an ad for a soap powder showed a picture of two identical garments. Purely visual antanaclasis can be seen in ads which show a picture of a person and his/her reflection in a mirror or in ads for film which show two pictures of the same scene, one a slide, the other a photographic print.

(b) In ads which contain *paradox* the text might indicate the real similarity which exists between two images of objects or persons which look dissimilar. In an ad for a make of beauty preparations, a picture of a glass with a toothbrush in it was placed next to a bottle of soap and face lotion. The same caption appeared above each of these separate images: 'Twice a day'. The implication of this message is that the facial cleansing products are as essential as brushing one's teeth twice a day. The ad for Colman's mint sauce (plate 22) is paradoxical because despite the obvious difference between fresh mint and bottled mint, the ad's question implies that there is no difference. In other words, the latter is the same as/as good as, the former.

Another version of paradox can be seen in ads which pose a problem or suggest a dilemma. An advertisement for a brand of lipstick asked the question: 'Which will win, the deep red or the light pink?' and then answered it by saying that it didn't matter very much as long as the product was Peggy Sage. The alternatives were false ones. The same mechanism is at work in this message from a

THE DIFFERENCE BETWEEN ORDINARY SOFT MARGARINE AND KRAFT LUXURY BLEND.

With everything there is the best and the rest.

And when it comes to soft margarines, Luxury Blend is, purely and simply, the best.

It has lightness, creaminess and above all purity, because it's made from 100% pure vegetable oils. To put it in a class of own.

And of course it also has something quite unique.

It's made by Kraft.

PURE UNADULTERATED LUXURY.

Plate 21 Double meaning

paint manufacturer: 'Which do you want, subtle shades or bold colours? Polycolour or Polyardent?' An interesting example of paradox can be found in those ads in which it is claimed that the product will be able to resolve a contradiction or provide an answer

168

THE ONLY WAY TO PICK FRESH NORFOLK MINT.

Straight off the shelf.
That's the only way to pick Colman's Garden Mint, fresh from the fields of Norfolk.

We harvest it and then prepare it within hours to keep it country fresh.

It's not only fresh though. It's the very best mint.

We looked at no less than 180 varieties before we chose the mint we grow today in the Norfolk fields.

So next time you're out, pick the finest, freshest mint.

Pick up a jar of Colman's Fresh Garden Mint.
THE PICK OF THE CROP.

Plate 22 A figure of paradox

to a supposedly insurmountable difficulty. In an ad for Outspan oranges the caption reads: 'How to gain a slender waist with the appetite of a horse — eat Outspan'. And one for 'SlimGard Protinets' declared 'How to lose weight by eating between meals'. In the caption for Evian water, 'Drink Evian and breathe fresh air', we can see the same figure — the implied message being that if you lead an unhealthy life a remedy can be found in Evian water.

Figures of suppression

These are much less common in advertising than figures of addition; probably because advertisements are more likely to exaggerate (add to, or expand) their case than to understate (lessen) it. It is difficult to argue a case by leaving something out and expecting spectators to notice this and supply the missing element themselves, although sometimes a play on absences is used in ads — the spectator has to fill in the missing object or person. As Judith Williamson suggests, 'in advertising, the exclusion of products, people or language, as opposed to their customary plenitude, works to give the subject the impression that he is "free" to produce a meaning for himself' (1978, p. 71). Of course, any *absence* in advertisements requires us to fill something in, usually along the lines suggested by the ad. Similarly understatement, humour, jokes and puzzles involve signification through absence. Certain gaps or oblique references can be deciphered and reached through the ad. This has the effect of making us think that meaningful reality lies directly behind the signs once we have succeeded in deciphering them.

1. *Ellipsis*. This figure may be seen as the opposite of repetition. In the latter the same element is present many times in succession, in the former an element is missing or left out. Usually ellipsis consists of the omission of an object or person such as we saw in the TU perfume ad. By leaving out an image of the product it is possible to give it extra value or an enigmatic quality. In its absence a product can be demonstrated to be indispensable or of even greater value.

2. *Circumlocution*. In this figure a part of an object is missed out, but it is linked to another element through a relationship of similarity. Visually we can see this in the ad for J'ai Osé (plate 23). A person is reflected in a mirror, but we can only see the reflection, not the person. Similarly in the Johnnie Walker ad (plate 23) the reflection is shown in full, the actual bottle is only half seen.

3. *Suspension*. This figure consists of holding back part of a message. Ads that cover two sides of the same page in a magazine, and which present an enigmatic image or a question on the first and the answer on the second, are examples of this figure. A television ad can also

170

be based on suspension or digression. A recent commercial was divided into two parts, the first appearing at the beginning of the 'natural break', the second after a series of other commercials but before the programme started again. It consisted of a presenter putting a product to a test and inviting the audience to stay tuned and wait for the results which were presented in the second half of the ad a minute or two later.

4. *Tautology.* In tautology a word is repeated, and although it is used in a different sense the second time it looks redundant because the different sense is not obvious: 'A Volkswagen is a Volkswagen'. An advertisement can employ visual tautology where the product itself is visually represented as if its mere presence dispenses with any further commentary. A product which is presented visually without benefit of commentary or caption is an example of a 'pure' advertisement. It is as if the ad doesn't need to say anything. Although they appear to be transparent, ads based on the image of a product exclusively are, nevertheless, signs.

5. *Preterition.* This can be seen in advertisements which feign a secret 'Don't tell your friends about X', in ads which say that the product has no need of publicity or which omit the name of the product on the assumption that it is so well known. A Schweppes campaign which mentioned only the first three letters of the product's name, 'Sch . . .', was a good example of this. Visually, preterition can be seen in gestures of false modesty: a woman's arms crossed in front of her breasts or a nude model covering her eyes with her hands; and in ads where the product is only half seen or presented in silhouette or outline only.

Figures of substitution

1. *Identical substitution.* The simplest example of substitution is where one thing replaces an identical one in a discourse. The difficulty with this figure is obviously that the substitution must be perceived despite the fact that the substituted element is identical. Sometimes the substitution can be a matter of degree. The use of exaggeration (hyperbole), accent, emphasis and understatement (litotes) are all devices whereby the element stays the same but is made a degree or two bigger, more emphatic or smaller. Accent has a number of visual equivalents in advertising: a black and white image can have a certain part of it picked out in colour in order to highlight it, or a product can be arrowed or circled to draw the audience's attention to it.

171

The only thing that changes
is how much you've got left.

Johnnie Walker—the world's
largest selling scotch whisky

Plate 23 Circumlocation

172

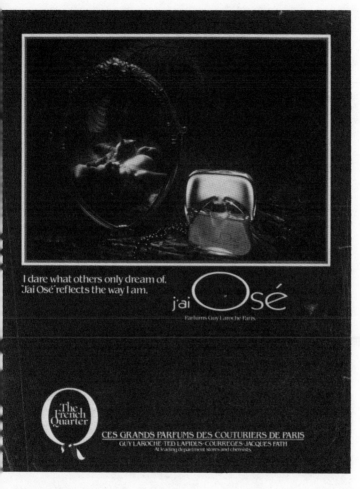

I dare what others only dream of.
'J'ai Osé' reflects the way I am.

j'ai Osé

Parfums Guy Laroche Paris

The French Quarter

CES GRANDS PARFUMS DES COUTURIERS DE PARIS
GUY LAROCHE·TED LAPIDUS·COURRÈGES·JACQUES FATH
At leading department stores and chemists.

Examples of hyperbole in advertising are almost too numerous to mention. As I mentioned in chapter 7, words such as 'big', 'bigger', 'most', 'gigantic', etc., are frequently used in advertisement copy. And hyperbole can also be encountered in the visuals and illustrations of ads. For example, the ad for Sansui hi-fi equipment (plate 24) shows an oversize image of the product dwarfing the small (and ordinary or understated) suburban houses next to it. The caption,

173

Plate 24 Hyperbole

'Way above the common or garden system', underlines the visual theme of superiority. Photographic techniques can be used to create hyperbole, such as when an object is shot in extreme close-up or blown up to fill the entire page or screen.

Meiosis is the opposite of hyperbole and similar to *litotes*. There are not many examples of this figure in advertising, since under-

174

statement or underselling a product are not usually used by advertisers. Nevertheless, one could argue that those ads which consist of precise, terse or objective statements are examples of meiosis. Understatement in ads can be so surprising or humorous that it is in fact very effective. In an ad for Burrough's business machines, an entire page was left blank. The accompanying text read: 'If you haven't got a Burrough's calculator yet, we are offering you this blank page to do your calculations'.

2. *Substitution of similar elements*. This is an important class of rhetorical figure, and the most common example is metaphor — the transference of ideas or meanings from one context to another. In the comparison of objects it allows abstract concepts to be expressed visually: freshness can be presented by a block of ice. When a comparison becomes conventional because it has been repeated so often, the thing which the object was originally compared to becomes a symbol: a feather symbolizes lightness, an egg can mean simplicity or novelty and a diamond can signify purity.

3. *Substitution of a different element*. Visual *metonymy* is frequently used in advertising. It occurs where an associated detail is used to invoke an idea or represent an object: in an ad for refrigerators, the product was replaced by a block of ice (the cause of the ice being the refrigerator). In a shoe ad, a shoe was replaced by its print. Substitution can also work the other way around: wool was replaced by a sheep in an ad for knitting yarns. An object can be replaced by its destination; thus in an ad for a radio, the product was replaced by a picture of an ear.

A *synechdoche* is another figure of speech based on replacement; in this case the part stands for the whole or the whole for the part (a car can be referred to as a motor, a policeman as the Law). In ads, a product can be represented by just one of its features or a person by a part of the body, as in the series of Flora margarine ads featuring a man's feet or his torso.

4. *Substitution of an opposing element*. This category includes *periphrasis* — a roundabout way of saying something — and *euphemism* — a mild or vague way of expressing something harsh or blunt. *Antonomasia* is a figure which substitutes an epithet for a proper name (the Iron Lady for Margaret Thatcher) or uses a proper name to express a general idea (a Solomon or a Jeremiah). Euphemism

may occur in advertising if the product relates to sensitive, personal or private matters.

5. *False homology*. Puns are plays on words involving the humorous use of words to suggest different meanings. Visual puns can be seen at work in the ads for White Horse whisky, where there is a continual interplay between the idea of taking the animal, a white horse, *and* the bottle of whisky to some rather unlikely places (plate 25). Two meanings of white horse are condensed to fit together perfectly in the same space.

Figures of exchange
These figures are more complicated to analyse because they concern a great number of elements.

1. *Inversion*. This figure is similar to repetition; the elements in a discourse may be identical but their order may be modified. It can be found in visual form in the advertisement for ball-point pens which shows a·person using the pen suspended upside down from a ceiling. Another example of inversion is seen in those ads which show a little person standing next to a giant version of the product, the normal size of the objects (elements) are inverted.

2. *Hendiadys*. This is the expression of a complex idea by two words connected by 'and', as in 'in goblets and gold' for 'in golden goblets'. One can see a visual version of this figure in ads where a formal similarity is established between a concrete object and an abstract idea, for example a type of light bulb and energy conservation. The abstract concept can be illustrated by an image in the shape of the bulb.

   Homology is the opposite of this. It is a figure based on similarity of content. The same meaning is presented in successive images but in different form. An ad for instant mashed potato showed a picture of raw steak and a packet of potato mix followed by a picture of the cooked steak and the prepared purée of mashed potato.

3. *Asyndeton*. In this figure one or more elements or things are unconnected. In verbal discourse a conjunction joining two sentences is missed out; the visual equivalent is an image which has been fragmented into parts. Ads for cosmetic products sometimes consist of a whole page showing the fragmented parts of a woman's body to

176

You can take a White Horse anywhere

Plate 25 False homology

highlight the application of the products: lips showing lipstick, nails showing nail polish, eyes showing eye shadow.

4. *Anacoluthon.* Here a sentence lacks a grammatical sequence. Visually this figure exists where an image appears to be an impossibility — it has probably been created by photo-montage. The ad for pasta

177

Everything about *Record Pasta* is naturally good. Made from the finest, specially-grown 'Durum' wheat, and full of golden sunshine, *Record Pasta* is marvellous for main courses, or as a starter, and perfect in puddings.

Spaghetti is the great family favourite. There are many different varieties of pasta, all delicious – there is never a dull meal with *Record Pasta*. And for even more goodness, there's the wholesome, whole wheat range, rich in dietary fibre (roughage).

Plate 26 Anacoluthon

(plate 26) shows a plate on which the spectator can see, not spaghetti, but a picture of a wheat field. One can often see improbable things in ads, such as baths in the middle of fields, people walking in and

178

out of television screens, and clever TV editing techniques allow 'magically' impossible feats to be executed.

5. *Chiasmus*. Another figure which involves the exchange of elements, although this time the 'grammar' may be correct. Visually this figure is present when, for example, two people are shown exchanging clothes: a father and son wearing each other's hats and carrying each other's newspapers, or a little girl in woman's clothing. In the ad for Smirnoff Silver vodka (plate 27) several huntsmen are shown in their 'pink' coats, but on the back of one we can see a Hell's Angel badge. In some respects this symbol is not out of place; it is displayed where one would expect to find it — on the back of a jacket worn by a man who is a member of a group who some would say are like Hell's Angels, violent and aggressive, they stalk their prey on horses instead of motorbikes. But of course, as the caption confirms, the audience is meant to read this as inappropriate behaviour.

6. *Antimetabole*. This is another figure of double meaning. An image can show a person the right way up and next to it the same person upside down looking uncomfortable.

7. *Oxymoron*. The reverse of paradox. Two elements remain contradictory, as in an ad which shows a basket of strawberries in the snow, and in another which shows a woman in a bathing suit against a wintry background.

You will often find several rhetorical figures in a single advertisement. This is especially true of television commercials. The following stills (plate 28) come from a TV commercial for bread, in which the loaf acts as a metaphor for a family photograph album. The slices of bread are turned over like the pages of an album revealing pictures of the family in various stages of growing up and involved in different 'family' activities. One shot shows a picture of a bottle of milk, cheese, fish and eggs, framed within a slice of bread. This is a visual synechdoche: the bread contains the attributes and qualities of the milk, cheese, fish, etc. In the final shot of this commercial we see a small image of the family group standing on top of an outsize loaf of bread (hyperbole) and in the caption there is an example of a pun in the double meaning of the word 'support'.

The examination of rhetoric in advertising is useful in that it draws attention to the constructed nature of advertisements and avoids some of the weaknesses associated with intuitive analysis.

179

Plate 27 Chiasmus

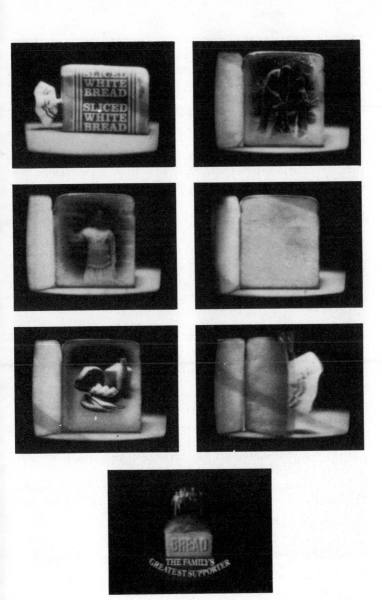

Plate 28 Rhetoric

Durand's work also calls into question the myth of creativity and inspiration which exists among advertisers. Far from being truly creative, Durand argues, all advertisements can be seen to be based on a limited number of rhetorical figures. However, in emphasizing the rhetorical devices of advertising there is a danger that analysis will be excessively formalistic and inward-looking, mystifying more than it clarifies. The formal rhetorical devices in advertisements should help us understand how ads work internally according to their own specific representational practice, but we also need to make connections outwards to a wider ideological field. To use terms first proposed by Winship (1981), ads should be analysed from the point of view of their means of representation, their mode of address and their 'ideological problematics'.

Suggestions for further work

1. Find five ads which use asyndeton visually. Why do you think this figure was used in your chosen ads? What does it lead us to think?
2. Choose an ad which contains more than one example of a visual figure of rhetoric. Name the different figures.
3. Why are paradoxes and double meanings popular with advertisers? Find some examples. Why is litotes less popular with advertisers? Try to find some examples.
4. Find some examples of ads which use
   (a) colour
   (b) numbers
   (c) jokes and puzzles
   in a rhetorical way. Name the precise figure used.
5. What is the link between rhetoric and connotation? (See Barthes, 1977.) Why do advertisers use rhetorical figures in ads? What do they expect to achieve by the use of rhetoric?
6. Why is metaphor particularly useful to advertisers? Find some examples of visual and verbal metaphor in TV commercials.

CONCLUSION

Advertisers play a major part in shaping society's values, habits and direction. They are also partly responsible for influencing the character and development of the media system. The traditional media are in decline as a result of advertising allocation, and advertising has encouraged the conservative domination of the press, orienting it more and more towards the young middle class and in the process depriving a substantial section of the population of a serious newspaper. Advertising threatens the UK public-service broadcasting institution and has caused both kinds of television service to limit their programming, 'play safe' and go for large, predictable audiences. Newspapers and magazines are increasingly forced into creating the right 'editorial environment' for advertisers, and in addition we can see a growing polarization between popular and quality newspapers.

The future of the media as organs of public communication looks extremely gloomy because of the narrow and competitive needs of large corporations. We might applaud the aesthetic and technical standards of many of the ads themselves or at worst regard them as superficial, unreliable and intrusive, but it is hard to get away from them and to resist the general temptations and advantages of the consumer society. It is often hard to pin down what is actually objectionable about ads. Who seriously believes, for instance, that 'Heineken reaches the parts that other beers can't reach' or that 'Four out of five people can't tell Stork from butter' or does 'The Daz blue whitener window test' with their washing?

183

To be fair, advertisements rarely perpetrate downright lies. The ads in magazines and newspapers, on posters and at the cinema are bound by a code of practice administered by the Advertising Standards Authority (see Appendix II for ASA guidelines). The IBA is responsible for television commercials and makes sure that they are not misleading or offensive and that they are confined to 'natural breaks'. The ASA judges the validity of complaints that come from the general public and publishes its verdicts in its own literature and in the press. (It also advertises itself in the press.) If a complaint is upheld the ASA can tell the advertiser to amend or remove offending material. It is particularly keen to uphold standards in sensitive areas such as those for slimming products, alcohol, tobacco and ads aimed at children. Ads for these products come in for special scrutiny, but as this book has argued, it is often not the overt message of an ad that is misleading or dangerous but its subtle, hidden message, which presumably the ASA is unable or unwilling to do much about.

As you might imagine, a lot of advertisements fall through the ASA's net. Many ads that might be seen as an attack on or demeaning to women are not considered so by the ASA. For instance, while many ads that appear in magazines, on posters and on television might not be too objectionable as far as women's roles in society are concerned, some ads that appear in trade or industrial journals, car, motorbike or girlie magazines often feature pictures of scantily-dressed or naked women, and captions such as 'Like a bit of spare' (from an ad for motorbike accessories), 'We'll never let you down' (an ad in a car magazine accompanying a picture of a woman with her knickers down) and 'Abbey carpets lay best' (alongside a woman lying down with few clothes on). Frequently the ASA dismisses complaints about these sorts of ads because 'they do not cause grave or widespread offence'; they have been known to dismiss complaints about the sexist portrayal of women in ads because they argue that the woman is there as decoration and is irrelevent to the product (and therefore presumably without significance), or because the ad is not addressed to women but to motorcycle enthusiasts, or long-distance lorry-drivers.

In general, the success of advertising depends not on its logical propositions but on the kinds of fantasies it offers. The world of ads is a dream world where people and objects are taken out of their material context and given new, symbolic meanings, placed on hoardings or on the screen where they become signs. Advertising

184

appropriates things from the real world, from society and history and sets them to its own work. In doing so it mystifies the real world and deprives us of any understanding of it. We are invited to live an unreal life through the ads. The more we are isolated from the real world by the media, the more we seek images from them to give us a sense of social reality. Advertising helps us to make sense of things. It validates consumer commodities and a consumer life-style by associating goods with personal and social meanings and those aspirations and needs which are not fulfilled in real life. We come to think that consuming commodities will give us our identities. In this sense advertising is capable of some success. People may admire us if we have made the right purchases within a system to which we are trained to respond. Ads may provide a magic which displaces our feelings and resolves our dilemmas but only at a personal and social cost. We become part of the symbolism of the ad world; not real people but identified in terms of what we consume: Raymond Williams sums this up when he says:

> Fantasy seems to be validated at a personal level but only at the cost of preserving the general unreality which it obscures: the real failures of society . . . if the meanings and values generally operative in society give no answers to, no means of negotiating, problems of death, loneliness, frustration, the need for identity and respect, then the magic system must come and mixing its charms and expedients with reality in easily available forms and binding the weakness to the condition which has created it. (1980, p. 191)

The condition which has need of this fantasy is one which isolates us, the consumers, from real information and decision-making about the production and distribution of goods. Advertising, according to Williams, has become 'a mimed celebration of other people's decisions', not the consumers'.

One of the ways in which advertising rebuffs criticism and validates its own existence is by appropriating hostile criticism and counter-ideologies. Some advertisers, aware of the objections of the feminist movement to traditional images of women in ads, have incorporated the criticism into their ads, many of which now present an alternative stereotype of the cool, professional, liberated woman. On the whole, however, advertising hasn't been able to keep pace with women's changing roles and aspirations and, unsure about what to do about criticism, has fallen back on tried and tested clichés. Some agencies,

185

trying to accommodate new attitudes in their campaigns, often miss the point and equate 'liberation' with a type of aggressive sexuality and very unliberated coy sexiness. So we have seen in the past few years campaigns like 'Underneath they're all Lovable' (for frilly underwear), or ads showing cool, professional women who really have weak spots, be they for a man's aftershave lotion, a gift of chocolates or 'sexy' underwear.

Another example of the way that ads escape real criticism is by self-reference; that is, by incorporating criticism or by showing up the ad system as rather dishonest and silly. The actor John Cleese's presentation of Sony products incorporates a kind of cynicism about the process of celebrities endorsing products — no doubt with great commercial success, since his image on his comedy programmes is that of a cynic. A shampoo commercial on TV shows a young couple running towards each other on a deserted beach in slow motion to the sound of an orchestra in full romantic flood; but instead of falling into each other's arms as we might have expected from watching countless similar ads and romantic films, they run past each other. The voice-over remarks that this shampoo will not get you a lover (as we have been led to believe from other shampoo ads) but will make your hair clean and beautiful. This is a parody of other, much criticized ads for beauty products. It is self-validating because we are disarmed by its honesty and its apparent self-criticism. Another example of an ad which refers to the genre of ads is a poster for sausages which says: 'I'm meaty. Fry me', a take-off of the offensive series of airline ads which said 'I'm Suzie/Cheryl/Lorraine. Fly me'. These kinds of ad often set themselves up as more aware, down-to-earth, honest and credible.

This leads us to a further point about advertising's resistance to criticism. The reason why ads are rarely dishonest in any 'legal' sense is that they don't function at the manifest level but at the level of the signifier. Few people believe or take seriously the (dishonest) slogans of ads: 'I was Mr Holmes of Household linens until I discovered Smirnoff', 'Fairy tales come true' (Martini), 'Daz with the blue whitener washes cleanest'. But the *signifiers* of the image of these ads are usually the kind of people who are seen using the product — smart, young people, caring mothers or happy families. And it is at this level that ads are hard to resist because they offer the chance to obtain perfect relationships, handsome lovers, luxurious surroundings, appreciative husbands and happy children. We remember these images

186

rather than the claims made on behalf of the product. We don't use a product for what it is; we identify with the result. The product can make us like the signifier in the ads.

It is possible to attempt to ban deceitful, sexist or racist slogans from ads. For instance, the ASA made the original 'I was only . . . until I discovered . . .' Smirnoff ads unlawful, because of the overt implication that drinking Smirnoff would bring sexual and material success. Some Smirnoff ads now show the successfully transformed Smirnoff person saying 'They say Smirnoff won't . . . I'll drink to that', referring to the old series of ads and to the restriction imposed on them. This again shows how 'daring' ads are and how they can rebut criticism by criticising themselves. It is impossible to ban the use of images and symbols in ads and the interconnections they make between things of value. It is ultimately the images that ads leave us with, and the images of the slogans, not the slogans themselves, that make ads so successful.

This is why it is important to be aware not just of the content, but also of the structure of signs in ads, the way meanings are exchanged, the way signifier and signified work, the way ads incorporate other referent systems and ideologies (even advertising itself), and the way they structure us into the ad and call upon us to create meaning. Only in this way can we understand the way ideology works and ties advertising to the existing conditions of society.

APPENDIX I

A central argument of the first part of this book was the importance of advertising to the general economic environment and how shifts and changes in the economy affect the role that advertising plays. Some people argue that the expenditure on advertising is a shocking waste of human and monetary resources and that the advantages of this expenditure, in terms of the expansion of the economy and technical progress, are outweighed by the disadvantages. Some understanding of the scale and type of expenditure in advertising can be gained from the following selection of statistics and information. It has been collected from trade journals and the financial pages of the quality press and can be updated with reference to these sources.

Tables 2–9 are taken from Advertising Association statistics

Table 2 *Total advertising expenditure and its relation to consumers' expenditure*

Year	Total expenditure	
	£m (in current prices)	*as a percentage of consumers' expenditure*
1952	123	1.23
1962	348	1.83
1972	708	1.78
1973	874	1.94
1974	900	1.74
1975	967	1.53
1976	1188	1.62
1977	1499	1.79
1978	1834	1.92
1979	2129	1.90

Table 3 *Total advertising expenditure by media*

Media	£m						Percentage of total					
	1960	1968	1973	1975	1977	1979	1960	1968	1973	1975	1977	1979
National newspapers	64	99	160	162	251	347	19.8	19.7	18.3	16.8	16.7	16.3
Regional newspapers	77	121	256	283	396	593	23.8	24.1	29.3	29.3	26.4	27.9
Magazines and periodicals	40	50	72	79	116	180	12.4	9.9	8.2	8.2	7.7	8.5
Trade and technical	31	46	73	86	133	203	9.6	9.1	8.4	8.9	8.9	9.5
Directories (inc. Yellow Pages)	2	8	17	20	43	54	0.6	1.6	1.9	2.1	2.9	2.5
Press production costs	15	23	46	49	73	119	4.6	4.6	5.3	5.1	4.9	5.6
Total press	229	347	624	679	1012	1496	70.9	69.0	71.4	70.2	67.5	70.3
Television	72	129	210	236	398	471	22.3	25.6	24.0	24.4	26.6	22.1
Poster and transport	16	20	31	35	54	93	5.0	4.0	3.5	3.6	3.6	4.4
Cinema	5	6	7	7	9	17	1.5	1.2	0.8	0.7	0.6	0.8
Radio	1	1	2	10	26	52	0.3	0.2	0.2	1.0	1.7	2.4
Total	323	503	874	967	1499	2129	100	100	100	100	100	100

189

Table 4 *Total advertising expenditure by type*

Type	£m						Percentage of total					
	1960	1968	1973	1975	1977	1979	1960	1968	1973	1975	1977	1979
Display advertising:												
Press[1]	151	193	322	361	533	795	46.7	39.3	36.8	37.2	35.6	37.3
Television	72	129	210	236	398	471	22.3	25.6	24.0	24.4	26.5	22.1
Other media[2]	22	27	40	52	89	162	6.8	5.4	4.6	5.4	5.9	7.6
Total	245	349	572	649	1020	1428	75.8	69.4	65.4	67.1	68.0	67.1
Financial notices etc.[3]	4	10	16	14	19	22	1.2	2.0	1.8	1.4	1.3	1.0
Classified advertising	43	98	213	218	327	476	13.3	19.5	24.4	22.5	21.8	22.4
Trade and technical journals	31	46	73	86	133	203	9.7	9.1	8.4	8.9	8.9	9.5
Total	323	503	874	967	1499	2129	100	100	100	100	100	100

[1] Excluding financial, classified and advertising in trade and technical journals.
[2] i.e. poster and transport, cinema, radio.
[3] Company reports, prospectuses and other notices, but excluding display advertising by financial institutions.

Table 5 Classified advertising expenditure by media

Media	£m						Percentage of total					
	1960	1968	1973	1975	1977	1979	1960	1968	1973	1975	1977	1979
National newspapers	8	22	41	38	57	75	19	22	19	17	17	16
Regional newspapers	34	68	154	160	230	350	79	69	73	73	70	73
Magazines and periodicals	1	4	7	7	8	12	2	4	3	3	2	3
Directories (inc. Yellow Pages)	–	4	11	13	32	39	0	4	5	6	10	8
Total	43	98	213	218	327	476	100	100	100	100	100	100

Table 6 *Newspaper advertising by category of newspaper*

| Year | National newspapers | | Regional newspapers | | Free sheets | |
	Dailies	*Sundays*	*Dailies*	*Weeklies*	*Newspaper format*	*Magazine format*
				£m		
1969	73	38	85	48	2	
1971	70	38	94	55	3	
1973	108	53	161	83	13	2
1975	108	54	176	89	18	1
1977	168	83	244	123	29	3
1979	242	105	359	181	53	6

Table 7 *Newspaper classified advertising by type*

Type	1971	1973	1975	1977	1979
			£m		
Recruitment	37	105	75	100	173
Property	17	27	34	45	58
Automotive	17	25	31	60	80
Other	34	27	44	65	92
	105	184	184	270	403

Table 8 *Index of Media Rates (1970 = 100)*

	1961	1966	1971	1973	1975	1977	1979
National dailies	76.9	84.4	107.7	116.1	172.4	257.6	333.7
National Sundays	80.0	87.7	107.1	120.3	161.2	242.9	294.7
Regional dailies	77.8	83.8	109.6	120.0	192.4	277.1	361.5
Weekly papers	74.1	80.7	104.3	117.0	176.5	243.3	315.4
Magazines/periodicals	72.0	83.4	108.9	113.3	160.2	214.6	277.8
Trade and technical	67.7	82.1	113.1	126.2	176.9	245.1	301.1
Total press	74.4	83.7	108.6	118.5	177.5	252.0	322.5
Year on year % change		+ 1.7	+ 8.6	+ 3.5	+28.9	+19.1	+13.8
TV	85.8	94.8	109.0	133.4	152.6	238.5	342.4
Year on year % change		+ 3.9	+ 9.0	+ 9.7	+21.3	+16.9	+19.5
Combined index	77.6	86.7	108.7	122.2	171.3	248.0	327.4
Year on year % change		+ 2.4	+ 8.7	+ 5.1	+26.9	+18.4	+15.2

Table 9 Estimated media expenditure by product group

Product group	£m Manufacturers' consumer advertising									
	1970	1971	1972	1973	1974	1975	1976	1977	1978	1979
Food	62	70	82	88	81	89	112	144	165	166
Clothing	13	12	13	12	10	12	15	18	21	23
Auto	19	18	23	29	23	33	43	56	75	93
Drink and tobacco	46	50	55	64	65	73	97	111	121	148
Toiletries and medical	32	35	39	48	50	53	66	77	86	98
Household and leisure	54	59	68	84	79	87	113	150	204	230
Publishing, books	9	11	13	16	17	16	20	26	32	34
Tourism, entertainment, foreign	22	24	26	30	32	34	39	47	63	75
Nationalized industries	12	14	16	19	18	18	23	28	34	41
Government	14	16	17	21	21	21	22	26	37	42
Retail	56	63	84	114	134	163	206	260	307	355
Savings, financial	23	28	39	39	36	36	44	57	70	84
Industrial	71	70	81	95	103	111	130	168	212	258
Charity, education	2	2	2	3	3	3	3	4	5	6
Classified	119	119	150	213	228	218	255	327	402	476

Table 10 *How the power is shared*
(extracted from *Campaign*, 2 January 1981)

Number of agencies in each billing category

£80 million and over 2
£70 million to £80 million. 2
£60 million to £70 million. 2
£50 million to £60 million. . . . . nil
£40 million to £50 million. 2
£30 million to £40 million. 7
£20 million to £30 million. 8
£10 million to £20 million. 35
£5 million to £10 million 52
Up to £5 million 141

Table 11 *The top ten agencies in 1980*
(extracted from *Campaign*, 2 January 1981)

		Billings in £m		Staff	
		1980	*1979*	*1980*	*1979*
1=	Saatchi and Saatchi	83.00	67.50	530	500
1=	J. Walter Thompson (London)	83.00	64.40	563	555
3=	D'Arcy MacManus and Masius	75.00	64.00	456	456
3=	McCann-Erickson Advertising	75.00	68.32	400	477
5	Ogilvy Benson and Mather	61.20	49.30	378	390
6	Collett Dickenson Pearce	60.89	54.96	272	265
7	Young and Rubicam	46.41	38.62	315	311
8	Foote Cone and Belding	45.22	32.80	282	259
9	Ted Bates	39.64	34.35	237	241
10	Allen Brady and Marsh	39.12	30.90	253	216

Table 12 *The top 99 advertisers for 1979*
(extracted from *Campaign*, 2 May 1980)

1 Procter and Gamble

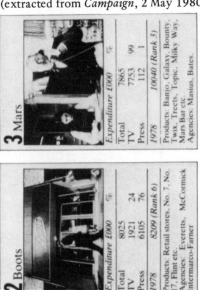

		Expenditure £000				
Total	1978	TV	%	Press	%	'78 Rank
10420	8227	10059	97	361	3	5

Products: Ariel, Daz, Tide, Fairy, Zest, Bold, Crest, Camay, Lenor etc.
Agencies: B and B, Saatchi, Y and R, Greys.

2 Boots

	Expenditure £000	%
Total	8025	
TV	1921	24
Press	6105	76
1978	8209 (Rank 6)	

Products: Retail stores, No. 7, No. 17, Flint etc.
Agencies: Everetts, McCormick Intermarco-Farmer.

3 Mars

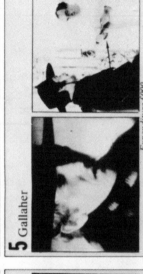

	Expenditure £000	%
Total	7865	
TV	7753	99
Press	112	1
1978	10040 (Rank 3)	

Products: Banjo, Galaxy, Bounty, Twix, Treets, Topic, Milky Way, Mars Bar etc.
Agencies: Masius, Bates.

4 W. D. and H. O. Wills

		Expenditure £000				
Total		TV	%	Press	%	'78 Rank
7583	1978					
	1979	184	2	7399	98	94

Products: Embassy, Castella, Lambert and Butler, Golden Virginia.
Agencies: Masius, Geers Gross, Royds.

5 Gallaher

		Expenditure £000				
Total	1978	TV	%	Press	%	'78 Rank
7390	6693	2342	32	5048	68	9

Products: Benson and Hedges cigarettes, cigars, tobacco, Kensitas, Manikin, Hamlet etc.
Agencies: CDP, KMP, JWT, Bates.

6 Rowntree Mackintosh

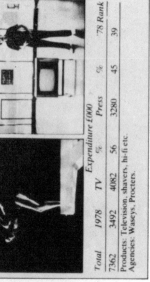

	1978	TV	%	Press	'78 Rank
Total	12124	6730	91	640	1
7371			9		

Products: After Eight, Rolo, Aero, Black Magic, Smarties, Dairy Box, Yorkie, Kit-Kat, Cabana, Toffo etc.
Agencies: JWT, OBM, Saatchi.

7 Philips Industries

	1978	TV	%	Press	'78 Rank
Total	3492	4082	56	3280	39
7362			45		

Expenditure £000

Products: Television, shavers, hi-fi etc.
Agencies: Waseys, Procters.

8 Cadbury Limited

	1978	TV	%	Press	'78 Rank
Total	11867	6331	88	838	2
7169			12		

Expenditure £000

Products: Bournville, Dairy Milk, Flake, Crunchie, Milk Tray, Buttons, Roses, Star Bar, Picnic etc.
Agencies: Burnetts, TBWA, Y and R, FCB.

9 Woolworth

Expenditure £000	%
Total 7089	
TV 3292	46
Press 3797	54
1978 5344 (Rank 16)	

Products: Retail Stores, Woolco, Tu cosmetics.
Agencies: ABM, Farmers, NCK.

10 Lever Bros

Expenditure £000	%
Total 6917	
TV 6065	88
Press 851	12
1978 8539 (Rank 4)	

Products: Persil, Surf, Vigor, Comfort, Shield, Jif, Sunlight etc.
Agencies: OBM, Limtas, JWT, DPBS.

11 British Rail Board

Total	1978	TV	%	Press	%	'78 Rank
				Expenditure £000		
6916	5873	2536	37	4380	63	12

Products: Inter-City, Awayday, Railcards, Sealink etc.
Agencies: ABM, Saatchi, Masius, Lonsdales.

12 Post Office

	Expenditure £000	%
Total	6354	
TV	3425	54
Press	2929	46
1978	5885 (Rank 11)	

Products: Call stimulation, postal services etc.
Agencies: BMP, Colmans, Dorlands, KMP.

13 Van den Berghs

	Expenditure £000	%
Total	6324	
TV	4838	77
Press	1485	23
1978	5846 (Rank 13)	

Products: Blue Band, Flora, Outline, Krona, Stork, Spry etc.
Agencies: McCanns, Lintas, DPBS, OBM.

14 Tesco

Total	1978	TV	%	Press	%	'78 Rank
				Expenditure £000		
5711	4941	1864	33	3847	67	19

Agency: McCanns.

15 Electricity Council

Total	1978	TV	%	Press	%	'78 Rank
				Expenditure £000		
5512	4063	2860	52	2652	48	29

Products: Appliances, central heating, industrial etc.
Agencies: Bates, JWT, Roles and Parker.

16 General Foods

| | | Expenditure £000 | | | | |
Total	1978	TV	%	Press	%	'78 Rank
5240	4536	4389	84	851	16	24

Products: Birds Coffee, Maxwell House, Apeel, Angel Delight, Birds Trifles, Birds Whisk and Serve, Dream Topping.
Agencies: B and B, Y and R, OBM.

17 Pedigree Petfoods

Mr. Dog
Dog

| | | Expenditure £000 | | | | |
Total	1978	TV	%	Press	%	'78 Rank
5217	5775	5131	98	64	1	14

Products: Kit-E-Kat, Whiskas, Pal, Frolic, Chum etc.
Agencies: Masius, Bates.

18 Heinz

Expenditure £000	%
Total	5054	
TV	4356	86
Press	698	14
1978	3248 (Rank 43)	

Products: Baby food, pasta, soups, salads etc.
Agencies: Y and R, CDP, DDB, Dorlands.

19 Austin Morris

Expenditure £000	%
Total	4953	
TV	2239	45
Press	2714	55
1978	7656 (Rank 7)	

Agencies: Burnetts, Saatchi.

20 Co-op Retail Societies

Bacon & Cooked Meats

| | | Expenditure £000 | | | | |
Total	1978	TV	%	Press	%	'78 Rank
4947	4729	571	12	4375	88	22

Agencies: Capra.

	Advertiser	Holding company	Expenditure £000s 1979	TV %	Press %
21	John Player (Players cigarettes, cigars and tobacco)	Imperial Tobacco	4826	15	85
22	Elida Gibbs (Denim, Signal, Sure, Pears, Sunsilk, SR, All Clear, Harmony, etc.)	Unilever	4782	83	17
23	MFI	—	4762	5	95
24	Renault	Regie Nationale Des Usines	4602	20	80
25	Birds Eye	Unilever	4564	83	17
26	Allied Retailers (Allied Carpet Stores, Williams Furniture)	—	4455	55	45
27	National Dairy Council (Milk, cream and cheese)	—	4422	68	34
28	Brooke Bond Oxo (Oxo, Haywards, Brooke Bond tea and coffee, Soya Mince)	Brook Bond Liebig	4321	79	21
29	Beecham Products (Medicines) (Beecham Powders, Venos, Fynnon, Eno, Night Nurse, Phensic, Mac Lozenges, Settlers, etc.)	Beecham Group	4199	66	32
30	Carreras Rothman (Piccadilly, Rothman, Dunhill, Erinmore)	Rothman International	4184	—	100
31	Kelloggs (All Bran, Corn Flakes, Extra, Frosties, Rise and Shine, Noodles, etc.)	Kellogg USA	4179	65	35
32	Cadbury Typhoo (Smash, Marvel, Typhoo, Pint Size, Snack, Kenco, Drinking Chocolate, etc.)	Cadbury Schweppes	4017	74	26
33	Fiat Motor Co. (UK)	Fiat SPA, Italy	3934	54	46
34	Co-Operative Wholesale Society	—	3765	34	66

	Advertiser	Holding company	Expen-diture £000s 1979	TV %	Pres %
35	Gillette (Papermate, RightGuard, Kalkitos, G11, Contour, Lightwave, Earthborn, etc.)	Gillette	3443	69	31
36	Allied Breweries (UK) (Arctic Lite Beer, DR, Double D, Burton Bot, Skol Lager, Tetley Bitter, etc.)	——	3348	71	29
37	McVitie and Cadbury Cakes	United Biscuits	3335	87	13
38	Arthur Guinness	—	3314	72	28
39	Book Club Associates (Arts Guild, Mystery Guild, World Books, Kaleidoscope, Book of the Month Club, etc.)	W. H. Smith and Sons (Holdings)/Doubeday	3286	—	100
40	Bass Marketing (Carling, Bass, Tennents, Tuborg, Worthington, Hemeling, Stones Best Bitter, etc.)	Bass Charrington	3273	95	5
41	The Nestle Company (Nescafe, Chef, Milky Bar, Dairy Crunch, etc.)	Nestle S. A.	3253	60	40
42	British Airways (Poundstretcher, Sovereign Airways, etc.)	——	3233	54	46
43	Volkswagen–Audi (GB) (Passat, Polo, Derby, Sirocco, Audi, Golf, etc.)	——	3216	21	79
44	Comet Discount	—	3191	—	100
45	Department of Transport (Drink and Drive, Seat Belts, Road Safety, Pedestrian Safety, etc.)	——	3110	95	5
46	Whitbread and Co. (Heineken, Stella Artois, Trophy, Heldenbrau, etc.)	——	3068	81	19
47	Debenhams	—	3045	18	83
48	Currys	—	2020	13	87
49	C and A Modes	C and A Nederland	2928	6	94

Advertiser	Holding company	Expenditure £000s 1979	TV %	Press %
50 Colgate Palmolive (Ajax, Palmolive, Fresh, Ultra-Brite, Woodleigh Green, etc.)	Colgate Palmolive (USA)	2924	93	7
51 Barclays Bank UK (Barclaycard, Barclay Trust, Barclay Unicorn 500, etc.)	Barclays Bank	2846	20	80
52 ICI (Paints) (Dulux Paints, Novamura, Vymura)	Imperial Chemical Industries	2791	68	32
53 W. H. Smith and Son	W. H. Smith (Holdings)	2787	2	98
54 Richardson-Merrell (Vick, Clearasil, Infacare, Oil of Ulay, Milgard, etc.)	Richardson-Merrell	2766	86	14
55 Jaguar–Rover Triumph (Daimler, Jaguar, Rover, Triumph, MG)	BL	2686	—	100
56 British-American Tobacco (State Express)	BAT Industries	2666	—	100
57 RHM Foods (Bisto, Paxo, McD, Atora, Saxa, Energen, Chesswood, etc.)	Rank Hovis McDougall	2602	90	10
58 Kodak (Cameras and films)	Eastman Kodak (USA)	2588	72	28
59 Milk Marketing Board (Milk, cream cakes, butter, etc.)	——	2568	78	22
60 Asda Stores	Associated Dairies Group	2552	37	63
61 Beecham Products (Proprietaries) (Aquafresh, Macleans, Silvikrin, Vosene, Bodymist, Badedas, etc.)	Beecham Group	2546	69	31
62 Talbot Cars (Alpine, Avenger, Horizon, Sunbeam)	P. S. A. Peugeot Citroen	2506	26	74
63 Lyons Groceries (Lyons Maid, Tetley and Lyons teas, Ready Brek, etc.)	J. Lyons	2441	77	23

	Advertiser	Holding company	Expenditure £000s 1979	TV %	Press %
64	Midland Bank	—	2418	32	68
65	Ministry of Defence (Army, Navy, RAF, TAVR, etc.)	—	2411	32	68
	Figures for COI Recruitment exclude advertisements on classified pages				
66	Fine Fare	Associated British Foods	2371	36	64
67	Halifax Building Society	—	2338	36	64
68	Bowater Scott (Andrex, Softex Toilet Tissue, Scotties, Libresse, Fiesta, etc.)	—	2322	67	33
69	Hedges and Butler (Bacardi, Hirondelle, Emva Cream, Bolla, Sandeman, etc.)	Bass	2314	24	76
70=	Abbey National Building Society	—	2309	46	54
70=	IPC Magazines (*Woman, Woman's Realm, Titbits, Woman's Own,* etc.)	Reed International	2309	46	54
72	Shell UK Oil	Shell UK	2282	28	72
73	British Gas Corporation (Appliances, corporate, Save-It etc.)	—	2275	63	37
74	Scottish and Newcastle Breweries (McEwan, Youngers, Newcastle Brown)	—	2236	87	13
75	Courage (Courage Colt 45 Malt, Courage JC, Hofmeister Lager, etc.)	Imperial Group	2229	91	9
76	Dixons Photographic Centres	Dixons Photographic	2228	19	81
77	J and J Colman (Colmans, Tom Caxton, Jif, Robinsons, etc.)	Reckitt and Colman	2213	46	54

	Advertiser	Holding company	Expenditure £000s 1979	TV %	Press %
78	Gilbey Vintners (Hennessy, Smirnoff Vodka, Croft Port, J and B Whisky, Baileys, Gilbey, etc.)	International Distillers Vintners	2199	38	62
79	Department of Health and Social Security (Child Benefits, Nursing, Pensions, Better Health, Health Education Council, Family Income Supplements, etc.)	—	2198	25	75
80	Status Stores	Status Discount	2185	51	49
81	Spillers (Homepride, Choosy, Winalot, Tyne Brand)	—	2153	73	27
82	Unigate (St Ivel, Cow and Gate, Farmers Wife, Gold Spinner, etc.)	Unigate	2119	79	21
83	Johnson and Johnson (Band Aid Plasters, Johnson Baby Products, Carefree, Vespré, etc.)		2108	53	47
84=	Ford Motor Co. (Capri, Cortina, Escort range, Fiesta range, Granada)	—	2104	61	39
84=	Martini and Rossi	—	2104	59	41
86	National Westminster Bank (National Westminster Bank, National Westminster UT range, etc.)	National Westminster Bank	2089	7	93
87	Citroen Cars	P. S. A. Peugeot Citroen	2075	47	53
88	EMI Records	EMI	2048	93	7
89	Rumbelows	Thorn Electrical Industries	2029	35	65
90	Bovril (Ambrosia, Bovril, Marmite, etc.)	Cavenham	2015	86	14

	Advertiser	Holding company	Expenditure £000s 1979	TV %	Press %
91	K-Tel International (UK)	K-Tel International NNC USA	1986	100	—
92=	Esso Petroleum	Exxon USA	1965	82	18
92=	Vauxhall Motors (Cavalier, Carlton, Chevette, Royale)	General Motors	1965	25	75
94	Findus	—	1961	85	15
95	Lentheric Morny (Cyclax, Lentheric)	BAT Industries	1958	100	—
96	British Mail Order Corp (Ace of Clubs, Marshall Ward, John England, John Noble, Trafford, Great Universal, etc.)	Great Universal Stores	1957	—	100
97	Black and Decker	—	1956	82	18
98	J. Sainsbury	—	1941	39	61
99=	American Express Int. Banking Corp.	—	1935	38	62
99	Peugeot Automobiles (UK)	P. S. A. Peugeot Citroen	1935	9	91

APPENDIX II

Rate cards for the different TV and radio stations can be obtained from BRAD (*British Rate and Data*). Here is one example of the sums of money that advertisers would be expected to pay for access to the air waves (Table 13).

Table 13 *London Region, Thames Television advertising rates*

Monday to Friday Time (p.m.)	£ per 10 secs	£ per 15 secs	£ per 20 secs	£ per 30 secs	£ per 40 secs	£ per 45 secs	£ per 50 secs	£ per 60 secs
up to 3.40	200	280	320	400	520	600	660	800
3.40 – 4.40	490	686	784	980	1274	1470	1617	1960
4.40 – 5.30	875	1225	1400	1750	2275	2625	2880	3500
5.30 – 6.30	1650	2310	2640	3330	4290	4950	5445	6600
6.30 – 10.35	3650	5110	5840	7300	9490	10950	12045	14600
10.35 – 11.35	1875	2625	3000	3750	4875	5625	6188	7500
11.35 – 12.05	600	840	960	1200	1560	1800	1980	2400
12.05 – close	255	357	408	510	663	765	842	1020

APPENDIX III

Laws affecting advertising

Accommodation Agencies Act, 1953
Adoption Act, 1958 (section I)
Advertisements (Hire-Purchase) Act, 1938 (1957)
Agriculture (Safety, Health and Welfare Provisions) Act, 1956
Betting and Lotteries Act, 1934 (section 26)
Betting and Gaming Act, 1960
Building Societies Act, 1960 (sections, 5, 7 and 10)
Business Names Registration Act, 1916
Cancer Act, 1939 (section 4)
Children and Young Persons (Harmful Publications) Act, 1955
Children Act, 1958 (section 37)
Cinematograph Films Act, 1938
Civil Aviation (Licensing) Act, 1960
Companies Act, 1948 (section 38 and the fourth schedule)
Copyright Act, 1956
Criminal Justice Act, 1925 (section 38)
Defamation Act, 1952
Food and Drugs Act, 1955, and *Labelling of Food Order* (SI 1953, No. 536)
Forgery Act, 1913
Geneva Convention Act, 1957 (section 6)
Hire Purchase and Credit Sales Agreements (Control) Order, 1960

Indecent Advertisements Act, 1889
Industrial Training Act, 1964
Labelling of Food Order, 1953 (1959)
Larceny Act, 1861 (section 102)
Merchandise Marks Acts, 1887–1953
Moneylenders Act, 1927 (sections 4 and 5)
Noise Abatement Act, 1960
Obscene Publications Act, 1959
Opticians Act, 1958
Patents Act, 1949 (section 92)
Pharmacy and Medicines Act, 1941 (sections 8–13 and 15–17)
Pharmacy and Poisons Act, 1933
Post Office Acts, 1908–1953 (sections 61 and 62)
Pre-Packed Food (Weights and Measures: Marking) Regulations, 1959
Prevention of Frauds (Investments) Act, 1958 (sections 13, 14 and 17)
Protection of Depositors (Contents of Advertisements) Regulations, 1963
Protection of Depositors (Exempted Advertisements) Regulations, 1963
Registered Designs Act, 1949
Representation of the People Act, 1949 (sections 63, 94 and 95)
Road Traffic Act, 1960 (twelfth schedule)
Sale of Goods Act, 1893
Sunday Observance Act, 1780 (section 3), Common Informer Act, 1951 and Sunday Entertainments Act, 1932
Television Act, 1964
Town and Country Planning Act, 1947 (sections 31 and 32) and Town and Country Planning (Control of Advertisements) Regulations, 1960 (SI 1960, No. 695)
Town Police Clauses Act, 1847 (section 28)
Trade Descriptions Act, 1968
Trade Marks Acts, 1887–1938
Unsolicited Goods and Services Act, 1971
Vagrancy Act, 1924 (section 4)
Venereal Diseases Act, 1917 (sections 2 and 3)
Weights and Measures Act, 1963 (schedules 4–8)

APPENDIX IV

The Advertising Standards Authority

How the British Code of Advertising Practice (sixth edition) affects alcohol advertising

Introduction

1.1 Moderate drinking is widely enjoyed and helps to make social occasions cheerful and pleasant.

1.2 The Alcoholic Drinks Industry, with others, is aware that a small, but significant minority cause harm to themselves and others through misuse of alcohol. They share the concern about this social problem, the causes of which are complex and varied. There is no evidence connecting such misuse with the advertising of alcoholic drinks.

1.3 The industry is concerned that its advertisements should not exploit the immature, the young, the socially insecure, or those with physical, mental or social incapacity. The industry accepts that its advertising should be socially responsible and should not encourage excessive consumption.

1.4 The industry believes that it is proper for advertisements for alcoholic drinks:

    1. to indicate that they give pleasure to many, are of high quality and are widely enjoyed in all classes of society;

2. to seek to persuade people to change brands and/or types of drinks;
3. to provide information on products;
4. to employ such accepted techniques of advertising practice as are employed by other product groups and are not inconsistent with the detailed rules.

Implementation and interpretation

2.1 The industry has therefore proposed the following rules for inclusion in the British Code of Advertising Practice. The CAP Committee has accepted this proposal and the Advertising Standards Authority has agreed to supervise the implementation of the rules.

2.2 The rules are to be interpreted in the light of the considerations set out in paragraphs 1.1 to 1.4 above. So far as the scope and general interpretation of the rules is concerned, the provisions of the British Code of Advertising Practice apply, as they do to those aspects of advertisements for drink not covered by the rules.

2.3 'Drink', for the purposes of this Appendix, is to be understood as referring to alcoholic beverages and their consumption.

Rules

Young people

3.1 Advertisements should not be directed at young people nor in any way encourage them to start drinking. Anyone shown drinking must appear to be over 21. Children should not be depicted in advertisements except where it would be usual for them to appear (e.g. in family scenes or in background crowds) but they should never be shown drinking alcoholic beverages, nor should it be implied that they are.

Challenge

3.2 Advertisements should not be based on a dare, nor impute any failing to those who do not accept the challenge of a particular drink.

Health

3.3 Advertisements should not emphasise the stimulant, sedative or tranquillising effects of any drink, nor imply that it can improve physical performance. However, references to the refreshing attributes of a drink are permissible.

Strength

3.4 Advertisements should not give the general impression of being inducements to prefer a drink because of its higher alcohol content or intoxicating effect. Factual information for the guidance of drinkers about such alcoholic strength may, however, be included.

Social success

3.5 Advertisements may emphasize the pleasures of companionship and social communication associated with the consumption of alcoholic drinks, but it should never be implied that drinking is necessary to social or business success or distinction, nor that those who do not drink are less likely to be acceptable or successful than those who do. Advertisements should neither claim nor suggest that any drink can contribute towards sexual success, or make the drinker more attractive to the opposite sex.

Drinking and machinery

3.6 Advertisements should not associate drink with driving or dangerous machinery. Specific warnings of the dangers of drinking in these circumstances may, however, be used.

Excessive drinking

3.7 Advertisements should not encourage or appear to condone overindulgence. Repeated buying of large rounds should not be implied.

How the British Code of Advertising Practice (sixth edition) affects advertising aimed at children

General

1.1 Direct appeals or exhortations to buy should not be made to children unless the product advertised is one likely to be of interest to them which they could reasonably be expected to afford for themselves.

1.2 Advertisements should not encourage children to make themselves a nuisance to their parents, or anyone else, with the aim of persuading them to buy an advertised product.

1.3 No advertisement should cause children to believe that they will be inferior to other children, or unpopular with them, if they do not buy a particular product, or have it bought for them.

1.4 No advertisement for a commercial product should suggest to children that, if they do not buy it or encourage others to do so, they will be failing in their duty or lacking in loyalty.

1.5 Advertisements addressed to children should make it easy for a child to judge the true size of a product (preferably by showing it in relation to some common object) and should take care to avoid any confusion between the characteristics of real-life articles and toy copies of them.

1.6 Where the results obtainable by the use of a product are shown, these should not exaggerate what is attainable by an ordinary child.

1.7 Advertisements addressed to children should where ever possible give the price of the advertised product.

Safety

2.1 No advertisement, particularly for a collecting scheme, should encourage children to enter strange places or to converse with strangers in an effort to collect coupons, wrappers, labels or the like.

2.2 Children should not appear to be unattended in street scenes unless they are obviously old enough to be responsible for their own safety; should not be shown playing in the road, unless it is clearly shown to be a play-street or other safe area; should not be shown stepping carelessly off the pavement or crossing the road without due care; in busy street scenes should be seen to use the zebra crossings when crossing the road; and should be otherwise seen in general, as pedestrians or cyclists, to behave in accordance with the Highway Code.

2.3 Children should not be seen leaning dangerously out of windows or over bridges, or climbing dangerous cliffs.

2.4 Small children should not be shown climbing up to high shelves or reaching up to take things from a table above their heads.

2.5 Medicines, disinfectants, antiseptics and caustic substances should not be shown within reach of children without close parental supervision, nor should unsupervised children be shown using these products in any way.

2.6 Children should not be shown using matches or any gas, paraffin, petrol, mechanical or mains-powered appliance which could lead to their suffering burns, electrical shock or other injury.

2.7 Children should not be shown driving or riding on agricultural machines (including tractor-drawn carts or implements), so as to encourage contravention of the Agriculture (Safety, Health and Welfare Provisions) Act 1956.

2.8 An open fire in a domestic scene in an advertisement should always have a fireguard clearly visible if a child is included in the scene.

APPENDIX V

Useful addresses

Advertising Agency Register, 62 Shaftesbury Avenue, London W1; (01) 437 3357.

The Advertising Association (and the CAM Foundation), Abford House, 15 Wilton Road, London SW1; (01) 828 2771.

Advertising Creative Circle, 82 Baker Street, London W1.

Advertising Standards Authority (also Code of Advertising Practice Committee), Brook House, Torrington Place, London WC1; (01) 580 5555.

Audit Bureau of Circulations, 13 Wimpole Street, London W1; (01) 631 1343.

British Rate and Data, 76 Oxford Street, London W1; (01) 637 7511/8.

The Central Office of Information, Hercules House, Hercules Road, London SE1; (01) 928 2345.

The History of Advertising Trust, 53 Goodge Street, London W1P 1FB.

Independent Broadcasting Authority, 70 Brompton Road, London SW3; (01) 584 7011.

Institute of Practitioners in Advertising, 44 Belgrave Square, London SW1; (01) 235 7020.

Institute of Public Relations, 1 Great James Street, London WC1; (01) 405 5505.

Trade Publications

Admap (monthly)
Advertisers Annual (yearly)
Advertising Magazine (quarterly)
Advertising and Marketing (quarterly)
BRAD (British Rate and Data) (monthly)
Broadcast (weekly)
Campaign (weekly)
Creative Handbook (yearly)
Designers and Art Directors Association Annual
IBA Yearbook
Marketing Weekly

REFERENCES

Adams, C. and Laurikiens, R. (1976) *Messages and Images (The Gender Trap*, Book 3), London: Virago.

Alvarado, M. (1980) 'Photographs and narrativity', *Screen Education*, 32/33.

Andren, G., Ericsson, L. O., Ohlsson, R. and Tännsjö, T. (1978) *Rhetoric and Ideology in Advertising*, Stockholm: Liber Förlag.

Arlen, M. J. (1981) *Thirty Seconds*, New York: Farrar Straus & Giroux.

Arnheim, R. (1967) *Art and Visual Perception*, London: Faber.

Baker, S. S. (1969) *The Permissible Lie*, London: Peter Owen.

Baran, P. and Sweezey, P. (1968) *Monopoly Capital*, Harmondsworth: Penguin.

Barnes, M. (ed.) (1975) *The Three Faces of Advertising*, London: The Advertising Association.

Barnouw, E. (1978) *The Sponsor*, New York: Oxford University Press.

Barthes, R. (1961) 'The photographic message', in Barthes, R. (1977).

— (1964) 'The rhetoric of the image', in Barthes, R. (1977).

— (1967a) *Elements of Semiology*, London: Jonathan Cape.

— (1967b) *Système de la Mode*, Paris: Editions du Seuil.

— (1973) *Mythologies*, St. Albans: Paladin.

— (1975) *S/Z*, London: Cape.

— (1977) *Image—Music—Text*, London: Fontana.

215

Berger, J. (1972) *Ways of Seeing*, Harmondsworth: Penguin.

Bonsiepe, G. (1961) 'Persuasive communication — towards a visual rhetoric', in Crosby, Theo. (ed.) *Upper Case 5*.

Boorstin, D. (1963) *The Image*, Harmondsworth: Penguin.

Bremond, J. (1977) *La Publicité*, Paris: Hatier.

Brown, J. A. C. (1963) *Techniques of Persuasion from Propaganda to Brainwashing*, Harmondsworth: Penguin.

Burgin, V. (1975) *Photographic Practice and Art Theory*, London: Studio International.

—— (1976) 'Art, common sense and photography', *Camerawork*, 3.

Caplin, R. (1967) *Advertising*, London: Business Publications Ltd.

Cleverly, G. (1976) *The Fleet Street Disaster*, London: Constable.

Cowie, E. (1977) 'Women: representation and the image', *Screen Education*, 23.

—— (1978) 'Woman and sign', *m/f* vol. 1.

Crompton, A. (1979) *The Craft of Copywriting*, London: Business Books.

Curran, J. (1978) 'Advertising and the press', in Curran (ed.) (1978).

—— (ed.) (1978) *The British Press: A Manifesto*, London: Macmillan.

—— (ed.) (1981a) 'Advertising', an issue of *Media, Culture and Society*, 3, 1.

—— (1981b) *Power and Responsibility*, London: Fontana.

Davies, D. (1960) *The Grammar of Television Production*, London: Barrie & Jenkins.

Dempsey, M. (ed.) (1978) *'Bubbles': Early Advertising Art from A. & F. Pears Ltd*, London: Fontana.

Dichter, E. (1960) *The Strategy of Desire*, New York: McGraw Hill.

Downing, J. (1980) *The Media Machine*, London: Pluto Press.

Durand, J. (1970) 'Rhetorique et image publicitaire', *Communications*, 15, Paris: Editions du Seuil.

Dyer, R. (1973) *Light Entertainment*, British Film Institute Television Monograph.

Eco, U. (1970a) 'Articulations of the cinematic code', in Nichols, B. (1976).

—— (1970b) 'Semiologie des messages visuels', *Communications*, 15, Paris: Editions du Seuil.

—— (1972) 'Towards a semiotic enquiry into the television message', *Working Papers in Cultural Studies*, 3, Centre for Contemporary Cultural Studies, University of Birmingham.

Ewen, S. (1976) *Captains of Consciousness: Advertising and the*

Social Roots of the Consumer Culture, New York: McGraw-Hill.

Fiske, J. (1982) *Introduction to Communication Studies*, London: Methuen.

— and Hartley, J. (1979) *Reading Television*, London: Methuen.

Friedan, B. (1965) *The Feminine Mystique*, Harmondsworth: Penguin.

Friendly, F. (1968) *Due to Circumstances Beyond Our Control*, New York: Vintage Books.

Galbraith, J. K. (1970) *The Affluent Society*, Harmondsworth: Penguin (first published in 1958 by Hamish Hamilton, London).

— (1968) *The New Industrial State*, Harmondsworth: Penguin (first published in 1967 by Hamish Hamilton, London).

Gauthier, G. (1976) *The Semiology of the Image*, British Film Institute Advisory Document.

Goffman, E. (1979) *Gender Advertisements*, London: Macmillan.

Golding, P. (1974) *The Mass Media*, London: Longman.

Golding, P. and Murdock, G. (1978) 'Confronting the market: public intervention and press diversity', in Curran, J. (ed.) (1978).

Gombrich, E. (1962) *Art and Illusion*, London: Phaidon (4th edition 1972).

Gramsci, A. (1971) *Selections from the Prison Notebooks*, London: Lawrence & Wishart.

Gregory, R. L. (1966) *Eye and Brain*, London: Weidenfeld & Nicolson.

Griff, M. (1969) 'Advertising — the central institution of mass society', *Diogenes*, 68.

Hall, S. (1972) 'The determinations of news photographs', *Working Papers in Cultural Studies*, 3, Centre for Contemporary Cultural Studies, University of Birmingham.

— (1973) 'Encoding and decoding in the television discourse', *Occasional Papers*, 7, Centre for Contemporary Cultural Studies, University of Birmingham.

Hall, S. and Whannel, P. (1964) *The Popular Arts*, London: Hutchinson.

Hartley, J. (1982) *Understanding News*, London: Methuen.

Hildick, E. W. (1969) *A Close Look at Advertising*, London: Faber & Faber.

Hoggart, R. (1957) *The Uses of Literacy*, London: Chatto & Windus.

— (ed.) (1967) *Your Sunday Paper*, London: University of London Press.

— (1970) 'The case against advertising', *Speaking to Each Other*, London: Chatto & Windus.

Hood, S. (1980) *On Television*, London: Pluto Press.

Inglis, F. (1972) *The Imagery of Power: A Critique of Advertising*, London: Heinemann.

Institute of Practitioners in Advertising (IPA) pamphlets.

ITV Handbook (annually).

Jakobson, R. (1971) *Studies on Child Language and Aphasia*, The Hague: Mouton.

Kaldor, N. H. (1950/1) 'The economic aspects of advertising', *Review of Economic Studies*, XVIII.

King, J. and Stott, M. (eds) (1977) *Is This Your Life? Images of Women in the Media*, London: Virago.

Kleinman, P. (1977) *Advertising Inside Out*, London: W. H. Allen.

Langholz Leymore, V. (1975) *The Hidden Myth*, London: Heinemann.

Leavis, F. R. and Thompson, D. (1933) *Culture and Environment*, London: Chatto & Windus.

Leech, G. (1966) *English in Advertising*, London: Longmans.

Lefebvre, H. (1971) *Everyday Life in the Modern World*, Harmondsworth: Penguin.

Lippa, M. and Newton, D. (1979) *The World of Small Ads*, London: Hamlyn.

Lukács, G. (1971) *History and Class Consciousness*, London: Merlin.

McGuinness, J. (1970) *The Selling of the President*, London: André Deutsch.

McLuhan, M. (1967) *Understanding Media*, London: Routledge & Kegan Paul.

—— (1967) *The Mechanical Bride*, London: Routledge & Kegan Paul.

Manstead, T. and McCullogh, C. (1981) 'Sex role stereotyping in British television ads', *British Journal of Social Psychology*, 20, 171–80.

Marcuse, H. (1968) *One-Dimensional Man*, London: Sphere.

Marmori, G. (1968) *Senso e Anagramma*, Rome: Feltrinelli.

Marland, M. (1974) *The Question of Advertising*, London: Chatto & Windus.

Masterman, L. (1980) *Teaching About Television*, London: Macmillan.

Mayer, M. (1961) *Madison Avenue*, Harmondsworth: Penguin.

Metz, C. (1974) *Film Language, A Semiotics of the Cinema*, New York: Oxford University Press.

Miliband, R. (1976) *The State in Capitalist Society*, London: Quartet.

Miller, J. (1971) *McLuhan*, London: Fontana.

Mills, C. W. (1956) *The Power Elite*, New York: Oxford University Press.

Millum, T. (1975) *Images of Women: Advertising in Women's Magazines*, London: Chatto & Windus.

Minns, R. (1980) *Bombers and Mash*, London: Virago.

Monaco, J. (1977) *How to Read a Film*, New York: Oxford University Press.

Morley, D. (1980) *The Nationwide Audience*, London: British Film Institute.

Mulvey, L. (1975) 'Visual pleasure and narrative cinema', *Screen*, 16, 3.

Neale, S. (1977) 'Propaganda', *Screen*, 18, 3.

— (1980) 'The same old story, stereotypes and difference', *Screen Education*, 32/33.

Nicholl, D. (1973) *Advertising: Its Purpose, Principles and Practice*, London: MacDonald & Evans.

Nichols, B. (ed.) (1976) *Movies and Methods*, Berkeley: University of California Press.

Ogilvy, D. (1963) *Confessions of an Advertising Man*, London: Longman.

Packard, V. (1970) *The Hidden Persuaders*, Harmondsworth: Penguin (first published in 1957 by Longman, London).

Photography/Politics: One (1979) London: Photography Workshop.

Panofsky, E. (1970) *Meaning in the Visual Arts*, Harmondsworth: Penguin.

Pearson, J. and Turner, G. (1965) *The Persuasion Industry*, London: Eyre & Spottiswoode.

Pilkington Committee (1962) *Report of the Committee on Broadcasting, 1960*, Cmnd 1753, London: HMSO.

Pollock, G. (1977) 'What's wrong with images of women?', *Screen Education*, 24.

Propp, V. (1968) *Morphology of the Folktale*, Austin: University of Texas Press.

De Saussure, F. (1966) *Course in General Linguistics*, New York: McGraw-Hill.

Savage, E. (1971) *Advertising*, London: Heinemann.

Schuwer, P. (1966) *History of Advertising*, Zurich: Leisure Arts.

Sharpe, S. (1976) *Just Like a Girl: How Girls Learn to be Women*, Harmondsworth: Penguin.

Sontag, S. (1979) *On Photography*, Harmondsworth: Penguin.

Spence, J. (1978) 'Class, gender, women', *Screen Education*, 25.

Thomas, D. (1967) *The Visible Persuaders*, London: Hutchinson.

Thompson, D. (ed.) (1965) *Discrimination and Popular Culture*, Harmondsworth: Penguin.

Tuchman, G., Kaplan Daniels, A. and Benet, J. (eds) (1978) *Hearth and Home: Images of Women in the Media*, New York: Oxford University Press.

Tunstall, J. (1964) *The Advertising Man*, London: Chapman & Hall.

Tuck, M. (1976) *How Do We Choose?*, London: Methuen.

Turner, E.S. (1952) *The Shocking History of Advertising*, Harmondsworth: Penguin.

Victoroff, D. (1978) *La Publicité et l'Image*, Paris: Denoël/Gonthier.

Webster, F. (1980) *The New Photography*, London: John Calder.

Welch, R., Huston-Stein, A., Wright, J. and Plehal, R. (1979) 'Subtle sex role cues in children's commercials', *J. of Communication*, 29:3, pp. 202–9.

White, C. (1970) *Women's Magazines*, London: Michael Joseph.

Whitehead, F. (1965) 'Advertising', in Thompson, D. (ed.) (1965).

Williams, R. (1965a) *Culture and Society*, Harmondsworth: Penguin.

—— (1965b) *The Long Revolution*, Harmondsworth: Penguin.

—— (1968a) *Communications*, Harmondsworth: Penguin.

—— (ed.) (1968b) *May Day Manifesto*, Harmondsworth: Penguin.

—— (1974) *Television: Technology and Cultural Form*, London: Fontana.

—— (1980) 'Advertising: the magic system', in *Problems in Materialism and Culture*, London: Verso.

—— (1981) *Culture*, London: Fontana.

Williamson, J. (1978) *Decoding Advertisements*, London: Marion Boyars.

Wilson, H. H. (1961) *Pressure Group: The Campaign for Commercial Television*, London: Secker & Warburg.

Winship, J. (1981) 'Handling sex', in Curran (ed.) (1981).

Wollen, P. (1969) *Signs and Meaning in the Cinema*, Cinema One, London: Secker & Warburg.

Women in Media (1976) *The Packaging of Women*, London: Women in Media.

BIBLIOGRAPHY

History

(Advertising has attracted surprisingly few historians.)

Begley, G. (1975) *Keep Mum! Advertising Goes to War*, London: Lemon Tree Press. An account of wartime advertising with some reproductions of wartime 'austerity' ads and propaganda posters against 'squanderbugs' etc.

Elliott, B. B. (1962) *A History of English Advertising*, London: London Business Publications Ltd.

Field, E. (1959) *Advertising: The Forgotten Years*, London: Ernest Benn. An anecdotal look at advertising campaigns during the first twenty-five years of this century. Quite interesting 'inside' detail and some nice illustrations but no depth.

Sampson, H. (1875) *A History of Advertising from the Earliest Times*, London: Chatto & Windus.

Schuwer, P. (1966) *History of Advertising*, Geneva: Edito-Service SA. Well illustrated.

Turner, E. S. (1965) *The Shocking History of Advertising*, Harmondsworth: Penguin. A lively account of advertising from the seventeenth century to the 1950s. Not much critical analysis but one of the very few books on the history of advertising.

de Vries, L. (1968) *Victorian Advertising*, London: John Murray.

Economics

(Consult also the business news sections of the quality press for a handy source of news of the economics and profession of advertising.)

Galbraith, K. (1962) *The Affluent Society*, Harmondsworth: Penguin. An entertaining yet profound account of the economics of Western society with many important insights into advertising and demand management. You don't need to be an economist to understand it.

Galbraith, K. (1969) *The New Industrial State*, Harmondsworth: Penguin. A study of advanced industrial economics, their 'techno-structures', and the way they reach out to control the consumer.

Kaldor, N. (1950/1) 'The economic aspects of advertising', in *The Three Faces of Advertising* (1975), London: The Advertising Association. Although written many years ago this is still a major contribution to the debate on economics and advertising. Recommended only for those who have some grasp of economic theory.

Effects

(See also advertising and marketing journals and also *Public Opinion Quarterly, Journalism Quarterly, Journal of Communication*.)

Krugman, H. (1975) 'The impact of TV advertising', *Public Opinion Quarterly*, XXIX, 3, 1965.

Morley, D. (1980) *The Nationwide Audience*, London: British Film Institute. A useful resumé of the various 'effects' research approaches, plus an attempt at a new kind of audience research based on group interviews.

Inside views, apologies and professional primers

(See also the business news sections of the 'quality' newspapers and the professional journals.)

Arlen, M. J. (1981) *Thirty Seconds*, New York: Farrar Straus & Giroux. A dryly humorous and cynical account of the machinations behind the making of a thirty second TV commercial for American Telephone and Telegraph by a New York advertising agency. The book charts every minute detail and the massive expense that went into the filming of a fleeting spot on American TV screens.

Baker, S. S. (1969) *The Permissible Lie*, London: Peter Owen. Subtitled *The Inside Truth About Advertising*, it was banned in the USA when it was first published.

Fletcher, W. (1973) *The Ad Makers*, London: Michael Joseph. Written by one of the top agency men, this 'defence' of advertising is entertaining and witty, and gives a good insight into the 'cynical' mind of advertising.

Mayer, M. (1961) *Madison Avenue, USA*, Harmondsworth: Penguin. A very straightforward account of the American advertising business.

Ogilvy, D. (1964) *Confessions of an Advertising Man*, London: Longman. A sensational kind of apology or defence of the system.

Pearson, J. and Turner, G. (1966) *The Persuasion Industry*, London: Eyre & Spottiswoode. An account of the way the advertising industry works. Well written and detailed but rather blind to its social and economic position and by no means critical.

Tunstall, J. (1964) *The Advertising Man in London Advertising Agencies*, London: Chapman & Hall. One of the very few socio-logical accounts of the work of advertising agencies and the people who work in them.

General cultural criticism

Barnouw, E. (1978) *The Sponsor*, New York: Oxford University Press. An investigation of the role played by advertising in American television, and its influence on news, documentaries and entertainment. Fascinating and frightening.

Berger, J. (1972) *Ways of Seeing*, London: BBC/Pelican. A collection of essays on the language and status of images, including a very illuminating one on publicity.

Boorstin, D. (1963) *The Image*, Harmondsworth: Penguin. General critique of the American 'moonshine' industries. A chapter on 'The search for self-fulfilling prophecies' shows how advertisers inflate nothing into something.

Ewen, S. (1976) *Captains of Consciousness: Advertising and the Social Roots of the Consumer Culture*, New York: McGraw-Hill. A history of the consumer culture, particularly of the early conditioning of consumers in the 1920s. A very good blend of theory and 'analysis' of advertisements against a background of social and economic change.

Hall, S. and Whannel, P. (1964) *The Popular Arts*, London: Hutchinson Educational. This book, written in the 1960s, examines film, television, magazines and advertising. The examples seem a bit

223

dated now, but the general theoretical framework and the approach are rigorous and pertinent. The section on advertising, 'The big bazaar', is a short but useful discussion of the cultural and 'moral' aspects of advertising and includes a closer look at its language, imagery and style.

Inglis, F. (1972) *The Imagery of Power*, London: Heinemann. A polemical critique of advertising bringing in historical politico-economic and cultural arguments. A chapter on the rhetoric of advertising examines a series of ads.

Leavis, F. R. and Thomson, D. (1933) *Culture and Environment*, London: Chatto & Windus. A 'classic' attack on advertising, originally intended as a manual for the training of 'critical awareness'. Very out of date and nostalgic but an interesting example of the Leavisite position on contemporary culture.

Packard, V. (1957) *The Hidden Persuaders*, Harmondsworth: Penguin. A very readable debunking of motivational research in American advertising. Probably a little out of date now. Despite its sinister and sensational revelations, in the end the book fails to consider why and how and for whose benefit advertising operates.

Williams, R. (1980) 'Advertising: magic system', in *Problems in Materialism and Culture*, London: Verso. This essay originally written for *The Long Revolution* (1961) turned up in *New Left Review*, 4, 1960, and has been rewritten for this collection. It is an acute and typically Williams attack on modern advertising, from historical, economic, social and cultural perspectives.

Methods and analysis

Andren, G. *et al.* (1978) *Rhetoric and Ideology in Advertising*, Stockholm: Liber Förlag. A content analysis of American advertising, written in English by a group of Swedish philosophers. Contains detailed discussion of content analysis as a method, and very thorough analysis of magazine ads.

Barthes, R. (1964) 'The rhetoric of the image', in *Image – Music – Text* (1977), London: Fontana. A major essay on semiotics and its application to the analysis of an advertising message.

Barthes, R. (1973) *Mythologies*, St Albans: Paladin. A key work of semiotics and cultural analysis, with several short essays on particular ads and publicity campaigns.

Durand, J. (1970) 'Rhetorique et image publicitaire', *Communications*

15, Paris: Editions du Seuil. A close study of rhetoric in advertising, which raises some interesting questions in relation to rhetorical analysis. No translation I know of, but easy French.

Fiske, J. (1982) *Introduction to Communication Studies*, London: Methuen. A companion to this volume with good general introduction to concepts and methods relating to communications in general.

Gauthier, G. (1976) *The Semiology of the Image*, British Film Institute Advisory Document. A good introduction to the application of semiotic theory to advertisements and other media images.

Langholz Leymore, V. (1975) *The Hidden Myth*, London: Heinemann. An original study applying the basic principles of structural analysis to modern television advertising. (Follows Levi-Strauss's *Structural Anthropology*.) Rather difficult to follow for the uninitiated and non-mathematical with rather disappointing conclusions.

Leech, G. (1966) *English in Advertising*, London: Longmans. A very comprehensive study of advertising style from a strictly linguistic point of view. Not too difficult for the non-linguist but no discussion of its cultural, economic or 'political' consequences.

McLuhan, M. (1951) *The Mechanical Bride*, London: Routledge & Kegan Paul. An early detailed discussion of contemporary advertising and visual communication. One of the first critics to consider the 'formal' properties of ads.

Webster, F. (1980) *The New Photography*, London: John Calder. A study of the social and political role of photography and of cultural/visual communication in general. References to advertising, photo-journalism, films and television.

Williamson, J. (1978) *Decoding Advertisements*, London: Marian Boyers. Interesting but sometimes complex analysis of advertisements using semiotics as a basis for ideological and psychoanalytic critique.

Women and advertising

Adams, C. and Laurikietis, R. (1976) *Messages and Images*, Book 3 of *The Gender Trap. A Close Look at Sex Roles*, London: Virago. Investigates the stereotypes of women and men in advertising, newspapers, jokes, cartoons, etc. Written for young people in school and college and their teachers and parents.

Goffman, E. (1979) *Gender Advertisements*, London: Macmillan. An elegant analysis and discussion of visual communication and gender display in advertising by a leading American social anthropologist.

King, J. and Stott, M. (eds) (1977) *Is This Your Life? Images of Women in the Media*, London: Virago. A look at the attitudes and images of women presented by advertising, with some useful advice on how to combat sexist and stereotypical portrayals of women.

Millum, T. (1975) *Images of Women: Advertising in Women's Magazines*, London: Chatto & Windus. A discussion of concepts of femininity and physical appearance which reveals the way women are presented in advertising from point of view of visual communication and cultural symbols.

Women in Media (1976) *The Packaging of Women: How Women are Portrayed in Advertisements*. Report of the proceedings of a Woman in Media Seminar on whether and how it might be possible to influence current business thinking and practice.

INDEX

accumulation, figures of, 162, 165
activity as a communication tool,
     101–4
Addison, Joseph, 22
addition, figures of, 161–70
advertisement tax, 17, 29
Advertisers' Protection Agency, 41
Advertisers Weekly, 47
Advertising Agency Register, 213
Advertising Standards Authority, 184,
     208, 213
age, influence of, 97
agencies, growth of, 34–5, 41, 56,
     74
alliteration, 155
allusion, 162
Alvarado, M., 129
ambiguity, 162, 167
anacoluthon, 162, 177–8
Andren, G., 109, 112
antanaclasis, 162
antilogy, 162
antimetabole, 162, 179
antiphrasis, 162
antithesis, 162
antonomasia, 175
appearance as a communication tool,
     97–9
art in advertising, 35–7
asyndeton, 162, 175

Ballyhoo, 47
Barnouw, E., 59–60, 70
Barthes, R., 81, 104, 127, 128, 129,
     130, 158, 159, 160
Berger, J., 92
billposting, growth of, 32
body, use of
     characteristics, 98
     movements, 101
Boorstin, D., 82
brand names, development of, 141
British Code of Advertising Practice,
     208–12
business advertising, characteristics
     of, 5
Byron, George G. (6th Baron), 56

calligraphy, 155–6
Carlyle, Thomas, 29
celebrities, use of, 10, 96, 113,
     145, 186
charity advertising, characteristics of,
     5
chiasmus, 162, 178–80
choice, consumer, 8–9
circulation figures, 42
circumlocution, 162, 170–1
class consciousness, 94
classification of advertising, 4–5,
     88–92

227

classified advertisements, characteristics of, 5, 88–9
codes, semiotic, 131–6 (*see also* signs)
coined words, 29, 150
colour, use of, 94, 107, 120, 129
commercial television
    establishment, 58–62
    future, 62–3
    relations with the press, 63–4
connotive signs, 127–31
consumer affairs
    choice, 8–9
    information, 6, 10
content analysis, 108–11
culture
    impact of advertising on, 79–81, 218–19
    traditions of, 97, 99, 115, 125, 135
Curran, J., 53, 66–7, 71

Daily Herald, 64, 68
Daily Mail, 42, 65
Daily Mirror, 68
Daily Sketch, 64
Daily Telegraph, 62
Deacon, Samuel, 35
definition of advertising, 2–3
denotive signs, 127–31
dialogue, use of, 130
display advertising, development of, 35
dubitation, 162
Durand, J., 159, 160, 162, 165

economic aspects, 3–4
editors, influence on, 66–8, 183
ellipsis, 162, 165, 170
emotions, exploitation of, 3, 6, 92, 150
epitrochasm, 165
Ericsson, L. C., *see* Andren, G.
euphemism, 162, 175–6
Ewen, S., 45
exchange, figures of, 176–82
expenditure on advertising, 188–91
expressions, use of facial, 99
eye contact, use of, 99–100

false homology, 176
female image, *see* women
figurative language, 151–5
financial advertising, characteristics of, 5
financial aspects of advertising, 42, 188–94, 216
Fiske, J., 108, 113
Ford, Henry, 41, 46
Foucault, M., 156
Frankfurt School, 81
Freud, S., 159
Friendly, F., 70

Galbraith, J.K., 6, 78
gender, influence of, 97 (*see also* sex)
gestures, use of, 101
Goffman, E., 97, 98, 99, 101, 112, 135
Golding, P., 53
Gombrich, E., 159
government advertising, characteristics of, 5
Gramsci, A., 46
Guardian, The, 63

Hall, S., 89
Harmsworth, Alfred (Lord Northcliffe), 42, 64
Hartley, J., 113
hendiadys, 162, 176
historical aspects of advertising, 15–37, 39–53, 55–60, 215–16
History of Advertising Trust, 213
homology, 162, 176
    false, 176, 177
homonymy, 153
hyperbole, 162, 173–5, 179

iconography
    analysis of, 93–4, 95, 105–6
    signs used in, 124–6, 128
illustrations, *see* imagery *and* images
imagery, use of visual, 82, 89, 93
images, creation of, 123–6
indexical signs, 124–6
information dissemination, 6–7, 89

228

Inglis, F., 2, 10, 80
Institute of Practitioners in Advertising, 213
International Advertising Corporation (IAC), 46
inversion, 162, 176

Jakobson, R., 127
jingles, 56
Johnson, Dr Samuel, 22

Kaldor, N.H., 6–7
key words, 149–51
Kipling, Rudyard, 37

Langholz Leymore, V., 2
language
    analysis of, 79–80, 81, 117–18, 151–5, 218–19
    role of, 139–40, 144–7
    style of, 142–3
Leavis, F.R., 80
Legal aspects, 147–9, 206–7
Lever Brothers advertising campaign, 40
Life, 46
Lippa, M., 48

McGregor Commission (1977), 65
McGuiness, J., 37
McLuhan, M., 82
male image, 78, 83, 92, 94, 97–8, 100, 105, 108–9
manufacturing patterns, 8–9, 39–40, 42
Marcuse, H., 81
market control, 8–9, 39–40, 42
market research, 50, 74–5
Marmori, G., 159
meanings, interchangeability of word, 116–17
media, role of mass communication, 9–11 (see also television)
meiosis, 174–5
metaphors, 127, 152, 162, 175
metonymy, 127, 153, 162, 175
Millais, Sir John Everett, 35
Mills, C.W., 8
Millum, T., 98, 104, 106

monopoly capitalism, 40
motivational research (MR), 83
Murdoch, Rupert, 65
music, 56

national advertisements, development of, 30
New York Evening Post, 43
News Chronicle, 64, 65
News of the World, 42, 62
newspaper advertising, development of, 42, 63–5
Newton, D., 48
Northcliffe, Alfred (1st Viscount) (Alfred Harmsworth), 42, 64

Observer, The, 62, 65
Ohlsson, L.O., see Andren, G.
opposition of rhetorical figures, 162, 165
oxymoron, 179

Packard, V., 83
Panofsky, E., 93, 94, 105
paradigmatic sign relations, 126–7
paradox, 162, 167–70
parallelism, 155
patent medicines, advertisements for, 24–7, 30, 46–7, 50
paternalism in advertising, growth of, 45–6
Pears advertising campaign, 33–4, 35–7, 40
periphrasis, 162, 175–6
persuasive techniques in advertising
    first instances of, 17
    growth of, 41, 89, 92–3, 109–10, 158–9
photographic techniques, 106–8, 124, 131
physical characteristics, influence of, 198
pictures, use of, 82, 89, 93, 106–8
poetry, 29, 56
political advertising, characteristics of, 11–12
positional communication, 100, 101–4
prestige advertising, characteristics of, 5

preterition, 162, 173
psychology in advertising
    first instances of, 43-5
    growth of, 74, 75, 83
public relations (PR), 11-12
puns, 153, 154, 162

racial characteristics, influence of, 98
Renault cars advertising campaign,
    120-3
repetition, figures of, 161-2
reticence, 162
rhetoric
    and language analysis, 152-5
    and visual analysis
        addition, 161-70
        exchange, 176-82
        substitution, 173-6
        suppression, 170-3
rhyme, 162, 163 (see also verse)
role borrowing in language, 146-7

Saussure, F. de, 115, 126
semiotics
    classification, 124-36
    definition, 115
    methods, 117-24
setting and staging, role of, 104-6
sex, in advertising, see male image, and
        women, image of (see also gender)
signs
    meanings, 127-31 (see also codes)
    relations, 126-7
    systems, 118-26
similes, 153, 162, 163
slogans, growth of, 32-3
small ads, 5, 88
Society for the Checking of Abuses in
        Public Advertising (SCAPA),
        37, 41
sociological effects of advertising, 75-7
spellings and misspellings, 150
structuralism, 117-18
substitution, figures of, 173-6
Sun, The, 62, 68
suppression, figures of, 170-3
suspension, 162, 170-2
symbolism, 91, 94, 105, 125
synechdoche, 175, 179

syntagmatic sign relations, 126-7

Tännsjö, T., see Andren, G.
tautology, 162, 173
tax on advertising, 17, 29
technical advertisements, character
        of, 4-5
television advertising
    analysis of, 10-11
    growth of, 57-63 (see also med
Thompson, D., 53
Thomson, K.R., 58
Times, The, 30, 35, 47, 63
trade advertising, characteristics of
Trade Descriptions Act (1968), 14
'truth in advertising' campaign, 46
Turner, E.S., 41

verse, use of, 29, 56 (see also rhym
visual imagery, 82, 89, 93, 123-6
visual perception, 94-6
visual rhetoric
    addition, 161-70
    exchange, 176-82
    substitution, 173-6
    suppression, 170-3
visual techniques, 106-8, 124, 131
voice, use of, 141-3

Welch, R., 107
Whannel, P., 89
Williams, R., 2, 5, 7, 10, 28, 37, 49
        73, 80, 185
Williamson, J., 1, 116, 117, 126, 156
Winship, J., 115, 182
women
    as sex objects, 92, 107, 124, 184
        185-6
    image of, 219-20
    domestic, 56, 78, 83, 92, 97-8,
        108-9, 117
    submissive, 99, 100, 101, 102, 1
    working, 52, 185-6
'word magic', 49, 50
words
    choice of, 140-3, 149-51
    meanings, 116-17

zeugma, 162